GOLDENEYE
GUIDEBOOKS

COTSWOLD
CLASSIC WALKS

WRITTEN AND PHOTOGRAPHED BY
WILLIAM FRICKER

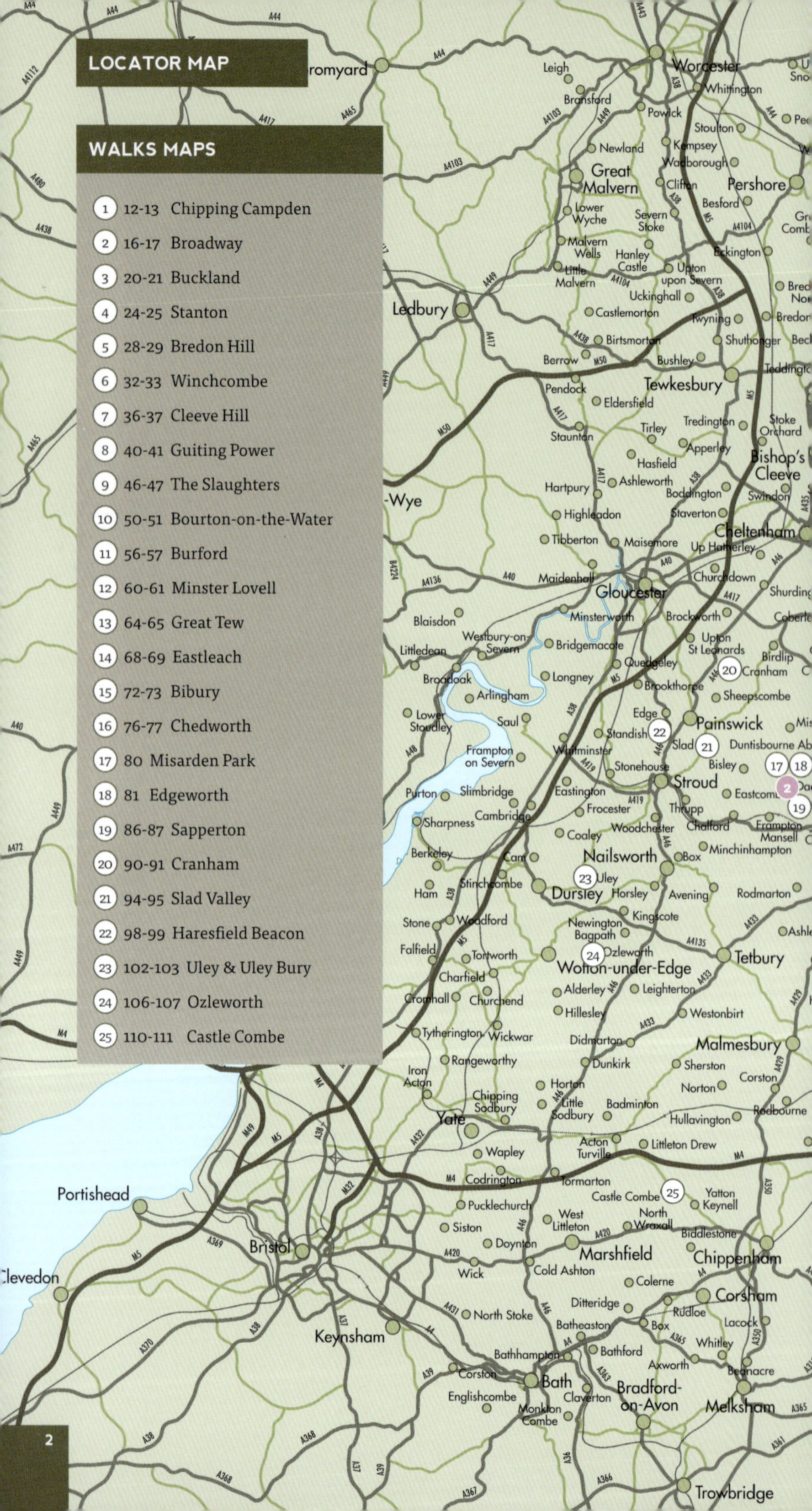

LOCATOR MAP

WALKS MAPS

1 12-13 Chipping Campden
2 16-17 Broadway
3 20-21 Buckland
4 24-25 Stanton
5 28-29 Bredon Hill
6 32-33 Winchcombe
7 36-37 Cleeve Hill
8 40-41 Guiting Power
9 46-47 The Slaughters
10 50-51 Bourton-on-the-Water
11 56-57 Burford
12 60-61 Minster Lovell
13 64-65 Great Tew
14 68-69 Eastleach
15 72-73 Bibury
16 76-77 Chedworth
17 80 Misarden Park
18 81 Edgeworth
19 86-87 Sapperton
20 90-91 Cranham
21 94-95 Slad Valley
22 98-99 Haresfield Beacon
23 102-103 Uley & Uley Bury
24 106-107 Ozleworth
25 110-111 Castle Combe

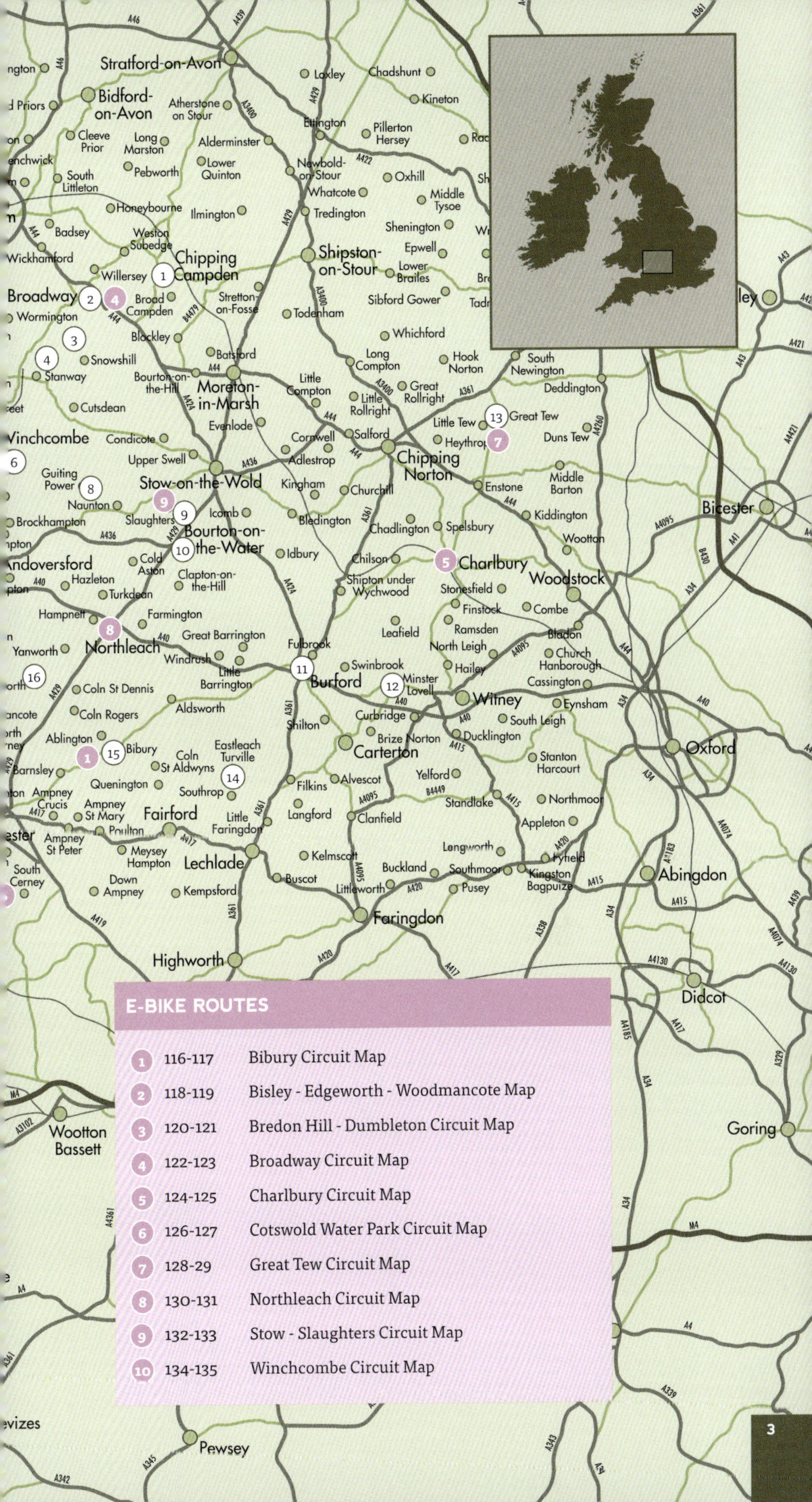

Stratford-on-Avon
Bidford-on-Avon
Priors
Cleeve Prior
Long Marston
Alderminster
enchwick
South Littleton
Pebworth
Lower Quinton
Loxley
Chadshunt
Kineton
Atherstone on Stour
Ettington
Pillerton Hersey
Rad
Newbold-on-Stour
Whatcote
Oxhill
Middle Tysoe
Honeybourne
Ilmington
Tredington
Shenington
Epwell
Badsey
Weston Subedge
Willersey
Chipping Campden
Shipston-on-Stour
Lower Brailes
Wickhamford
Broadway
Broad Campden
Stretton-on-Fosse
Todenham
Sibford Gower
Tadr
Wormington
Blockley
Whichford
Snowshill
Batsford
Long Compton
Hook Norton
South Newington
Stanway
Bourton-on-the-Hill
Little Compton
Great Rollright
Deddington
Cutsdean
Moreton-in-Marsh
Little Rollright
Evenlode
Salford
Little Tew
Great Tew
Duns Tew
Vinchcombe
Condicote
Cornwell
Heythrop
Upper Swell
Adlestrop
Chipping Norton
Guiting Power
Naunton
Stow-on-the-Wold
Kingham
Churchill
Enstone
Middle Barton
Brockhampton
Icomb
Bledington
Chadlington
Spelsbury
Kiddington
Bicester
Slaughters
Bourton-on-the-Water
Idbury
Wootton
pton
Cold Aston
Chilson
Andoversford
Hazleton
Clapton-on-the-Hill
Shipton under Wychwood
Charlbury
Woodstock
Turkdean
Stonesfield
Hampnett
Farmington
Finstock
Combe
Yanworth
Northleach
Great Barrington
Leafield
Ramsden
Bladon
Windrush
Little Barrington
North Leigh
Church Hanborough
orth
Fulbrook
Hailey
Cassington
Coln St Dennis
Swinbrook
Burford
Witney
Eynsham
Coln Rogers
Aldsworth
Minster Lovell
Ablington
Shilton
Curbridge
South Leigh
Barnsley
Bibury
Coln St Aldwyns
Eastleach Turville
Brize Norton
Ducklington
Stanton Harcourt
Quenington
Southrop
Carterton
Yelford
Oxford
Ampney Crucis
Filkins
Alvescot
Northmoor
Fairford
Langford
Clanfield
Standlake
Appleton
Ampney St Mary
Poulton
Little Faringdon
Meysey Hampton
Kelmscott
Longworth
Fyfield
Abingdon
ester
Ampney St Peter
Buckland
Southmoor
Kingston Bagpuize
South Cerney
Down Ampney
Kempsford
Lechlade
Buscot
Littleworth
Pusey
Faringdon
Highworth
Didcot
M4
Wootton Bassett
Goring
evizes
Pewsey
3

E-BIKE ROUTES

1 116-117 Bibury Circuit Map
2 118-119 Bisley - Edgeworth - Woodmancote Map
3 120-121 Bredon Hill - Dumbleton Circuit Map
4 122-123 Broadway Circuit Map
5 124-125 Charlbury Circuit Map
6 126-127 Cotswold Water Park Circuit Map
7 128-29   Great Tew Circuit Map
8 130-131 Northleach Circuit Map
9 132-133 Stow - Slaughters Circuit Map
10 134-135 Winchcombe Circuit Map

ACKNOWLEDGEMENTS

To my Cotswold Walking Companions: Caroline, Isabella, Harry, Flora, Alice & Salar (ESS)

Research & Text by William Fricker. Photography by William Fricker (unless credited with an initial ss - supplied by subject). First published in the United Kingdom, in 2010, Fifth Edition, 2023 by: Goldeneye, Broad Street, Penryn TR10 8JL

Text copyright © 2023, William Fricker. Photographs copyright © 2023 William Fricker.

Maps supplied by Goldeneye's Digital Database. Maps copyright © Goldeneye, 2023.

Cartography by Cox Cartographic Ltd. Sub Editor: Isabella Fricker E-Bike Routes Researched by Al Churcher. Design and layout by Camouka. All Rights Reserved. Printed in the Czech Republic.

Inside Flap Images: Clockwise from the top right hand tent image:. Westley Farm - Chalford, The Slaughters Manor House - Lower Slaughter, Buckland Manor - Broadway, Russell's of Broadway, Lords of the Manor - Upper Slaughter, Buckland Manor - Broadway, The Painswick Hotel - Painswick and Abbots Grange B&B - Broadway. All Supplied By Subjects.

Correct Information. The contents of this publication were believed to be correct and accurate at the time of printing. However, Goldeneye accepts no responsibility for any errors, omissions or changes in the details given, or for the consequences arising thereto, from the use of this book. However, the publishers would greatly appreciate your time in notifying us of any changes (to way-marking and physical detriments) or new attractions (or places to eat, drink and stay) that you consider merit inclusion in the next edition.

Your comments are most welcome for we value the views, suggestions and feedback of our readers.

CONTENTS

The Cotswolds epitomise the romantic notion of the traditional English scene: picture-postcard images of rolling green hills overlooking villages of golden stone cottages, manor houses and majestic churches. This image is no dream but is clearly evident when you walk the routes described in this book. And, no better way to experience the setting of this dramatic architecture than to walk from village to village, or along the western escarpment that affords spectacular views across the Severn Vale and towards the Welsh hills. But, first you must explore and savour the village from whence your walk begins and stroll through this rolling landscape of sheep pastures, trout streams and dry-stone walls.

The Cotswold landscape was formed by geological upheaval and by the interference of Man; i.e. by the limestone and wool. The Cotswold hills are the highest part of a band of oolitic limestone which tilts in a south east direction running from near the Dorset coast to south Lincolnshire. From the steep escarpments in the west, the Cotswold hills gently descend in an easterly direction, bisected by fast-flowing trout streams feeding the River Thames.

This limestone is a superb building material and is malleable and easily cut into beautiful shapes, it weathers extreme climate and looks attractive in all light. The wool merchants of the Middle Ages developed the fleece and laid the foundations of prosperity and it was these merchants who built the great 'Wool' churches, manor houses and tithe barns so splendidly evident in Broadway, Burford, Chipping Campden and Winchcombe.

These walks are categorised as easy, moderate or strenuous. A modicum of fitness is required. Waterproof footwear is advised and a light rucksack with cagoule, refreshments and spare jumper will not go amiss. I always carry a flask of hot chocolate - a life saver! The topography is of an undulating landscape and to link various routes we have used the Cotswold Way which can be hard-going in places and can resemble the South West coastal footpath as an energy sapping device. A number of the routes do join up and can make an interesting figure-of-eight for those looking for an all-day walk.

Our mapping has been tried and tested these past twenty-two years. You don't need to be an experienced map-reader to follow these routes. The maps illustrate regular points of reference to make you feel secure: water troughs, stiles, a special tree. And, you should also be able to follow the routes just by reading the boxes of text. Of course, landmarks do disappear and stiles or gates move from time to time so please let me know if you encounter any such changes. For this new edition the routes have been re-walked. The major change has been the replacement of stiles to gates

I have also included a few suggestions for accommodation and eating/drinking venues. This list is by no means exhaustive but I have tried to provide oases that are used to walkers, children and dogs. In the last couple of years my (and my walking companions) movements have been restricted due to having a young daughter bed bound with Severe M.E. It occurred to me that walking and visiting pubs was a privilege I had always taken for granted. Indeed, these sentiments have deepened by the day as I note the endless misery of families seeking to survive in Afghanistan, Eastern Europe and Syria. Coupled with these tragedies the restrictions of COVID (and other influences) on the hospitality industry with all that that has upset peoples lives.

So, be with good cheer, and a hearty breakfast inside you. Go forth and take advantage of these English combes and hills while you can.

Why have we included E-Bike Routes? You yearn to walk but your dodgy knees and aching hips tell you, No! But, with an E-Bike the Great Outdoors is suddenly open to you again....Life ain't so bad after all...The spirit of adventure beckons...

Happy Walking, Happy Cycling,

William Fricker

◄ *Two English Spring Spaniels, Saltridge Woods, Sheepscombe*

WHICH WALK TO UNDERTAKE

With 25 circular walks, this book will help you find a base to escape from your car and enjoy a weekend of fresh air and exercise. Some walks offer various route options or links to other walks. How to decide which walk to undertake? Which walks are best for kids, dogs or pub lunches? Where are the best views? Where to find solitude? We have made some suggestions to help guide you in your choice. These are by no means the only options in this book but might help you get started.

1. Pushchairs

Misarden Park walk. At just 1.5miles and with only about 20 metres of rough track and one stile, this walk is suitable for pushchairs. Furthermore, the surroundings are beautiful, ranging from woodland to lakes with abundant wildlife – plenty of interest for both parents and kids.

2. Families

The Eastleach-Leach Valley walk provides plenty of interest to all ages. If 4.5 miles is too long for smaller children, there is a handy shortcut. Alternatively, Guiting Power is a mostly flat, wooded walk of 3 miles with plenty of flora and fauna.

3. Dogs

Cleave Common is popular with dog walkers as dogs can run free. With only a few stiles once you leave Cleave Common and great views for the humans, this is by far the best dog walk in this book. Note of caution: If you prefer to walk your dog away from the madding crowd, Haresfield Beacon and Sapperton are good alternative walks.

4. Pubs

If you like to get the hard work out of the way and finish your walk with a well-earned rest at a local pub, the Sapperton walk provides you with a delightful watering hole in the Bell Inn. If you need something to spur you on to the halfway point, the Cranham walk provides a rest stop in the Butcher's Arms, Sheepscombe, as well as a walker's pit stop a little further on at the Foston's Ash.

5. Views

For a variety of views from far reaching landscapes to views overlooking quaint Cotswold villages, the Painswick-Slad Valley walk provides beautiful English landscapes in all directions. For more dramatic tastes, the views from Broadway Tower take in 13 counties or there are fine views towards the River Severn and Welsh Hills from Uley Bury Hill Fort.

Misarden Park

Eastleach

Cleeve Hill

The Bell at Sapperton

Slad Valley

Laverton Hill

Haresfield Beacon

Saltridge Wood

Broadway Tower

Ozleworth Church

6. Weekends Away

If you want to avoid using the car, there are plenty of towns to make your base for a weekend away with great eating places and a choice of places to stay. Based in Broadway, you could undertake the Broadway-Broadway Tower walk and the Buckland-Laverton walk. Chipping Campden and Painswick also provide a choice of walks, as does Winchcombe.

7. Public Transport

If you base yourself in Painswick which has bus links to Stroud Railway Station, you will have a choice of two walks on your doorstep. The Painswick-Slad Valley walk which starts in the town and the Haresfield Beacon walk which is connected to Painswick by a short link route.

8. Woodland

Cranham - Sheepscombe walk. Plenty of interest including Saltridge Wood Nature Reserve. The route is mainly through or along the edge of woodland which is particularly beautiful in early summer and autumn. Sapperton, Stanton and Ozleworth, too.

9. Bluebells and Springtime

The descent from Broadway Tower passes through a wood carpeted in wild flowers and abundant with bluebells in spring. Delightful after the open vistas from Broadway Tower.

10. Peace and Quiet

For wild, beautiful and remote landscapes, the deep combes of Ozleworth Bottom are for you. The isolated landscape teems with wildlife and flowers.

The route picks up the start of the Cotswold Way in Chipping Campden and follows it up to Dover's Hill, scene of the Cotswold Olympick Games. It then follows the edge of the Scarp to provide splendid views over the Vale of Evesham, before climbing up through enchanting woodland and then descending back into Chipping Campden.

Distance
4.25 miles/6.8km.
Minimum Time
2 hours.
Grade/Level of Difficulty
Easy/Moderate.
Terrain/Paths
Tarmac, stone tracks, woodland paths.
Landscape
Arable fields, woodland and sheep pastures.
Dogs
Keep under control - beware livestock. Short section along road has grass verges.

Public Toilets
Chipping Campden High Street.
Parking (P)
Hoo Lane P.
Recommended Start/Finish
Market Hall, Chipping Campden or Dover's Hill.
Location
On the B4081, off the A44 Broadway to Moreton in Marsh road.
Link to other walks in this Guide
Broadway Walk via Fish Hill.

  Seymour House, Chipping Campden

FEATURES OF INTEREST...

Almshouses. You will pass these on your left as you make your way toward the Parish Church. Built about the same time as the Market Hall (in 1627) by the town's wealthy benefactor, Sir Baptist Hicks.

Chipping Campden. The Jewel of the Cotswolds, indeed the architectural gem of this region with a superb harmony of honey-coloured stone houses. A major wool centre in the Middle Ages between the C14 and C17s. The village's prosperity is mirrored by the handsome buildings such as St James' Church, the Lodges at Campden House, Almshouses, Grevel's House, the Woolstaplers Hall and Market Hall. If you choose to visit just one Cotswold village, make sure it's this one. There is no better introduction.

Court Barn Museum. Set opposite the Almshouses, a celebration of the town's association with the "Arts & Crafts Movement". An exhibition of silver, jewellery, ceramics, sculpture, industrial design and more, all beautifully laid out by the Guild of Handicraft Trust. Open Apr-Sept Tu-Su 10-5 & BH Ms (- 4 Oct-Mar). courtbarn.org.uk

Dover's Hill. A natural amphitheatre on a spur of the Cotswolds with magnificent views over the Vale of Evesham. The 'Olympick Games & Scuttlebrook Wake' have been held here since 1612, and take place the Friday and Saturday following Spring Bank Holiday.

Grevel's House. William Grevel, one of the wealthiest wool merchants, is remembered in the church on a brass transcription which reads: 'the flower of the wool merchants of all England'. Built by him, the house has exquisitely decorated windows, gargoyles and sundial.

Hart Silversmiths, The Old Silk Mill. Founded in 1888 as part of the 'Arts & Crafts' movement. The Harts gold and silversmith workshop is the last operating remnant of the Guild of Handicraft which C R Ashbee established in 1888, And which moved to this village in 1902. Café. Open all year. 01386 841100 hartsilversmiths.co.uk

Market Hall. This iconic image of Chipping Campden was funded by Sir Baptist Hicks (merchant banker) in 1627 for the cheese and butter markets. It is Jacobean.

St James' Church. Famous 'Wool' church of Norman origins but restored in the C15. Perpendicular nave, elegant tower, C15 cope, and a unique pair of C15 altar hangings. Superb brasses of the Woolstaplers. C15 falcon lecturn. Open daily.

WHERE TO EAT, DRINK & STAY...

Badgers Hall (B&B). Charming C15 house with mullioned windows and exposed beams housing a B&B and tearoom. Light lunches or substantial afternoon cream teas available to visitors and guests. No pets or young children. 01386 840839 badgershall.com

Bantam Tea Rooms. C17 building situated opposite the old Market Hall. Afternoon teas available inside or in the tea garden. B&B with private guest lounge and off street parking. 01386 840386 bantamtea-rooms.co.uk

Cotswold House Hotel & Spa, The Square. Boutique hotel in the centre of the village with two restaurants, two bars and 6 treatment rooms and hydro pool if your weary limbs are in need of a revival. 01386 840330 cotswoldhouse.com

Eight Bells Inn (B&B), Church Street. C14 inn full of rustic charm contrasts well with modern cuisine and bright bedrooms. Fresh fare. 01386 840371 eightbellsinn.co.uk

Michaels Mediterranean Restaurant. Greek and modern Mediterranean cuisine, served in a relaxed setting. Open for coffee, lunches, takeaways and evening meals. 01386 840826 michaelsmediterranean.co.uk

Noel Arms Hotel, High Street. C16 coaching inn transformed into a luxurious hostelry. 01386 840317 bespokehotels.com/ noelarmshotel

The Volunteer B&D, Lower High St., Named The Volunteer in the mid 1800's because local men used to visit to 'sign on' for the volunteer armies (mercenaries). A popular local specialising in curries. 01386 840688 thevolunteerinn.net

William Grevel's House

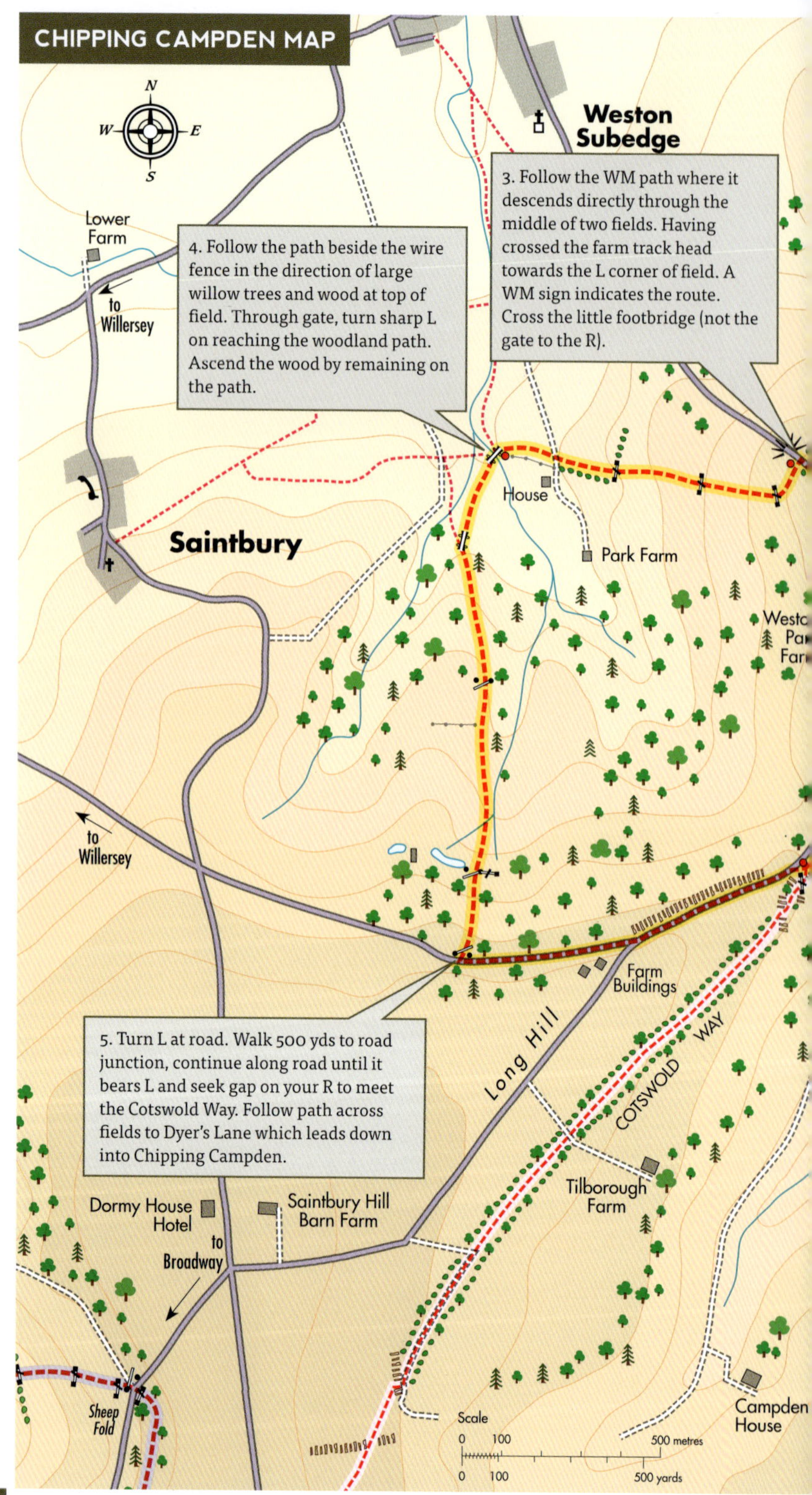
N
W E
S

Lower Farm

to Willersey

Weston Subedge

4. Follow the path beside the wire fence in the direction of large willow trees and wood at top of field. Through gate, turn sharp L on reaching the woodland path. Ascend the wood by remaining on the path.

3. Follow the WM path where it descends directly through the middle of two fields. Having crossed the farm track head towards the L corner of field. A WM sign indicates the route. Cross the little footbridge (not the gate to the R).

Saintbury

House

Park Farm

Westo
Pa
Far

to Willersey

Farm Buildings

Long Hill

COTSWOLD WAY

5. Turn L at road. Walk 500 yds to road junction, continue along road until it bears L and seek gap on your R to meet the Cotswold Way. Follow path across fields to Dyer's Lane which leads down into Chipping Campden.

Tilborough Farm

Dormy House Hotel

Saintbury Hill Barn Farm

to Broadway

Sheep Fold

Campden House

Scale
0   100   500 metres
0   100   500 yards

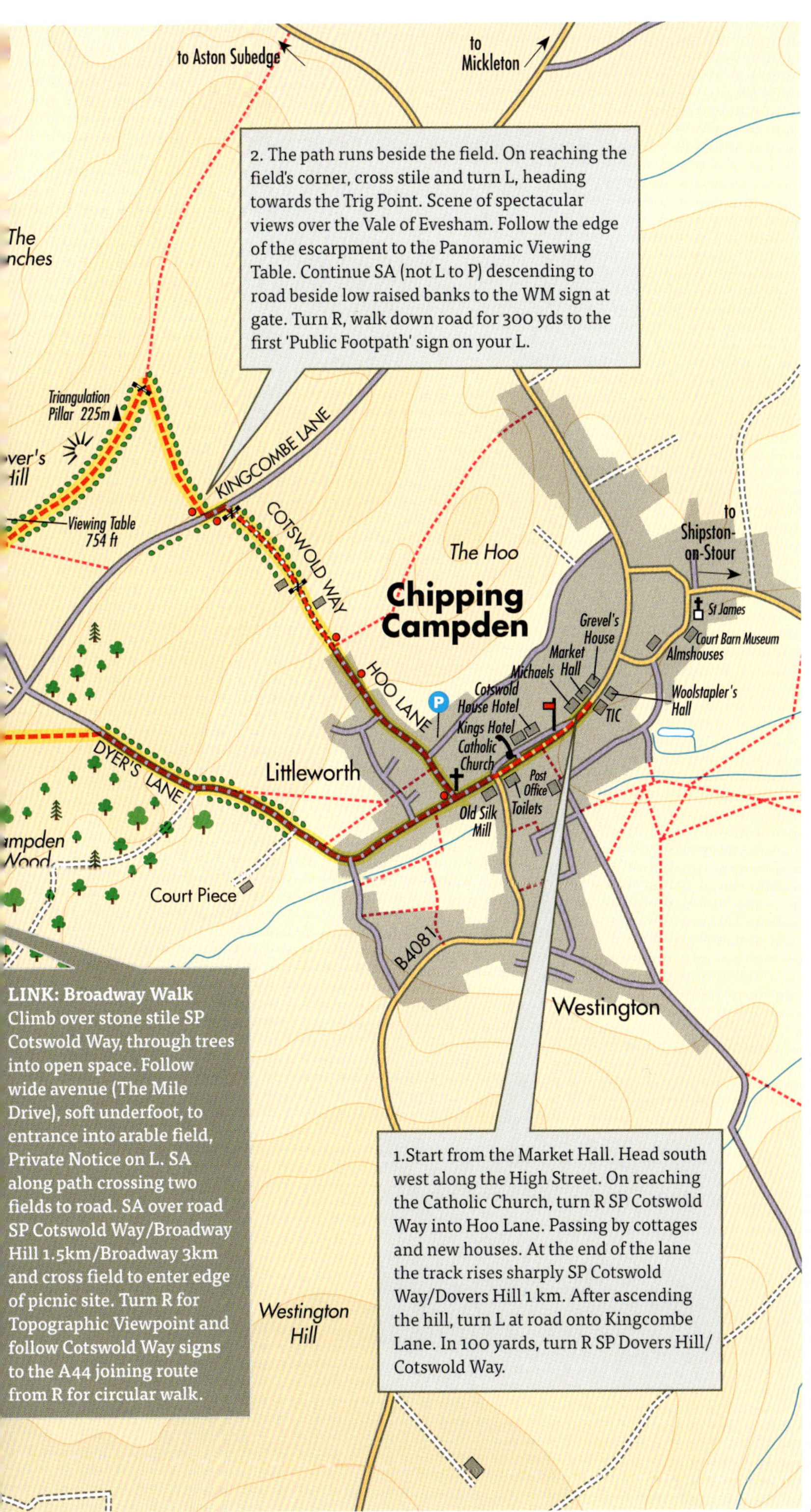

2. The path runs beside the field. On reaching the field's corner, cross stile and turn L, heading towards the Trig Point. Scene of spectacular views over the Vale of Evesham. Follow the edge of the escarpment to the Panoramic Viewing Table. Continue SA (not L to P) descending to road beside low raised banks to the WM sign at gate. Turn R, walk down road for 300 yds to the first 'Public Footpath' sign on your L.

LINK: Broadway Walk
Climb over stone stile SP Cotswold Way, through trees into open space. Follow wide avenue (The Mile Drive), soft underfoot, to entrance into arable field, Private Notice on L. SA along path crossing two fields to road. SA over road SP Cotswold Way/Broadway Hill 1.5km/Broadway 3km and cross field to enter edge of picnic site. Turn R for Topographic Viewpoint and follow Cotswold Way signs to the A44 joining route from R for circular walk.

1. Start from the Market Hall. Head south west along the High Street. On reaching the Catholic Church, turn R SP Cotswold Way into Hoo Lane. Passing by cottages and new houses. At the end of the lane the track rises sharply SP Cotswold Way/Dovers Hill 1 km. After ascending the hill, turn L at road onto Kingcombe Lane. In 100 yards, turn R SP Dovers Hill/ Cotswold Way.

Broadway epitomises English domestic architecture at its finest, and so it is worth spending some time here before you venture forth out of the village up a relatively steep climb followed by a woodland walk and superb views over the vale. From Broadway Tower, it is possible, on a clear day, to see 13 counties. The descent is through a wood carpeted in wild flowers (bluebells in spring).

Distance
4.5 miles/7.2km.
Minimum Time
2.5 hours.
Grade/Level of Difficulty
Easy/Moderate.
Terrain/Paths
Grass, farm tracks, paths.
Landscape
Rolling countryside, woodland.
Dogs
Fairly good for dogs - can run free in woodland. Keep under control around livestock.
Public Toilets
Broadway P & Broadway Tower Country Park.

Parking (P)
Broadway - behind High Street. There are two car parks in the village.
Recommended Start/Finish
Broadway P.
Location
Broadway lies off the A44 midway between Evesham and Stow on the Wold, or on the B4632 midway between Cheltenham and Stratford upon Avon.
Link to other walks in this Guide
35 minute link from Fish Hill to join Chipping Campden walk. 40 minute link to Buckland, return via Cotswold Way and Lydbrook.

Broadway Tower, Broadway

FEATURES OF INTEREST...

Broadway. 'The Painted Lady of the Cotswolds' is a term often used to describe this beautiful village. The honey-coloured stone captivates the visitor today as it did in the C19 when William Morris and his pre-Raphaelite friends settled here. A slow walk up the High Street will reveal some large and impressive houses that have been homes to Edward Elgar, JM Barrie (Peter Pan), Ralph Vaughan Williams, Sir Gerald Navarro MP and Laura Ashley. These great houses with bow windows, dormers & finely graduated stone roofs are usually hidden behind statuesque gates. There are a number of fine hotels, restaurants, tearooms, art galleries and a splendid bookshop.

Broadway Tower Country Park. A unique Cotswold attraction: an C18 folly tower with historical and geographical exhibitions. Country retreat of the pre Raphaelite, William Morris. Nature walks. Morris & Brown cafe with quality gift shop. Superb views from the Tower - a clear day gives a view of 12 counties. Nuclear Bunker open Apr-Oct W/Es & BHs 10-4.45. E-bike hire and new Visitor Centre in Tower Barn 10-4.30. The M & B Cafe opens from 9-5, Tower 10-5, all year 01386 852390 broadwaytower.co.uk

Fish Hill Woods. Attractive woodland providing superb views.

Gordon Russell Design Museum. Displays the work of the renowned C20 furniture designer who started in 1920. Open daily from 10, all year except Ms & closed in January. gordonrusselldesignmuseum.org

St Eadburgh's Church. A rare architectural gem of almost perfect proportions with a mix of C12-C18 additions. Superb brass work, topiary in churchyard, interesting tombstones and a welcome retreat from the hustle and bustle of Broadway.

WHERE TO EAT, DRINK...

Broadway Deli, 29 High Street. For those who are self-catering, treat yourself to a trip to this excellent deli with a passion for organic and ethically produced food. Great for picnics, late breakfasts and delish snacks to sustain you on your walk. 01386 853040 broadwaydeli.co.uk

Crown & Trumpet Inn, Church Street. A necessary pit stop as you enter Broadway from the Cotswold Way. Music Sa evenings. Monthly jazz and blues nights. B&B. 01386 853202 crownandtrumpet.co.uk

Market Pantry, 31 High Street. A cute café ideal for a late breakfast prior to walking the Cotswold Way. 01386 858318 marketpantry.co.uk

No 32 Broadway, 32 High Street. Primi or Pizza, and a menu for Vegetarians, too. A quiet corner of Italian style to assuage your hunger for antipasti, and a glass of Chianti. Open daily. 01386 306670

Russell's Fish & Chips. You can't get away from the fact that this staple diet has kept families in clover for years. It's a pretty little restaurant, too, and a wee bit classy. Open daily. russellsfishandchips.co.uk

The Horse and the Hounds, 54 High Street. Ideal stop off point for a drink at the end of a day walking. Dog friendly. B&B. 01386 852287

Tisanes, 21 The Green. A friendly tea room set in a C17 Cotswold stone building full of charm and overlooking the Village Green. Garden. Homemade cakes. 01386 853296 tisanes-tearooms.com

WHERE TO STAY...

Abbots Grange B&B, Church St. One of the Cotswolds most romantic and historic retreats. Step back into Medieval England with C21 comforts: 4-poster beds, log fires, Great Hall, croquet lawn, tennis court. Breakfast, no dinner. 020 8133 8698 abbotsgrange.com

Mill Hay House, Snowshill Road. Imposing Queen Anne house provides luxurious B&B on the outskirts of Broadway. No children U-12. No dogs. 01386 852498 millhay.co.uk

Olive Branch Guest House, 78 High Street. A B&B of long standing, and one that has traded for 50 + years. Convenient, comfortable with 2/3 day break deals. 01386 853440 theolivebranch-broadway.com

Russell's, 20 High Street. A popular North Cotswold destination; whether it be lunch, or dinner. So, feast on their food, then settle into one of their comfortable bed-rooms with all the latest mod cons. 01386 853555 russellsofbroadway.co.uk

St Eadburgh's Church

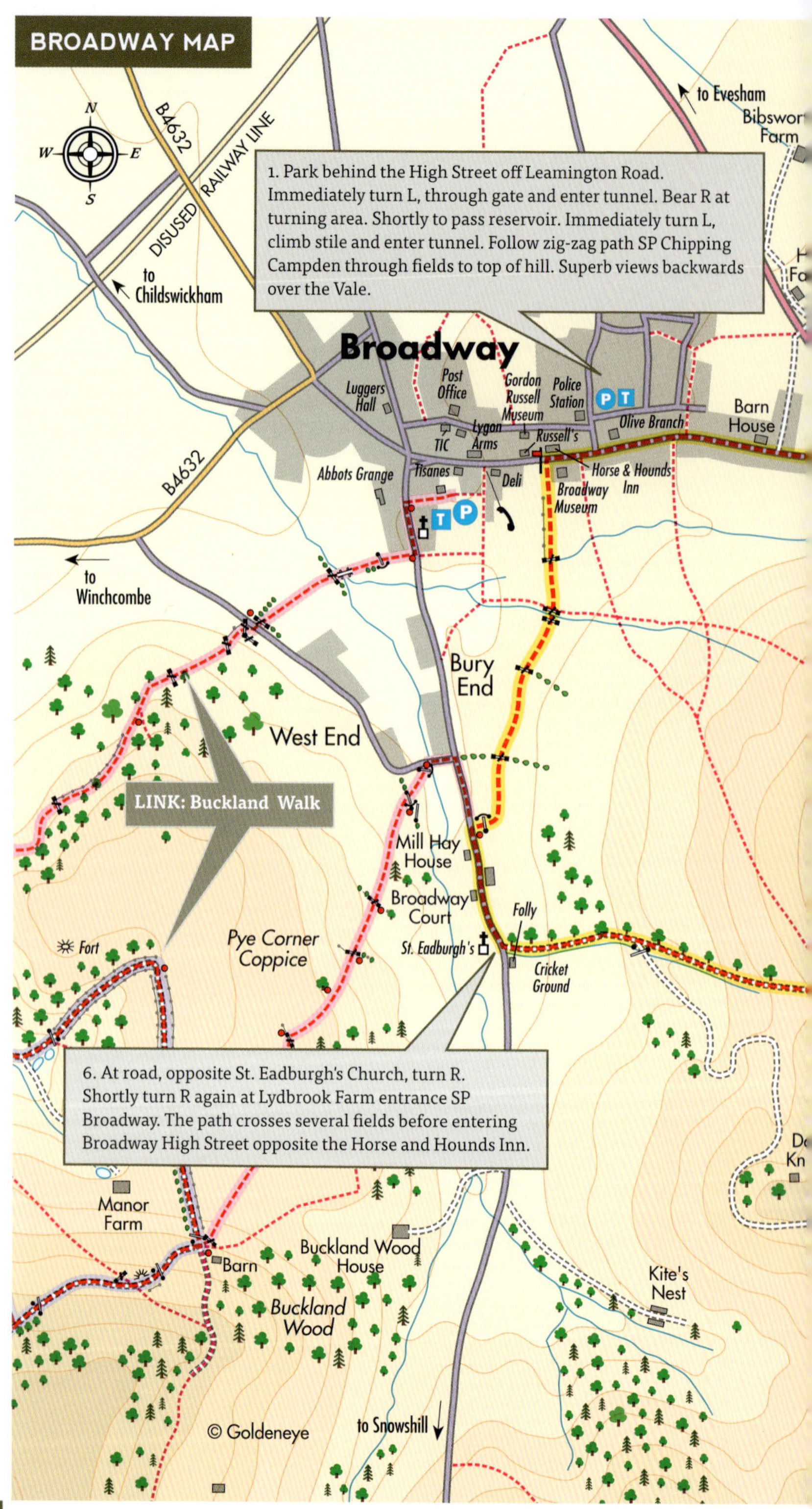

BROADWAY MAP

N
W E
S

B4632
DISUSED RAILWAY LINE

to Childswickham

to Evesham
Bibsworth Farm

1. Park behind the High Street off Leamington Road. Immediately turn L, through gate and enter tunnel. Bear R at turning area. Shortly to pass reservoir. Immediately turn L, climb stile and enter tunnel. Follow zig-zag path SP Chipping Campden through fields to top of hill. Superb views backwards over the Vale.

Broadway

Luggers Hall
Post Office
Gordon Russell Museum
Police Station
P T
Barn House
Lygon Arms
TIC
Russell's
Olive Branch
B4632
Abbots Grange
Tisanes
Deli
Broadway Museum
Horse & Hounds Inn
T P

to Winchcombe

Bury End

West End

LINK: Buckland Walk

Mill Hay House

Broadway Court

Folly

St. Eadburgh's

Cricket Ground

Fort

Pye Corner Coppice

6. At road, opposite St. Eadburgh's Church, turn R. Shortly turn R again at Lydbrook Farm entrance SP Broadway. The path crosses several fields before entering Broadway High Street opposite the Horse and Hounds Inn.

Manor Farm

Barn

Buckland Wood House

Buckland Wood

Kite's Nest

© Goldeneye

to Snowshill

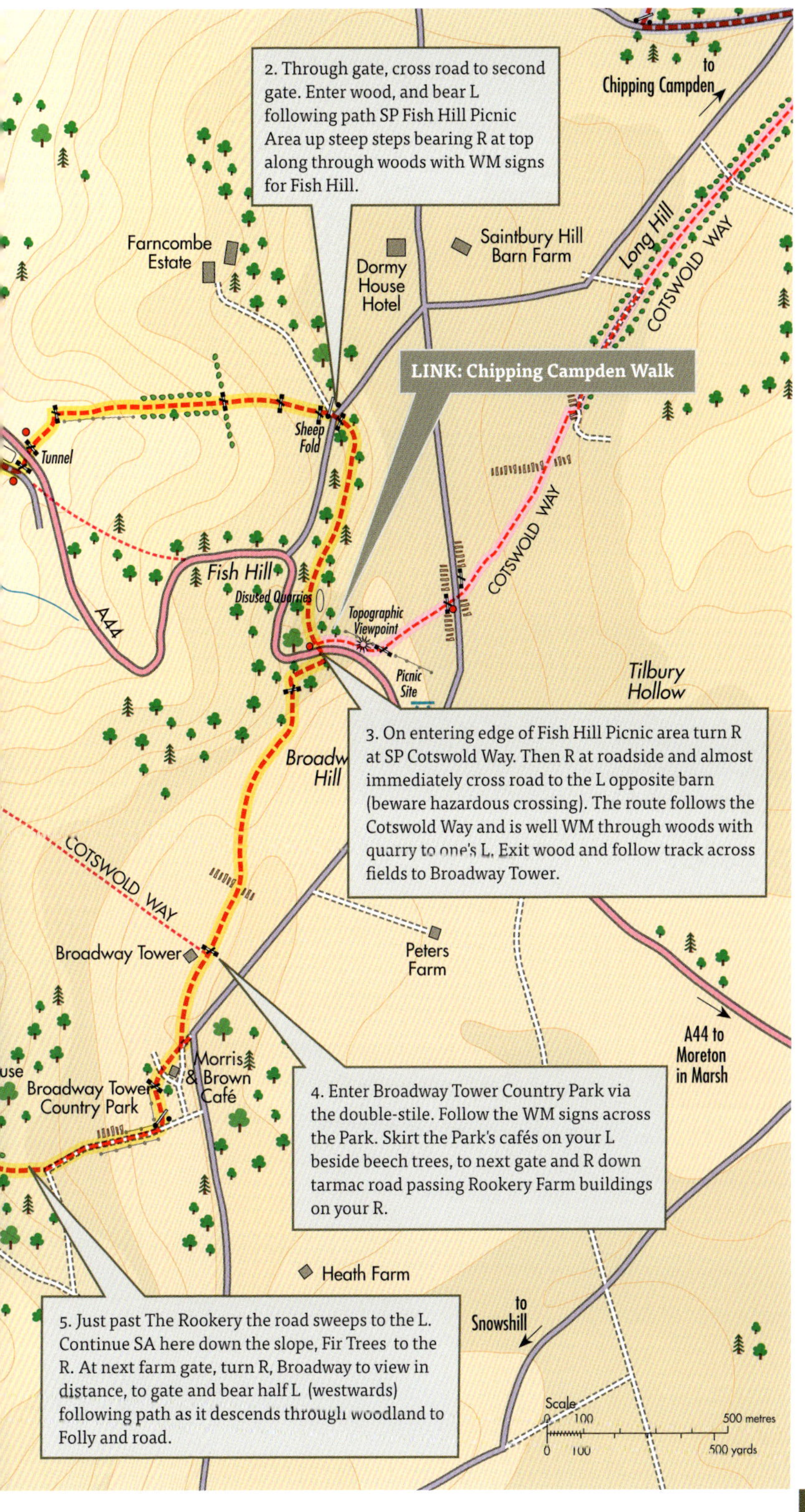

2. Through gate, cross road to second gate. Enter wood, and bear L following path SP Fish Hill Picnic Area up steep steps bearing R at top along through woods with WM signs for Fish Hill.

to Chipping Campden

Long Hill

COTSWOLD WAY

Farncombe Estate

Dormy House Hotel

Saintbury Hill Barn Farm

LINK: Chipping Campden Walk

Sheep Fold

Tunnel

COTSWOLD WAY

Fish Hill

Disused Quarries

A44

Topographic Viewpoint

Picnic Site

Tilbury Hollow

3. On entering edge of Fish Hill Picnic area turn R at SP Cotswold Way. Then R at roadside and almost immediately cross road to the L opposite barn (beware hazardous crossing). The route follows the Cotswold Way and is well WM through woods with quarry to one's L. Exit wood and follow track across fields to Broadway Tower.

Broadway Hill

COTSWOLD WAY

Broadway Tower

Peters Farm

A44 to Moreton in Marsh

use

Broadway Tower Country Park

Morris & Brown Café

4. Enter Broadway Tower Country Park via the double-stile. Follow the WM signs across the Park. Skirt the Park's cafés on your L beside beech trees, to next gate and R down tarmac road passing Rookery Farm buildings on your R.

Heath Farm

to Snowshill

5. Just past The Rookery the road sweeps to the L. Continue SA here down the slope, Fir Trees to the R. At next farm gate, turn R, Broadway to view in distance, to gate and bear half L (westwards) following path as it descends through woodland to Folly and road.

Scale
0   100   500 metres
0   100   500 yards

Buckland to Laverton is a short walk connecting two quiet villages via a steep climb up to and along, the Cotswold Way. The views make up for the steep climb and the descent to Laverton is easy-going. Broadway to Buckland is easy-going across fields and through pretty woodland. Climbing steeply up to the Cotswold Way with a gentle descent providing fine views to Broadway.

Distance
2.75 miles/4.4km.
Minimum Time
1.5 hours.
Grade/Level of Difficulty
Easy/Moderate.
Terrain/Paths
Farm track, rough path, grass.
Landscape
Undulating escarpment, sheep pastures.
Dogs
Lots of farm fields so dogs to be kept under control throughout. Beware livestock.

Public Toilets
Broadway.
Parking (P)
Beside church.
Recommended Start/Finish
Buckland Church.
Location
Buckland is 2 miles south of Broadway, just off the B4632.
Link to other walks in this Guide
Stanton to Stanway Walk. Circular route from edge of Laverton to Stanton via Cotswold Way and Shenberrow Farm.

Buckland Church

FEATURES OF INTEREST...

Buckland. A tranquil, linear village where time appears to have stood still. Noted for its Country House Hotel, stone cottages, stables, nursery and holiday cottage complex.

Buckland Rectory. The oldest and most complete rectory in the county. Notable Great Hall with timbered roof. Open occasionally for village events.

St Michael's Church, Buckland. An exquisite church preserved with an almost undisturbed history from the C13 to the C17. Beautiful roof, painted and wood panelled. C14 tower with gargoyles. C15 stained glass in East window restored by William Morris. Not to be missed, the wainscotting: medieval wooden benches along the far wall as you enter, the Hazel Bowl made in 1607 of Dutch maple with a silver rim, the Buckland Pall and C15 embroidered vestments from the V&A Museum, London. Sadly, the medieval frescoes were removed by the restorer FS Waller in 1885.

WHERE TO STAY...

Buckland Manor Hotel. The benchmark for the Country House Hotel, so if you seek quiet, understated luxury, and a haven of relaxation, none better. You will have to splash the cash starting from £200+ per night but it will be worth it for that special occasion, and after all, you will have the memories. There is a formal dress code for dinner - the exquisite cuisine deserves your respect. Open all year. Non-residents welcome for cream teas. 01386 852626 bucklandmanor.co.uk

Nearby **Broadway** has a wealth of tea rooms and inns for alternative dining and To Stay options.

Buckland Manor ss

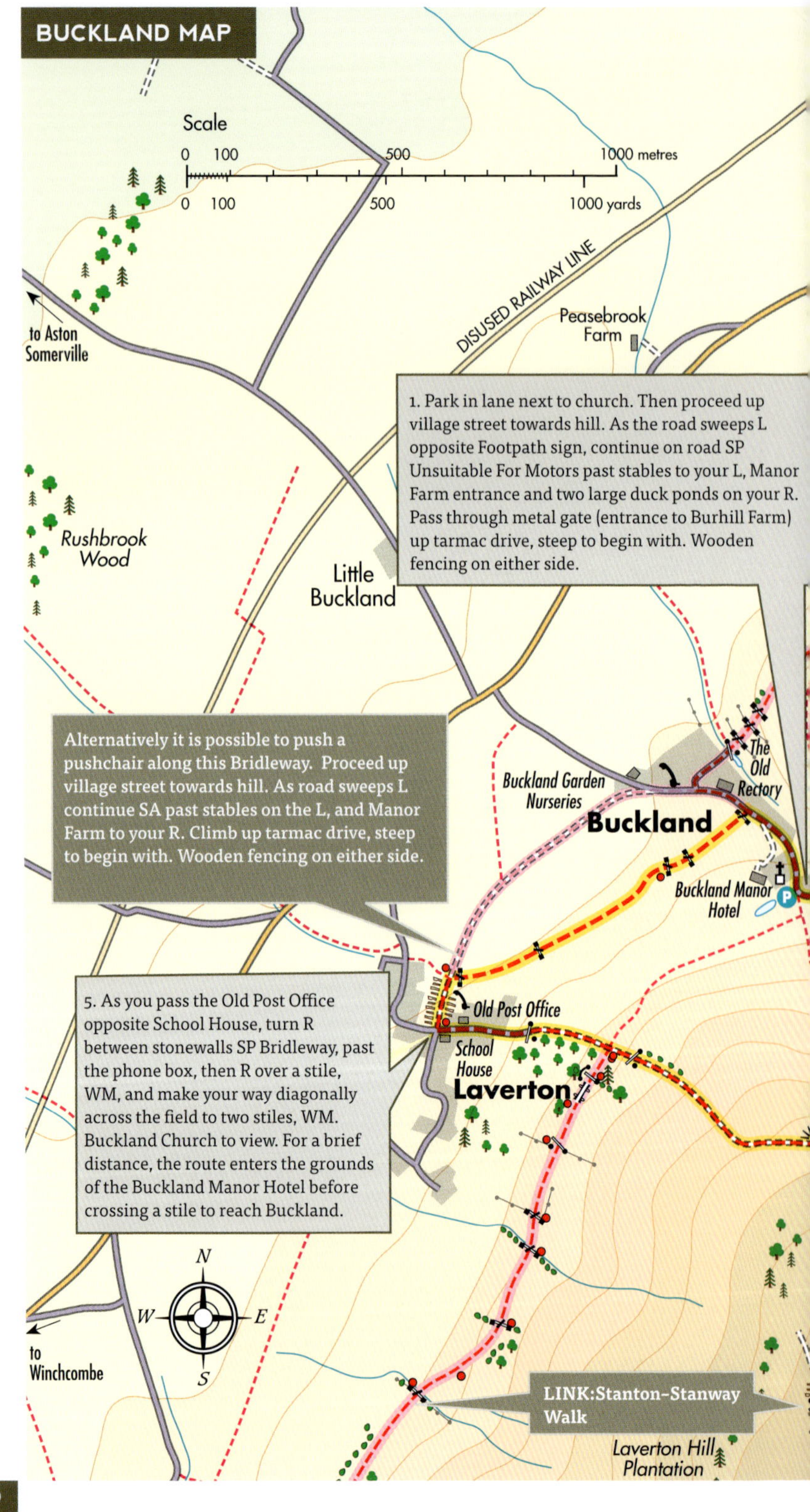

BUCKLAND MAP

Scale
0   100   500   1000 metres
0   100   500   1000 yards

to Aston
Somerville

DISUSED RAILWAY LINE

Peasebrook
Farm

Rushbrook
Wood

Little
Buckland

1. Park in lane next to church. Then proceed up village street towards hill. As the road sweeps L opposite Footpath sign, continue on road SP Unsuitable For Motors past stables to your L, Manor Farm entrance and two large duck ponds on your R. Pass through metal gate (entrance to Burhill Farm) up tarmac drive, steep to begin with. Wooden fencing on either side.

Alternatively it is possible to push a pushchair along this Bridleway. Proceed up village street towards hill. As road sweeps L continue SA past stables on the L, and Manor Farm to your R. Climb up tarmac drive, steep to begin with. Wooden fencing on either side.

Buckland Garden
Nurseries

The
Old
Rectory

Buckland

Buckland Manor
Hotel

5. As you pass the Old Post Office opposite School House, turn R between stonewalls SP Bridleway, past the phone box, then R over a stile, WM, and make your way diagonally across the field to two stiles, WM. Buckland Church to view. For a brief distance, the route enters the grounds of the Buckland Manor Hotel before crossing a stile to reach Buckland.

Old Post Office

School
House
Laverton

N
W   E
S

to
Winchcombe

LINK:Stanton–Stanway
Walk

Laverton Hill
Plantation

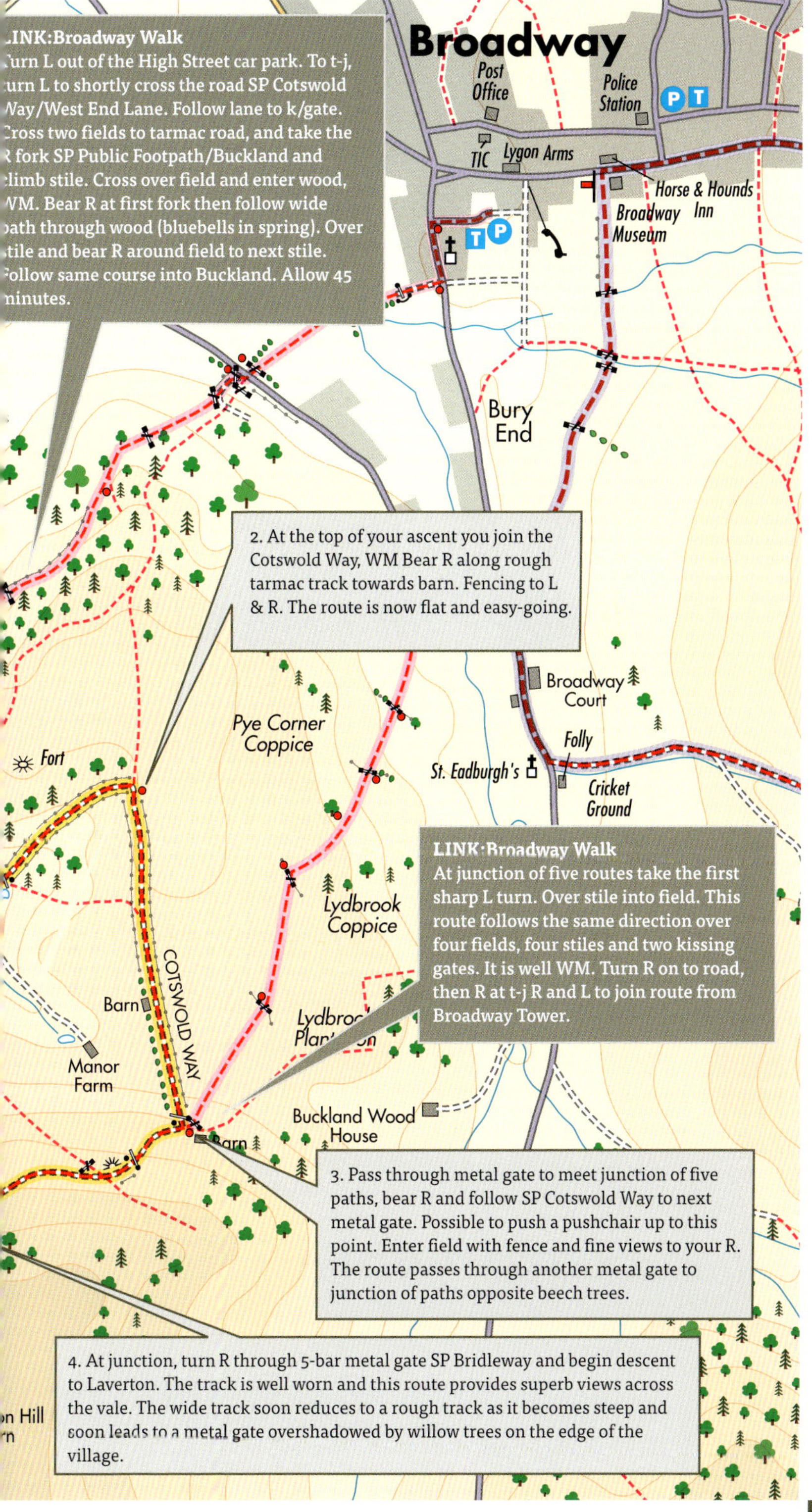

LINK:Broadway Walk
Turn L out of the High Street car park. To t-j, turn L to shortly cross the road SP Cotswold Way/West End Lane. Follow lane to k/gate. Cross two fields to tarmac road, and take the R fork SP Public Footpath/Buckland and climb stile. Cross over field and enter wood, WM. Bear R at first fork then follow wide path through wood (bluebells in spring). Over stile and bear R around field to next stile. Follow same course into Buckland. Allow 45 minutes.

Broadway
Post Office
Police Station
TIC
Lygon Arms
Horse & Hounds Inn
Broadway Museum
Bury End

2. At the top of your ascent you join the Cotswold Way, WM Bear R along rough tarmac track towards barn. Fencing to L & R. The route is now flat and easy-going.

Broadway Court
Folly
St. Eadburgh's
Cricket Ground
Pye Corner Coppice
Fort
Lydbrook Coppice

LINK:Broadway Walk
At junction of five routes take the first sharp L turn. Over stile into field. This route follows the same direction over four fields, four stiles and two kissing gates. It is well WM. Turn R on to road, then R at t-j R and L to join route from Broadway Tower.

COTSWOLD WAY
Barn
Manor Farm
Lydbrook Plantation
Buckland Wood House
Barn

3. Pass through metal gate to meet junction of five paths, bear R and follow SP Cotswold Way to next metal gate. Possible to push a pushchair up to this point. Enter field with fence and fine views to your R. The route passes through another metal gate to junction of paths opposite beech trees.

4. At junction, turn R through 5-bar metal gate SP Bridleway and begin descent to Laverton. The track is well worn and this route provides superb views across the vale. The wide track soon reduces to a rough track as it becomes steep and soon leads to a metal gate overshadowed by willow trees on the edge of the village.

n Hill
n

The Stanton to Stanway route at first follows the Cotswold Way with a steady climb up to Shenberrow Hill. Thereafter, the route descends through pretty woodland passing by Estate workers' cottages and an orchard, then from Stanway through beautiful parkland and arable fields. The Stanton to Laverton route travels north through open fields to join the Buckland to Laverton Walk returning via the Cotswold Way and Shenberrow Hill with a link to Snowshill at Shenberrow.

Distance
Walk 1: 4.5 miles/7.2 km. Walk 2: 3 miles.

Minimum Time
Walk 1: 3 hours. Walk 2: 2 hours.

Grade/Level of Difficulty
Moderate.

Terrain/Paths
Stone paths, woodland, grassy turf.

Landscape
Rolling escarpment, woodland, domestic architecture.

Dogs
Large section of woodland where dogs can run free. Keep under control around livestock. Popular with local dog walkers.

Public Toilets
None.

Parking (P)
Stanton P.

Recommended Start/Finish
Stanton P. or Stanway.

Location
Situated between Winchcombe and Broadway just off the B4632.

Link to other walks in this Guide
Buckland to Laverton & Snowshill Walks.

 Lidcombe Wood

FEATURES OF INTEREST...

Shenberrow Hill fort. Iron Age settlement inhabited around 2,000 BC. Superb viewpoint at 280 ft.

Snowshill. This charming and unspoilt hilltop village is a short distance by car from Broadway. There's a striking church, a pub and a row of much photographed cottages opposite Snowshill Manor.

Snowshill Manor (NT). A Cotswold manor house containing Charles Paget Wade's extraordinary collection of craftsmanship and design amounting to some 22,000 items from toys to musical instruments, Samurai armour to clocks and bicycles. Open daily mid-Mar to 30 Oct 11-5.30. House from 11. 01386 852410 nationaltrust.org.uk

Stanton. Charming village with houses of warm honey-coloured stone. Restored by Sir Philip Scott, 1903-37. Centre for equine excellence in the Vine, a popular horse riding centre.

Stanway. Estate village owned by the Earl of Wemyss and March and dominated by Stanway House in the grounds of which stand one of the country's finest tithe barns. The C17 gatehouse is exceptional, and behind the church, across the road is the thatched cricket pavilion set on staddle stones. The little Church of St Peter has C14 origins.

Stanway House & Water Garden. This exquisite Jacobean Manor House and Gatehouse is built from the local stone known as Guiting Yellow which lights up when the sun touches it. All is set within an enchanting and ancient park designed by a numerologist. The partially restored C18 Cascade and Canal was designed by the highly respected Charles Bridgman. Open as locally advertised. Dogs on lead. 01386 584469 stanwayfountain.co.uk

St Michael's Church, Stanton. Impressive Perpendicular tower. Much is C12 -15 with wall paintings, Jacobean pulpit, but its fame was associated with the many visits of John Wesley, the Methodist preacher.

WHERE TO EAT AND DRINK...

Mount Inn, Stanton. Situated on a rise at the edge of Stanton the Inn's unique position provides the most spectacular panoramic views across the Vale of Evesham towards the Malvern Hills & even the Black Welsh mountains beyond. On a summer's evening it is the most perfect spot to watch the sunset & enjoy a pint of Donnington Brewery's traditional ale. Used to walkers and their dogs, the Inn serves a range of excellent food to suit all levels of hunger. Now considered to be one of the Cotswold's culinary high spots. 01386 584316 themountinn.co.uk

Snowshill Arms, Snowshill. Traditional, unpretentious Cotswold pub with old settles and a large garden. Not your gastro-pub, more your ploughman's lunch, Sunday Roasts and Donnington Ales. Children and dog friendly. 01386 852653 snowshillarms.co.uk

WHERE TO STAY...

The Vine, Stanton. B&B designed for horse lovers. Riding lessons for all levels available. The owner's popular pub rides include an hour's lunch stop at a traditional pub. Has had mixed reviews! 01386 584250 cotswoldsriding.co.uk

The Gatehouse, Stanway

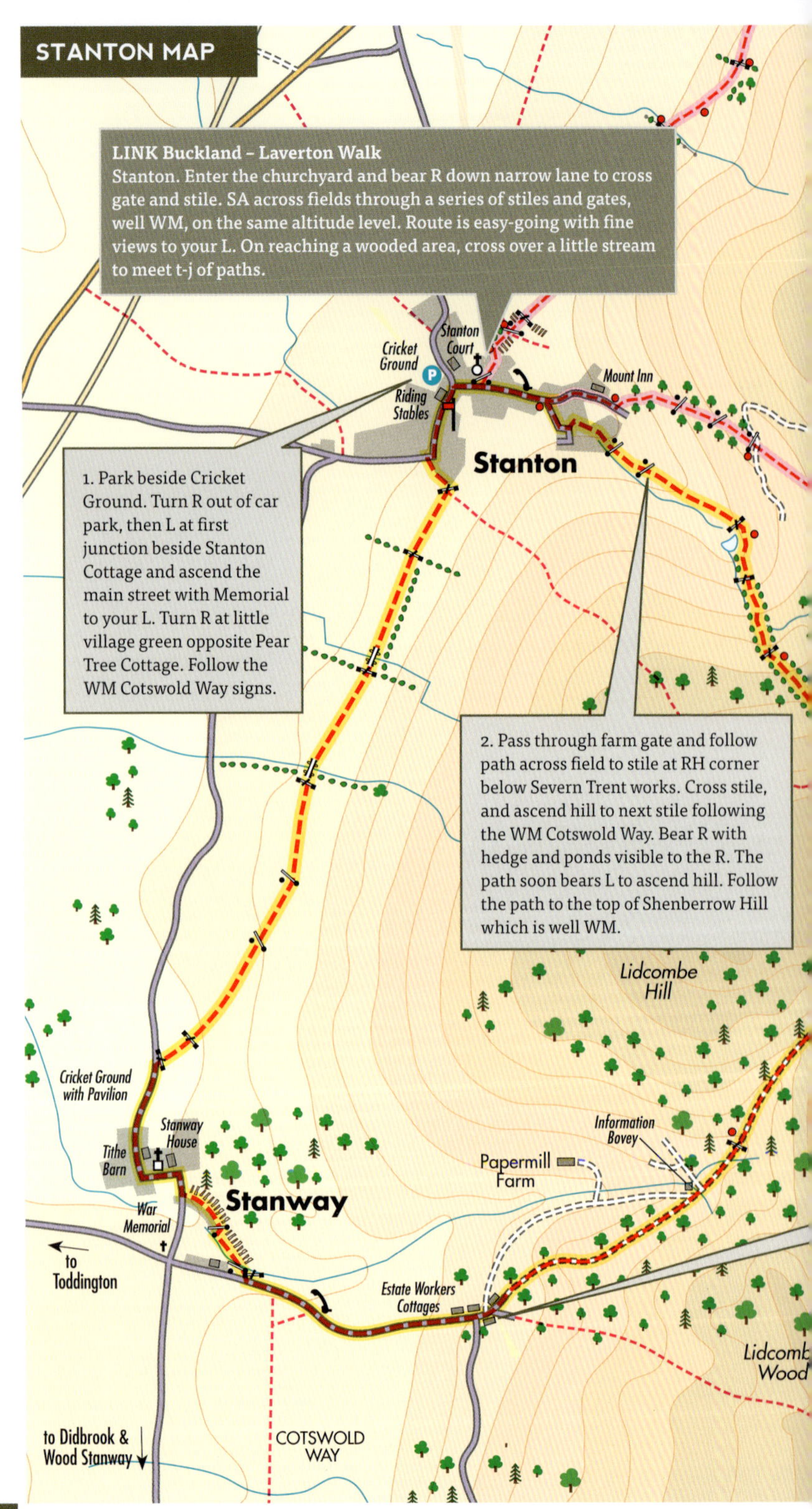

LINK Buckland – Laverton Walk
Stanton. Enter the churchyard and bear R down narrow lane to cross gate and stile. SA across fields through a series of stiles and gates, well WM, on the same altitude level. Route is easy-going with fine views to your L. On reaching a wooded area, cross over a little stream to meet t-j of paths.

1. Park beside Cricket Ground. Turn R out of car park, then L at first junction beside Stanton Cottage and ascend the main street with Memorial to your L. Turn R at little village green opposite Pear Tree Cottage. Follow the WM Cotswold Way signs.

2. Pass through farm gate and follow path across field to stile at RH corner below Severn Trent works. Cross stile, and ascend hill to next stile following the WM Cotswold Way. Bear R with hedge and ponds visible to the R. The path soon bears L to ascend hill. Follow the path to the top of Shenberrow Hill which is well WM.

Cricket Ground
Stanton Court
Mount Inn
Riding Stables
Stanton

Cricket Ground with Pavilion
Stanway House
Tithe Barn
War Memorial
Stanway
to Toddington

Lidcombe Hill
Information Bovey
Papermill Farm
Estate Workers Cottages
Lidcomb Wood

to Didbrook & Wood Stanway
COTSWOLD WAY

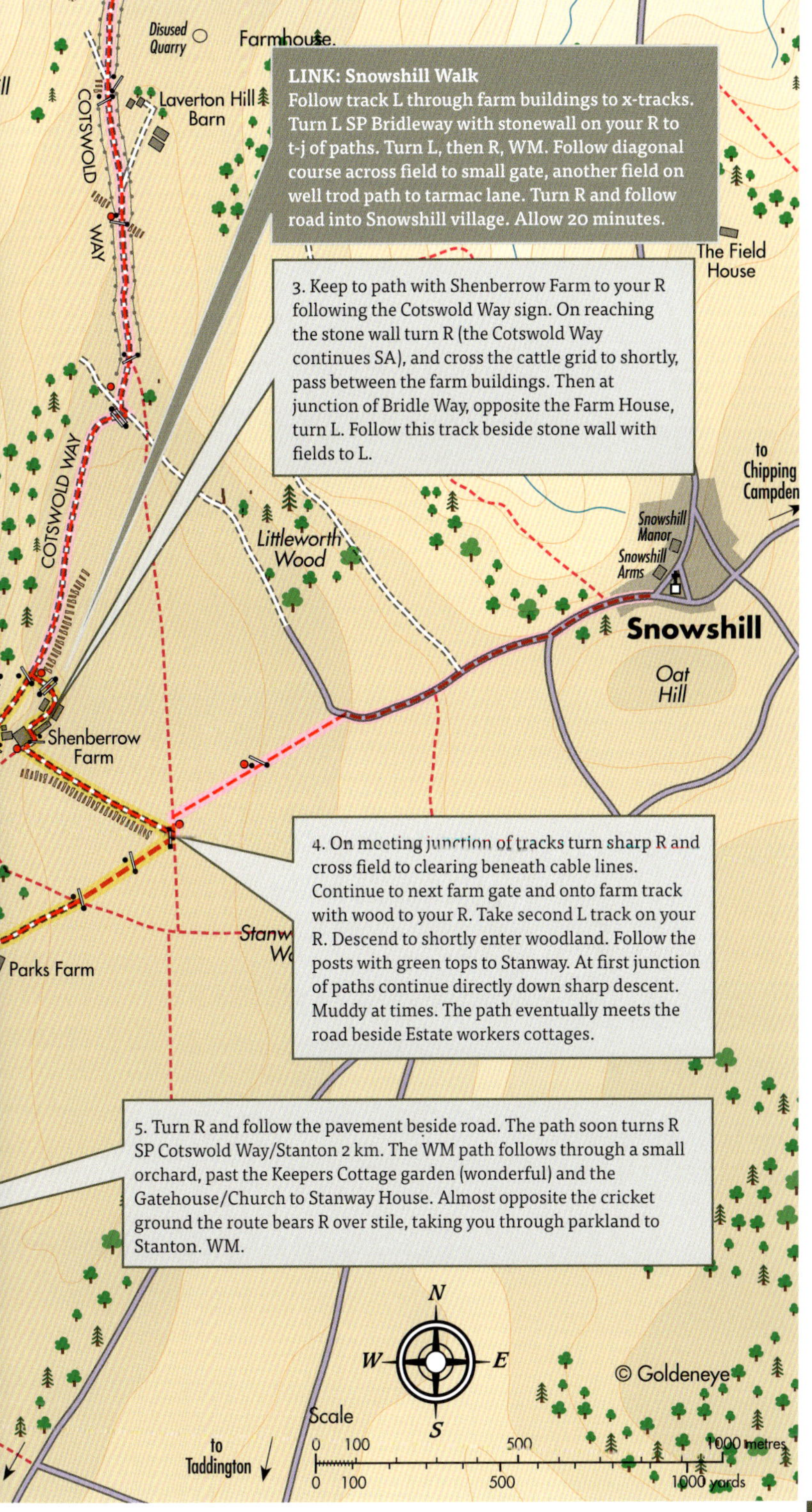

LINK: Snowshill Walk
Follow track L through farm buildings to x-tracks. Turn L SP Bridleway with stonewall on your R to t-j of paths. Turn L, then R, WM. Follow diagonal course across field to small gate, another field on well trod path to tarmac lane. Turn R and follow road into Snowshill village. Allow 20 minutes.

3. Keep to path with Shenberrow Farm to your R following the Cotswold Way sign. On reaching the stone wall turn R (the Cotswold Way continues SA), and cross the cattle grid to shortly, pass between the farm buildings. Then at junction of Bridle Way, opposite the Farm House, turn L. Follow this track beside stone wall with fields to L.

4. On meeting junction of tracks turn sharp R and cross field to clearing beneath cable lines. Continue to next farm gate and onto farm track with wood to your R. Take second L track on your R. Descend to shortly enter woodland. Follow the posts with green tops to Stanway. At first junction of paths continue directly down sharp descent. Muddy at times. The path eventually meets the road beside Estate workers cottages.

5. Turn R and follow the pavement beside road. The path soon turns R SP Cotswold Way/Stanton 2 km. The WM path follows through a small orchard, past the Keepers Cottage garden (wonderful) and the Gatehouse/Church to Stanway House. Almost opposite the cricket ground the route bears R over stile, taking you through parkland to Stanton. WM.

A circumnavigation of Bredon Hill is a fine introduction to the beautiful villages of Kemerton, Overbury, Conderton, Ashton-under-Hill and Elmley Castle. The villages are scattered with a lovely mixture of Cotswold stone and black-and-white timbered buildings with many fine inns and peaceful churchyards. Various footpaths lead up to the summit from Elmley and Kemerton. Superb views from this isolated limestone hill at 961 ft. This walk features a fairly lengthy ascent through fields and pretty woodland to the top of Bredon Hill. But the climb is rewarded with superb views of the Welsh and Malvern Hills, the River Severn and Avon, and the Cotswolds. Listen for the singing of the Skylark. The walk is best undertaken on a clear day to benefit from the views.

A shorter pushchair walk is possible through Overbury Park, up to the Plateau of the hill (park in Overbury village). This is not a circular walk but the outward journey does provide different views to the homeward one.

Distance
Overbury walk: 3.25 miles/5.2km,
Elmley Castle walk: 5.5 miles/8.8km.
Minimum Time
Elmley Castle walk: 3.5 hours.
Grade/Level of Difficulty
Easy/Moderate.
Terrain/Paths
Grass, woodland, tracks, roads.
Landscape
Fields and woodland.
Dogs
To be kept under control at all times.
Beware livestock.

Public Toilets
None.
Parking (P)
Outside St Mary's Church, Elmley Castle.
Recommended Start/Finish
Elmley Castle.
Location
Elmley Castle/Bredon Hill is located north of Tewksbury and can be accessed via the A46, A44 and B4080.

FEATURES OF INTEREST...

Banbury Stone. Associated with legends, witchcraft and superstitions.

Bredon Hill & surrounding villages. Immortalised by John Moore's Brensham Trilogy and by Houseman's poem 'See the Coloured Counties and Hear the Larks so High'. The hill and villages are detached from the Cotswold range but share characteristics of the Cotswolds and Middle England; stone and half-timbered buildings. These villages are well kept and proud of their churchyards, country pubs and tended cottage gardens.

Bredon Hill Fort. Iron Age fort with two ramparts. Scene of great battle at the time of Christ, possibly against the Belgic invaders. The hacked remains of 50 men were found near the entrance. Superb views over to Wales, Vale of Evesham, the rivers Severn and Avon, and to the Cotswolds.

Conderton Pottery, The Old Forge. Distinctive salt-glaze stoneware pots by specialist country potter, Toff Milway. Open M-Sa 9-5. 01386 725387 toffmilway.co.uk

Elmley Castle. Village named after the C11 site on Castle Hill. Elmley means 'Elm tree by the field'. A pretty village green. Refurbished The Queens Inn.

Elmley Castle Ruins. Castle Hill, built in late C11, and refortified in C14. Little remains today.

Overbury. One of Worcestershire's most attractive villages. A mix of Cotswold stone and half-timbered houses - Stuart and Georgian. C18 Overbury Court.

Parson's Folly. Inside fort, short tower, late C18.

St Mary's Church, Elmley. Saxon and mix of the C12, C13 and C14. C17 monument of Savage Family inside. Superb sundial.

WHERE TO EAT & DRINK...

The Queen Elizabeth Inn, Elmley Castle. C16 (community run) Inn serving breakfast, lunch and dinner; pub-grub and local ales. 01386 710251 elmleycastle.com Within is the The Polka Dot Tearoom, serving cup cakes, teas and coffees.

The Star Inn, Ashton-under-Hill. Perfect rest stop for walkers. Children and dogs welcome. Large garden. Delicious home-cooked food to eat in or takeaway. 01386 881325 thestar-ashtonunderhill.co.uk

Yew Tree Inn, Conderton. One of the most popular local pubs around Bredon Hill. Conveniently situated for pre- or post-walk drinks. Basic pub grub. 01386 725364 yewtreepub.com

WHERE TO STAY JUST OFF THE MAP...

Lower End House B&B, Manor Road, Eckington. Believed to be one of the oldest houses in Worcestershire. A 12th Century period house full of character, renovated with the emphasis on quality and style. Perfectly located for walking the nearby Bredon or Malvern Hills. Garden Bar and Restaurant open for lunch, afternoon teas and dinner. Self-catering, too. Cookery School. 01386 751600 eckingtonmanor.co.uk

Meadows Home Farm, Bredons Norton. Family run working farm in a quiet setting. One ensuite double bedroom and one ensuite room with a double and a single bed. Garden and patio area, TV lounge, ample parking. Farm shop and cottage to rent. 01684 772322 meadowshomefarm.co.uk

Below Bredon Hill

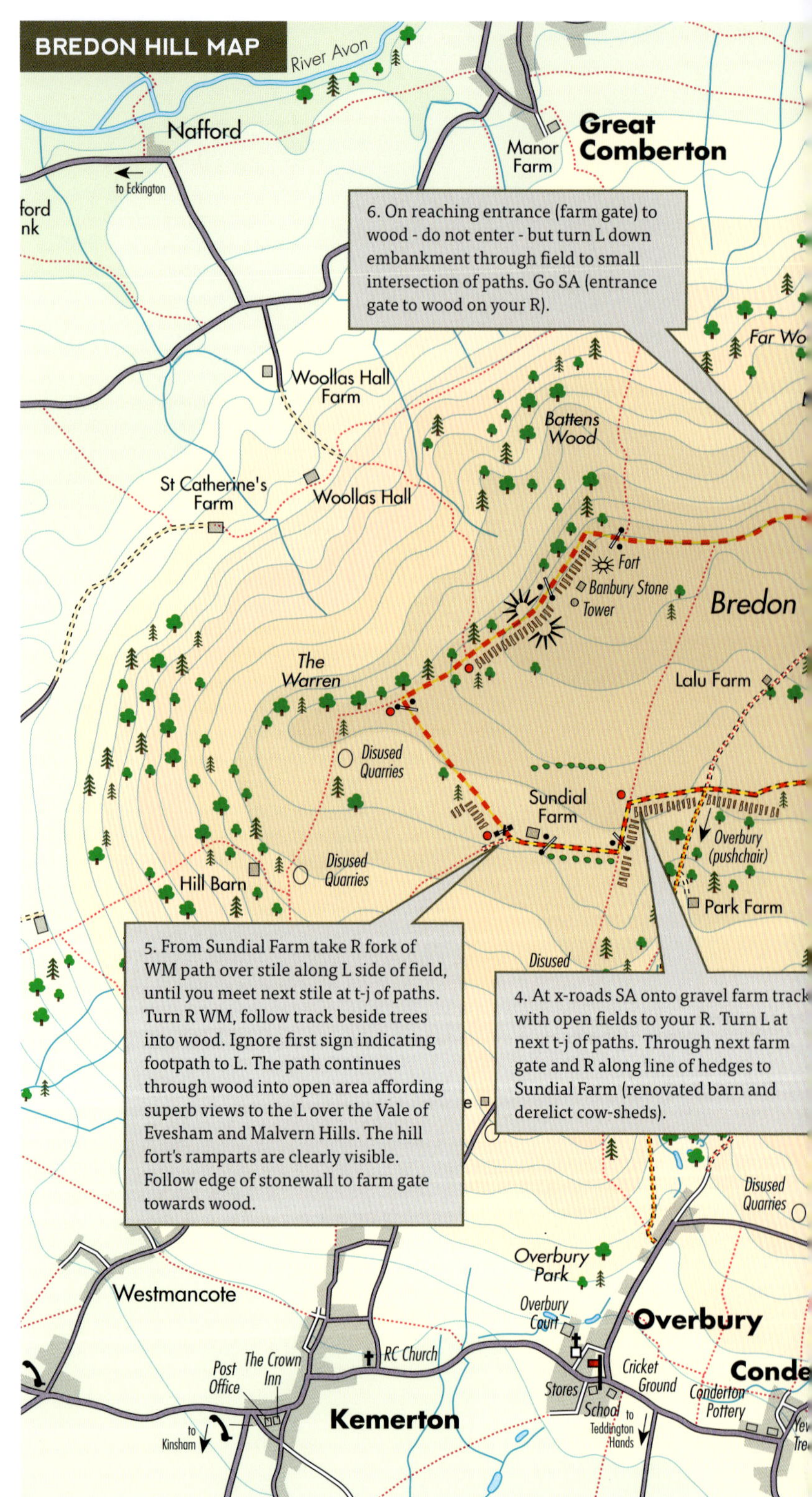

6. On reaching entrance (farm gate) to wood - do not enter - but turn L down embankment through field to small intersection of paths. Go SA (entrance gate to wood on your R).

5. From Sundial Farm take R fork of WM path over stile along L side of field, until you meet next stile at t-j of paths. Turn R WM, follow track beside trees into wood. Ignore first sign indicating footpath to L. The path continues through wood into open area affording superb views to the L over the Vale of Evesham and Malvern Hills. The hill fort's ramparts are clearly visible. Follow edge of stonewall to farm gate towards wood.

4. At x-roads SA onto gravel farm track with open fields to your R. Turn L at next t-j of paths. Through next farm gate and R along line of hedges to Sundial Farm (renovated barn and derelict cow-sheds).

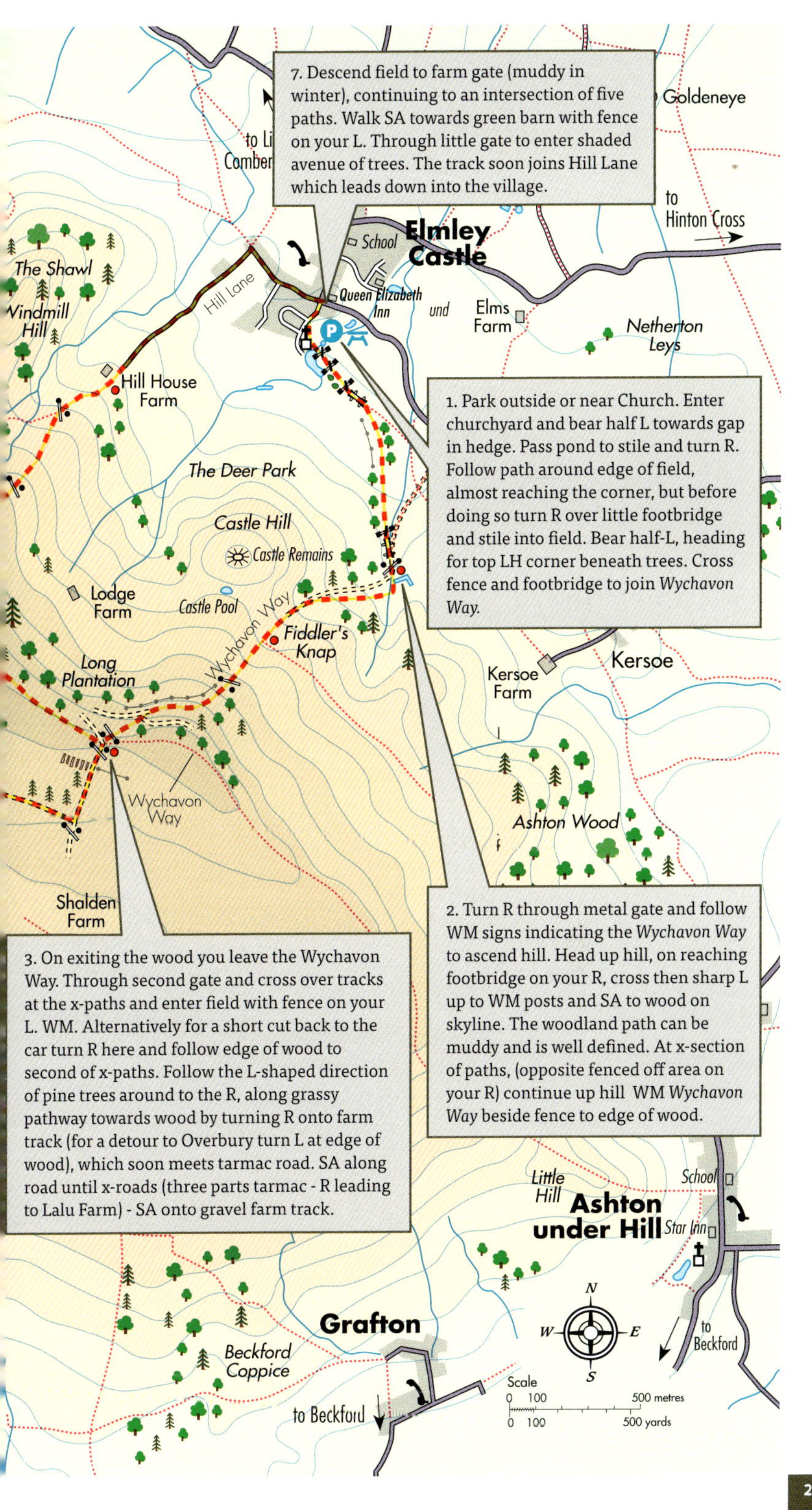

7. Descend field to farm gate (muddy in winter), continuing to an intersection of five paths. Walk SA towards green barn with fence on your L. Through little gate to enter shaded avenue of trees. The track soon joins Hill Lane which leads down into the village.

The Shawl
Windmill Hill
Hill Lane
Hill House Farm
The Deer Park
Castle Hill
Castle Remains
Lodge Farm
Castle Pool
Wychavon Way
Fiddler's Knap
Long Plantation
Wychavon Way
Shalden Farm

to Li
Comber
School
Elmley Castle
Queen Elizabeth Inn
und
Elms Farm
Goldeneye
to Hinton Cross
Netherton Leys
Kersoe Farm
Kersoe
Ashton Wood
Little Hill
Ashton under Hill
Star Inn
School
to Beckford
Grafton
Beckford Coppice
to Beckford

1. Park outside or near Church. Enter churchyard and bear half L towards gap in hedge. Pass pond to stile and turn R. Follow path around edge of field, almost reaching the corner, but before doing so turn R over little footbridge and stile into field. Bear half-L, heading for top LH corner beneath trees. Cross fence and footbridge to join Wychavon Way.

2. Turn R through metal gate and follow WM signs indicating the Wychavon Way to ascend hill. Head up hill, on reaching footbridge on your R, cross then sharp L up to WM posts and SA to wood on skyline. The woodland path can be muddy and is well defined. At x-section of paths, (opposite fenced off area on your R) continue up hill WM Wychavon Way beside fence to edge of wood.

3. On exiting the wood you leave the Wychavon Way. Through second gate and cross over tracks at the x-paths and enter field with fence on your L. WM. Alternatively for a short cut back to the car turn R here and follow edge of wood to second of x-paths. Follow the L-shaped direction of pine trees around to the R, along grassy pathway towards wood by turning R onto farm track (for a detour to Overbury turn L at edge of wood), which soon meets tarmac road. SA along road until x-roads (three parts tarmac - R leading to Lalu Farm) - SA onto gravel farm track.

N
W   E
S
Scale
0   100   500 metres
0   100   500 yards

It is worth a wander around the historic village of Winchcombe before the climb up Salters Hill. At first this is a fairly energetic ascent. Thereafter, the route is comparatively easy. The views north towards the Vale of Evesham are a delight. And as you cross the Salt Way and bear down on Parks Farm (now part of the overbearing Farmcote Estate) the views towards Cleeve Common and left up the valley are magnificent. Return to Winchcombe through the parkland of Sudeley Castle.

Distance
7 miles/10km.

Minimum Time
3 hours.

Grade/Level of Difficulty
Moderate.

Terrain/Paths
Stone paths, farm tracks, grass.

Landscape
Patchwork of arable fields, sheep pastures, rolling hills, woodland.

Dogs
Quite a lot of farm tracks through sheep pastures. Keep under control at all times.

Public Toilets
Winchcombe High Street.

Parking
Gloucester Street opposite Church, or in Long Stay beside County Library.

Recommended Start/Finish
Winchcombe High Street.

Location
Midway between Cheltenham and Broadway on the B4632.

**Link to other walks
in this Guide**
Cleeve Hill Walk via The Cotswold Way. To Guiting Power from Deadmanbury Gate.

 Sudeley Castle, Winchcombe

FEATURES OF INTEREST...

Folk & Police Museum, Town Hall. History of the town, police and weapons. TIC. Open East/Apr-Oct M-Sa 10-1, 2-4.30. 01242 609151

Salt Way. This prehistoric track runs east of Winchcombe from Hailes, south towards Hawling along Sudeley Hill. It was used in medieval times to carry salt from Droitwich and coastal salt towns, salt being the essential meat preservative.

St Peter's Church. One of the great 'Wool' churches. It is of a C15 Perpendicular design but is strangely plain, yet dignified. Not as elaborate as some of the other 'Wool' churches. For example, it has no Chancel Arch. The gargoyles are the one notable feature, and a circumnavigation of the exterior is advised. The weathercock is the county's finest.

Sudeley Castle. A Tudor house and the original home of the Seymour family. Katherine Parr, widow of Henry VIII, lived here and lies buried in the chapel. There is a fine collection of needlework, furniture and tapestries plus paintings by Van Dyck, Rubens and Turner. All surrounded by award-winning gardens and open parkland. The Castle is open daily mid-Mar to 31 Oct 10.30-5. 01242 602308 sudeleycastle.co.uk

Winchcombe. This small Cotswold town lies cradled in the Isbourne Valley. It was an ancient Saxon burh (small holding) and famous medieval centre visited from far and wide for the market, horse fair and monastery which was destroyed in the C16. You can still walk the narrow streets beside the C16 and C18 cottages, but do look up and admire the many fine gables above the shop fronts. There's a local saying: Were you born in Winchcombe? This is directed at those of us who leave doors open as it can be a wee bit drafty.

WHERE TO EAT, DRINK & STAY...

William's of Winchcombe, 12 North Street. A deli and coffee shop serving quiches, cheeses, pates, pastries and cold meats. Open daily. 01242 604466

5 North Street Street. Set in a low-beamed, quaint C17 building, this is a small and well-run restaurant which provides a relaxed and friendly atmosphere and has gained a healthy respect from fellow restaurateurs in the Cotswolds. 01242 604566 5northstreetrestaurant.co.uk

The Lion Inn, 33 North Street. A traditional hostelry that's retained many original features; stone walls, open fires...coupled with real ales, comfy chairs, and if you desire, bedrooms with all the mod cons. A fine Inn, that won't disappoint you. 01242 603300 butcombe.com/the-lioninn

North Farmcote. A working family farm producing sheep and cereals situated high on the Cotswold escarpment. Built around 1840 as a dower house for Lord Sudeley's mother, the house is surrounded by a large garden where guests can have afternoon tea. Visit their specialist herb garden (open mid-Apr to mid-Sept F-Su & BHs 10-5). 01242 602304 northfarmcote.co.uk

Sudeley Hill Farm. Comfortable C15 listed farmhouse with panoramic views over a working sheep and arable farm of 800 acres. Three en-suite bedrooms. 01242 602344 cotswoldfarmstay. co.uk/sudeley-hill-farm

Wesley House, High Street. Deserved reputation for excellent food. Locals travel miles to this gastronomic oasis and wine. Now, Five bedrooms. 01242 602366 wesleyhouse.co.uk

White Hart, High Street. Variously viewed as a hostelry, the White Hart offers food and a bed for this C16 inn has eight en-suite bedrooms and a bar plus restaurant. 01242 602359 whitehartwinchcombe.co.uk

Winchcombe Gargoyle

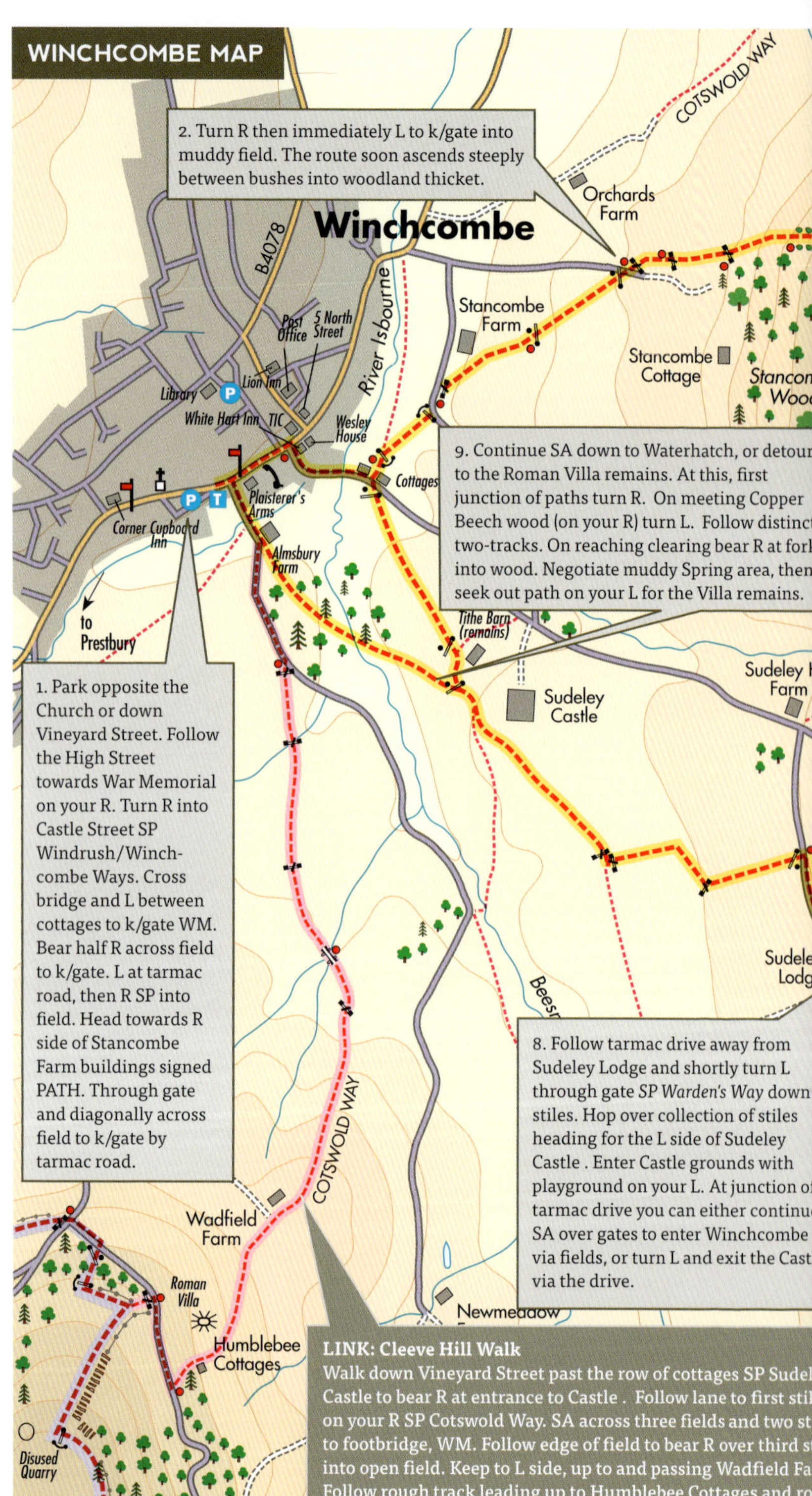
Winchcombe
COTSWOLD WAY
Orchards Farm
B4078
Post Office
5 North Street
Stancombe Farm
Stancombe Cottage
Stancombe Wood
River Isbourne
Library
Lion Inn
White Hart Inn
TIC
Wesley House
P
Corner Cupboard Inn
Plaisterer's Arms
Cottages
Almsbury Farm
Tithe Barn (remains)
Sudeley Castle
Sudeley Farm
to Prestbury
P T
Beesmoor
COTSWOLD WAY
Wadfield Farm
Sudeley Lodge
Roman Villa
Humblebee Cottages
Newmeadow
Disused Quarry
2. Turn R then immediately L to k/gate into muddy field. The route soon ascends steeply between bushes into woodland thicket.
9. Continue SA down to Waterhatch, or detour to the Roman Villa remains. At this, first junction of paths turn R. On meeting Copper Beech wood (on your R) turn L. Follow distinct two-tracks. On reaching clearing bear R at fork into wood. Negotiate muddy Spring area, then seek out path on your L for the Villa remains.
1. Park opposite the Church or down Vineyard Street. Follow the High Street towards War Memorial on your R. Turn R into Castle Street SP Windrush/Winchcombe Ways. Cross bridge and L between cottages to k/gate WM. Bear half R across field to k/gate. L at tarmac road, then R SP into field. Head towards R side of Stancombe Farm buildings signed PATH. Through gate and diagonally across field to k/gate by tarmac road.
8. Follow tarmac drive away from Sudeley Lodge and shortly turn L through gate SP Warden's Way down stiles. Hop over collection of stiles heading for the L side of Sudeley Castle . Enter Castle grounds with playground on your L. At junction of tarmac drive you can either continue SA over gates to enter Winchcombe via fields, or turn L and exit the Castle via the drive.
LINK: Cleeve Hill Walk
Walk down Vineyard Street past the row of cottages SP Sudeley Castle to bear R at entrance to Castle . Follow lane to first stile on your R SP Cotswold Way. SA across three fields and two stiles to footbridge, WM. Follow edge of field to bear R over third stile into open field. Keep to L side, up to and passing Wadfield Farm. Follow rough track leading up to Humblebee Cottages and road.

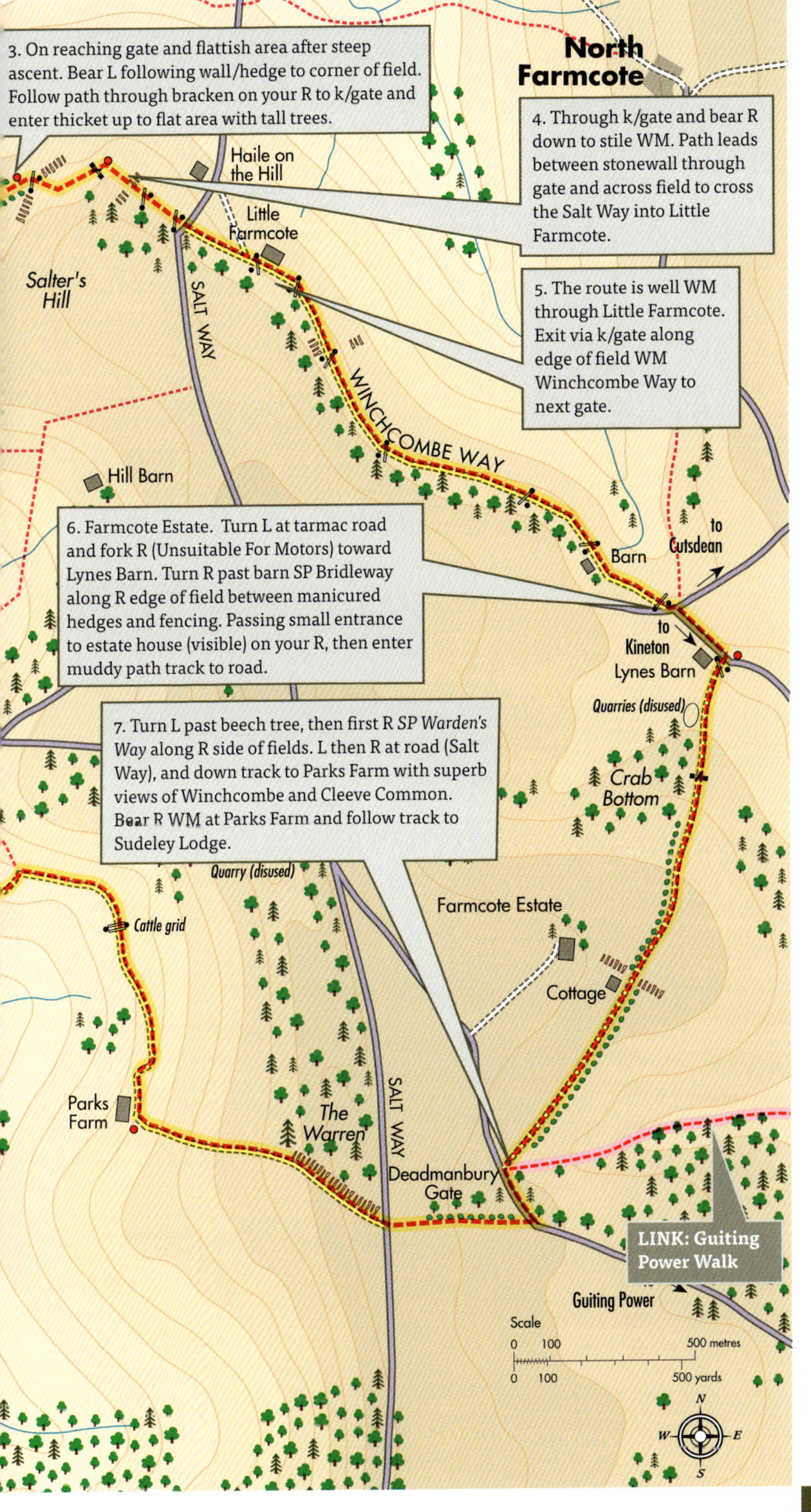

3. On reaching gate and flattish area after steep ascent. Bear L following wall/hedge to corner of field. Follow path through bracken on your R to k/gate and enter thicket up to flat area with tall trees.

North Farmcote

4. Through k/gate and bear R down to stile WM. Path leads between stonewall through gate and across field to cross the Salt Way into Little Farmcote.

5. The route is well WM through Little Farmcote. Exit via k/gate along edge of field WM Winchcombe Way to next gate.

Haile on the Hill

Little Farmcote

Salter's Hill

SALT WAY

WINCHCOMBE WAY

Hill Barn

6. Farmcote Estate. Turn L at tarmac road and fork R (Unsuitable For Motors) toward Lynes Barn. Turn R past barn SP Bridleway along R edge of field between manicured hedges and fencing. Passing small entrance to estate house (visible) on your R, then enter muddy path track to road.

Barn

to Cutsdean

to Kineton
Lynes Barn

Quarries (disused)

7. Turn L past beech tree, then first R SP Warden's Way along R side of fields. L then R at road (Salt Way), and down track to Parks Farm with superb views of Winchcombe and Cleeve Common. Bear R WM at Parks Farm and follow track to Sudeley Lodge.

Crab Bottom

Quarry (disused)

Farmcote Estate

Cattle grid

Cottage

Parks Farm

The Warren

SALT WAY

Deadmanbury Gate

LINK: Guiting Power Walk

Guiting Power

Scale
0   100   500 metres
0   100   500 yards

N
W   E
S

Undertake this bracing walk on a clear day and you will be richly rewarded with spectacular views of the Severn Valley, Malvern and Welsh Hills, Winchcombe and Sudeley Castle. From the Cotswolds highest viewpoint (1084ft/317metres) you cross Cleeve Common, an open space of moorland like quality, along part of the Cotswold Way to a Stone Age Long Barrow, and onto a Jacobean Manor.

Distance
7 miles/11.2km. Short walk 1.5miles/2.4km.

Minimum Time
4 hours. Short walk 40 minutes.

Grade/Level of Difficulty
Easy/Moderate.

Terrain/Paths
Springy turf, wide farm tracks.

Landscape
Flat open moorland, undulating hills. Sheep pastures.

Dogs
Very popular dog walking area. Dogs can run free on Cleeve Common. Otherwise keep under control.

Public Toilets
Cleeve Hill.

Parking (P)
Cleeve Hill P beside toilets or by golf club.

Recommended Start/Finish
Cleeve Hill P.

Location
On the B4632 between Cheltenham and Winchcombe.

Link to other walks in this Guide
Access Winchcombe walk; from Belas Knap Long Barrow to Winchcombe via Humblebee and Wadfield Farm.

FEATURES OF INTEREST...

Belas Knap Long Barrow. In Old English translates as 'beacon mound'. A burial chamber, 4,000 years old. Opened in 1863 to reveal 38 skeletons. In superb condition and good viewpoint. Steep footpath from road.

Cleeve Cloud. Site of Iron Age hill fort. Superb views of Severn Valley, Malvern and Welsh hills. The Ring, a site of religious/pagan rituals is just below the scarp, 100ft in diameter. Castle Rock is a popular site for the rock climbing novice.

Cleeve Common. A vast expanse of common land where you are free to roam, with dog and friends. It is more like a piece of wild moorland with its extensive horizons, and you may be forgiven for believing you are in the midst of a National Park. There are wild flowers, the Gallops (for exercising race horses) and tracks that lead off in all directions. Park in the golf course, or in the lay-byes, on the B4632.

Cleeve Hill. At 1,083 feet this is the highest point in the Cotswolds and thus a superb viewpoint across to the Malvern Hills, Welsh Mountains, and northwards across the Cotswold landscape. A popular dog walking area and, in winter snow, ideal for toboggan runs. In 1901 a tramway was built from Cheltenham to Cleeve Cloud but sadly closed in 1930.

Postlip Hall & Tithe Barn. A former Jacobean Manor House set in fifteen acres, Postlip Hall has been for the past 44-years a co-housing idyll. Eight families live in separate dwellings, working the organic kitchen garden and

Belas Knapp Long Barrow

grounds, and pursuing their own creative pleasures, be it writing, painting, sculpting or inventing. The original tithe barn is also in continual use except when it is hired out as a venue for weddings, parties and beer festivals. postliphall.org.uk

WHERE TO EAT, DRINK & STAY...

Cleeve Hill Golf Club. Public golf club perched near the top of Cleeve Hill and welcoming to non-golfers who fancy a bite to eat. Bar and Restaurant opens 8am-6pm (F-Sa to 10pm). 01242 672025 cleevehillgolfclub.co.uk

Cleeve Hill Hotel. Ideally situated to tackle the Cotswold Way, and or, two or three walks in this book over an energetic weekend. You will enjoy stunning views from their light and airy rooms. And, sleep the dreams of rambling over hills and dales. 01242 672052 cleevehillhotel.co.uk

Rising Sun Hotel, Cleeve Hill. Situated close to the top of Cleeve Hill, the highest point in the Cotswolds, the views from the large beer garden are magnificent. Restaurant and bar offering seasonal menus 7am-9.45pm. Children and dog friendly. B&B. Perfect spot for a drink and sandwich on a sunny day but you may not want to start walking again! 01242 676281 greeneking-pubs.co.uk

Castle Rock

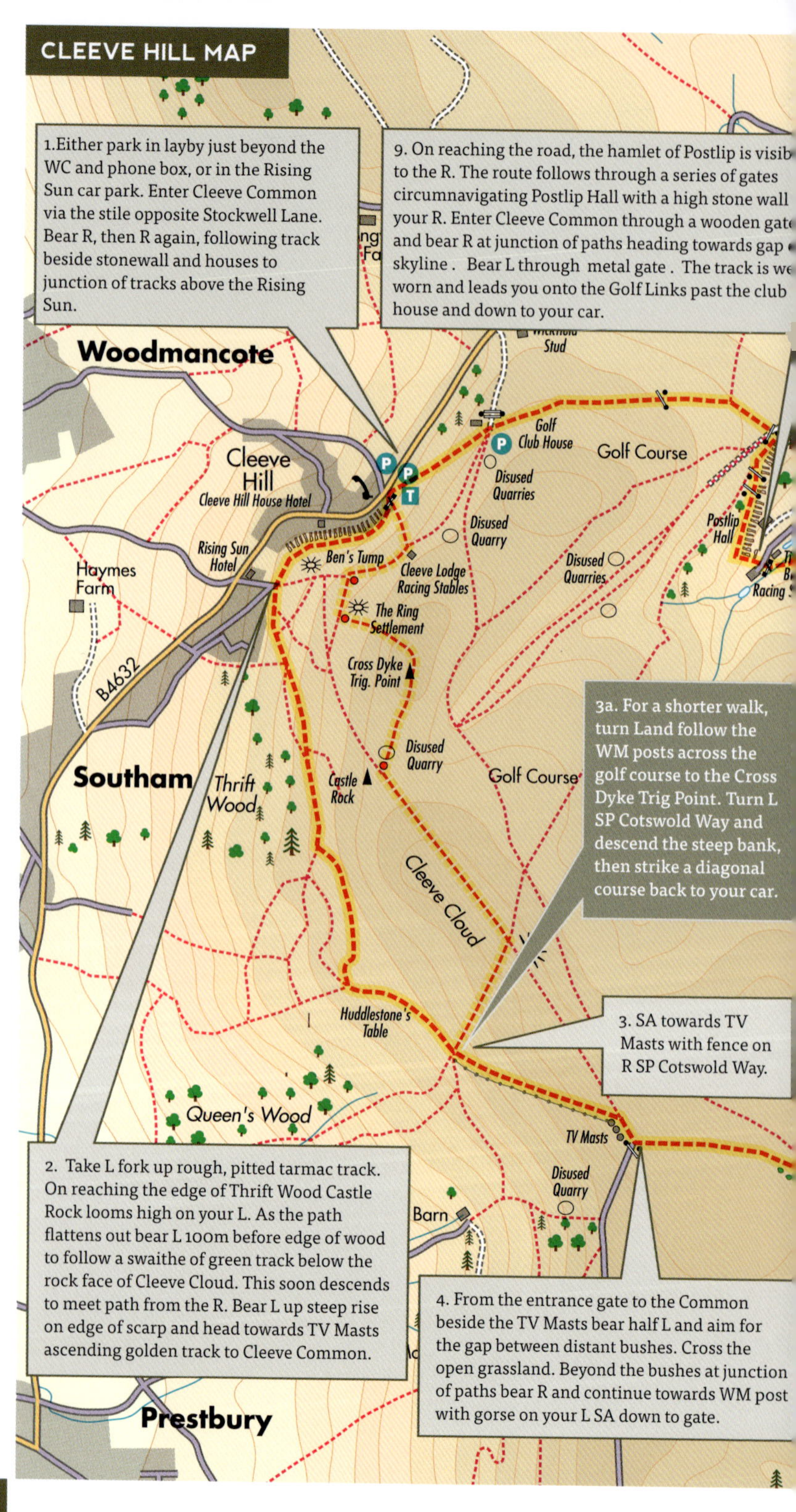

1.Either park in layby just beyond the WC and phone box, or in the Rising Sun car park. Enter Cleeve Common via the stile opposite Stockwell Lane. Bear R, then R again, following track beside stonewall and houses to junction of tracks above the Rising Sun.

9. On reaching the road, the hamlet of Postlip is visib to the R. The route follows through a series of gates circumnavigating Postlip Hall with a high stone wall your R. Enter Cleeve Common through a wooden gate and bear R at junction of paths heading towards gap skyline . Bear L through metal gate . The track is we worn and leads you onto the Golf Links past the club house and down to your car.

3a. For a shorter walk, turn Land follow the WM posts across the golf course to the Cross Dyke Trig Point. Turn L SP Cotswold Way and descend the steep bank, then strike a diagonal course back to your car.

3. SA towards TV Masts with fence on R SP Cotswold Way.

2. Take L fork up rough, pitted tarmac track. On reaching the edge of Thrift Wood Castle Rock looms high on your L. As the path flattens out bear L 100m before edge of wood to follow a swaithe of green track below the rock face of Cleeve Cloud. This soon descends to meet path from the R. Bear L up steep rise on edge of scarp and head towards TV Masts ascending golden track to Cleeve Common.

4. From the entrance gate to the Common beside the TV Masts bear half L and aim for the gap between distant bushes. Cross the open grassland. Beyond the bushes at junction of paths bear R and continue towards WM post with gorse on your L SA down to gate.

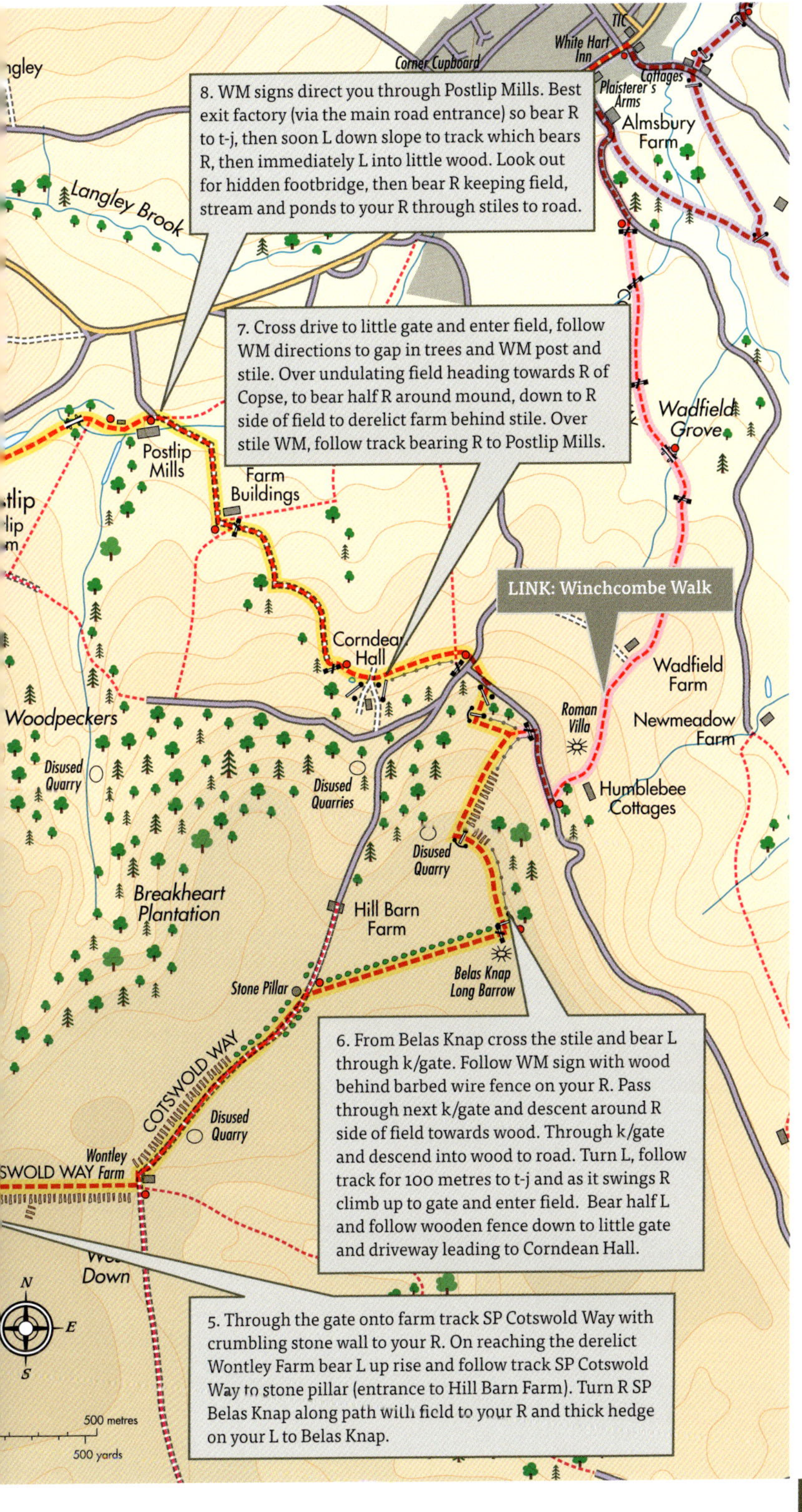

ngley

Langley Brook

Corner Cupboard

White Hart Inn

TIC

Plaisterer's Arms

Cottages

Almsbury Farm

8. WM signs direct you through Postlip Mills. Best exit factory (via the main road entrance) so bear R to t-j, then soon L down slope to track which bears R, then immediately L into little wood. Look out for hidden footbridge, then bear R keeping field, stream and ponds to your R through stiles to road.

7. Cross drive to little gate and enter field, follow WM directions to gap in trees and WM post and stile. Over undulating field heading towards R of Copse, to bear half R around mound, down to R side of field to derelict farm behind stile. Over stile WM, follow track bearing R to Postlip Mills.

Wadfield Grove

Postlip Mills

Farm Buildings

tlip
lip
m

LINK: Winchcombe Walk

Corndean Hall

Wadfield Farm

Woodpeckers

Roman Villa

Newmeadow Farm

Disused Quarry

Disused Quarries

Humblebee Cottages

Disused Quarry

Breakheart Plantation

Hill Barn Farm

Belas Knap Long Barrow

Stone Pillar

COTSWOLD WAY

6. From Belas Knap cross the stile and bear L through k/gate. Follow WM sign with wood behind barbed wire fence on your R. Pass through next k/gate and descent around R side of field towards wood. Through k/gate and descend into wood to road. Turn L, follow track for 100 metres to t-j and as it swings R climb up to gate and enter field. Bear half L and follow wooden fence down to little gate and driveway leading to Corndean Hall.

Disused Quarry

Wontley Farm

SWOLD WAY Farm

Down

N
E
S

5. Through the gate onto farm track SP Cotswold Way with crumbling stone wall to your R. On reaching the derelict Wontley Farm bear L up rise and follow track SP Cotswold Way to stone pillar (entrance to Hill Barn Farm). Turn R SP Belas Knap along path with field to your R and thick hedge on your L to Belas Knap.

500 metres

500 yards

A short walk from one of the Cotswolds' pretty Estate villages. Rich in wildlife, with an abundance of wild flowers and evidence of wild animals: deer, badgers, rabbits, and in summer, a profusion of butterflies. Following heavy rain the footpaths can be muddy and slippery, so wear stout footwear. These woods are managed by the Farmcote Estate (Shoot).

Distance
3 miles/4.8km.
Minimum Time
1.5 hours.
Grade/Level of Difficulty
Easy.
Terrain/Paths
Farm tracks, woodland paths. Muddy at times.
Landscape
Cultivated farmland, farm tracks, woodland.
Dogs
Keep dogs under control from car park to woods - some livestock.
Public Toilets
None.

Parking (P)
Beside barn as indicated on map, or in village.
Recommended Start/Finish
From P or in village.
Location
Between Winchcombe and Stow on the Wold, west of Temple Guiting. Easiest access from Winchcombe.
Link to other walks in this Guide
Winchcombe Walk via bridle path on western edge of Guiting Wood.

 Exit from St Michael's Church

FEATURES OF INTEREST...

Guiting Power. A hidden, somnolent estate village that surprisingly manages to support two pubs, a village shop/post office serving tea and coffees, a nursery school and an active village hall. The blue-grey cottages belong to the Cochrane Estate (or Guiting Manor Amenity Trust) that has thankfully saved this village from greedy developers and second homeowners.

Guiting Wood. Well tended wood full of flowers, wild animals and pheasants grown for the Farmcote Estate shoot.

St Michael's Church. Of Norman origins - both the North and South doorways are Norman. C12 chancel, C13 nave and roof. C15 Perpendicular West Tower. Severe alterations in the early C20. Interesting tombs/tablets in the churchyard. Isolated position beside ancient Anglo-Saxon settlement called Gyting Broc. Views of rolling Cotswold landscape are unforgettable.

WHERE TO EAT & DRINK...

The Cotswold Guy, Church Lane. This is a new boutique farm shop with a passion for fresh, locally sourced produce. Takeaway Meals and a bespoke food distribution service: dinner parties etc. Open M-Su 9-4, 01451 851955 thecotswoldguy.co.uk

The Farmers Arms, Winchcombe Road. A proper locals country pub whose untarnished exterior does not do justice to the welcome, or home-cooked food served. My children used to love coming here. Donnington Ales. 01451 850358 farmersarmsguiting.co.uk

The Halfway at Kineton. Two hospitality crazy/foodie nuts Nathan and Liam, along with their families now run this cosy pub. B&B. 074259 70507 thehalfwayatkineton.com

Hollow Bottom. Out on the road to Winchcombe, herewith this foodie-friendly pub, popular with the racing fraternity. 01451 509890 hollowbottom.com

WHERE TO STAY...

Guiting Guest House, Post Office Lane. C16 Cotswold stone former farmhouse which has been tastefully modernised. Candlelit and tasty evening meals by arrangement. Garden. Children and dogs welcome. B&B. 01451 850470 guitingguesthouse.com

WHERE TO STAY JUST OFF THE MAP...

Fox Hill, Naunton. Originally a coaching inn, the Fox Hill offers annexed B&B. Children and dogs welcome. 01451 850496

Overlooking Guiting Power

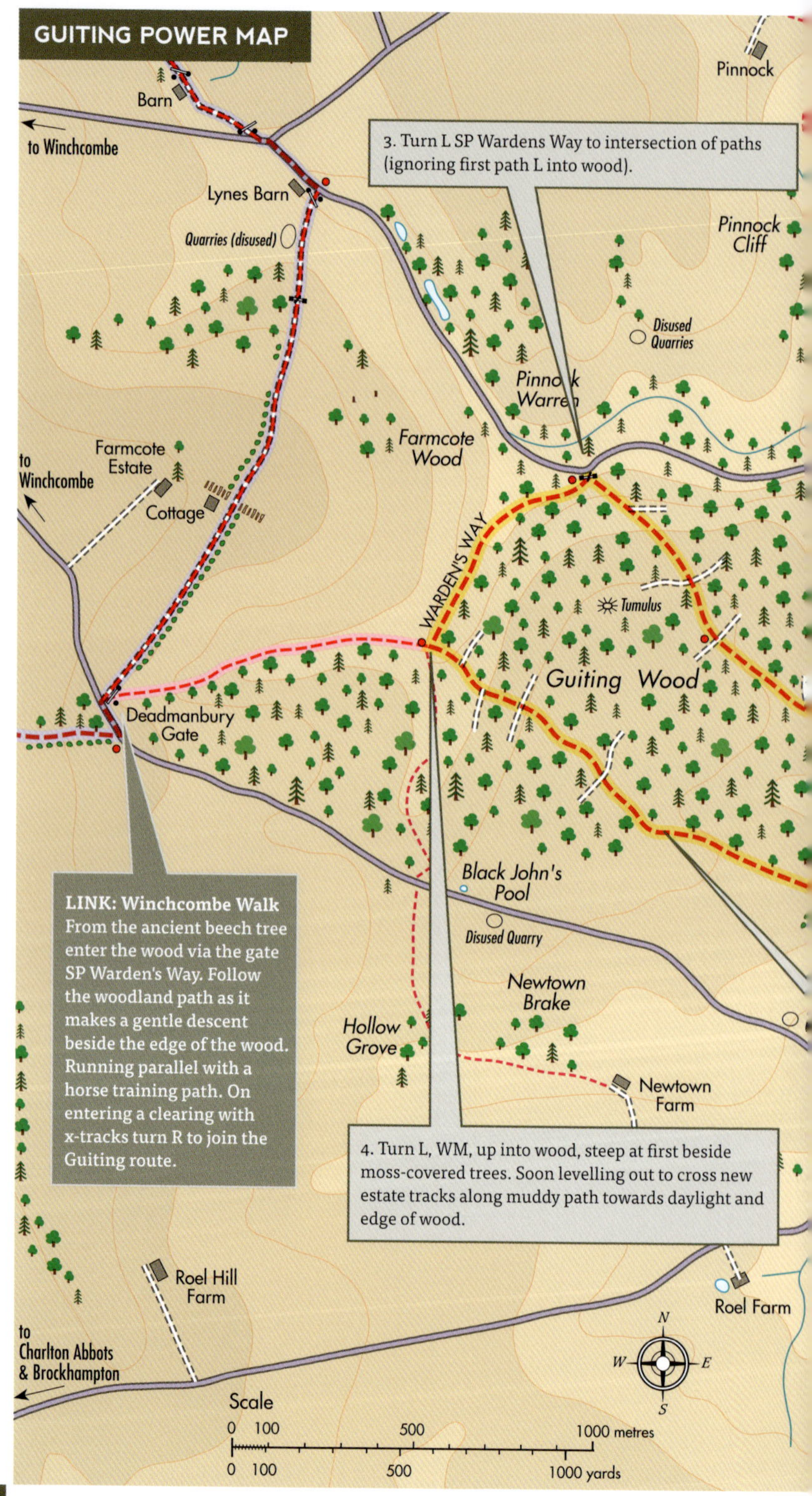

GUITING POWER MAP
to Winchcombe
Barn
Lynes Barn
Quarries (disused)
Farmcote Estate
Cottage
to Winchcombe
3. Turn L SP Wardens Way to intersection of paths (ignoring first path L into wood).
Pinnock
Pinnock Cliff
Disused Quarries
Pinnock Warren
Farmcote Wood
WARDEN'S WAY
Tumulus
Guiting Wood
Deadmanbury Gate
LINK: Winchcombe Walk
From the ancient beech tree enter the wood via the gate SP Warden's Way. Follow the woodland path as it makes a gentle descent beside the edge of the wood. Running parallel with a horse training path. On entering a clearing with x-tracks turn R to join the Guiting route.
Black John's Pool
Disused Quarry
Newtown Brake
Hollow Grove
Newtown Farm
4. Turn L, WM, up into wood, steep at first beside moss-covered trees. Soon levelling out to cross new estate tracks along muddy path towards daylight and edge of wood.
Roel Hill Farm
Roel Farm
to Charlton Abbots & Brockhampton
N
W
E
S
Scale
0   100   500   1000 metres
0   100   500   1000 yards

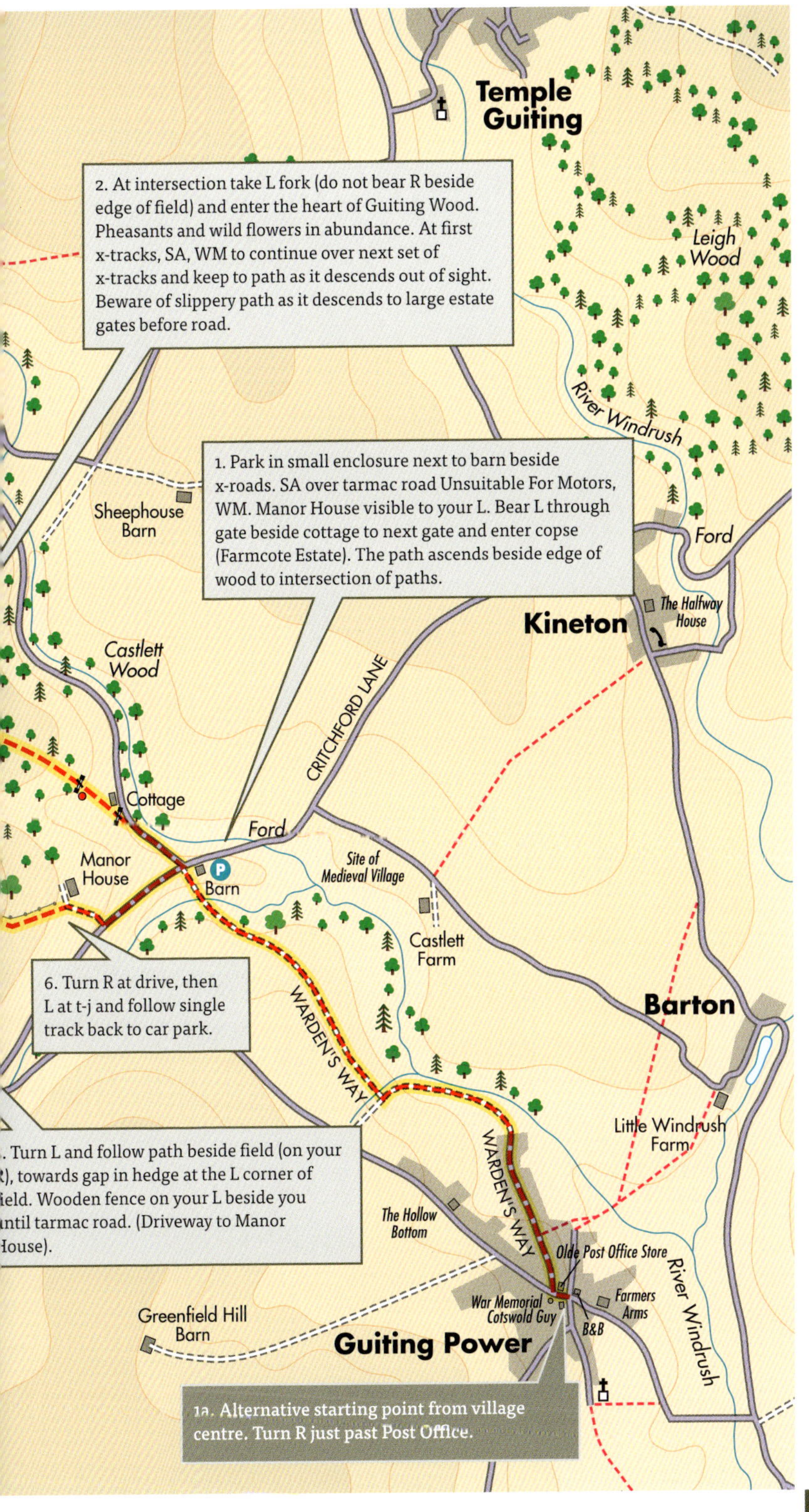

Temple Guiting
Leigh Wood
River Windrush
Sheephouse Barn
Ford
Castlett Wood
The Halfway House
Kineton
CRITCHFORD LANE
Cottage
Ford
Manor House
Barn
Site of Medieval Village
Castlett Farm
Barton
WARDEN'S WAY
Little Windrush Farm
WARDEN'S WAY
The Hollow Bottom
Olde Post Office Store
River Windrush
War Memorial
Cotswold Guy
Farmers Arms
B&B
Greenfield Hill Barn
Guiting Power

2. At intersection take L fork (do not bear R beside edge of field) and enter the heart of Guiting Wood. Pheasants and wild flowers in abundance. At first x-tracks, SA, WM to continue over next set of x-tracks and keep to path as it descends out of sight. Beware of slippery path as it descends to large estate gates before road.

1. Park in small enclosure next to barn beside x-roads. SA over tarmac road Unsuitable For Motors, WM. Manor House visible to your L. Bear L through gate beside cottage to next gate and enter copse (Farmcote Estate). The path ascends beside edge of wood to intersection of paths.

6. Turn R at drive, then L at t-j and follow single track back to car park.

. Turn L and follow path beside field (on your), towards gap in hedge at the L corner of ield. Wooden fence on your L beside you ntil tarmac road. (Driveway to Manor ouse).

1a. Alternative starting point from village centre. Turn R just past Post Office.

This good half-days walk joins two of the Cotswolds most famous villages, known jointly as The Slaughters. Home to Cotswold stone cottages and beautifully tended gardens, and some enchanting Country House hotels. The route enters, for many, unknown territory and follows the upper reaches of the Eye Stream and River Windrush. It cuts through a rich meadow of wild flowers beside the Eye Stream and crosses undulating farmland and picturesque woodland.

Distance
7.25 miles/11.6km.
Minimum Time
3 hours.
Grade/Level of Difficulty
Moderate.
Terrain/Paths
Muddy paths, springy turf, farm track.
Landscape
River valleys, rolling farmland, woodland.
Dogs
Keep under control across farmland. Despite some sections along roadside grass verges, this walk is away from the crowds so quite suitable for dogs.

Public Toilets
None.
Parking (P)
Beside Eye Stream, Lower Slaughter, or outside church at Upper Slaughter.
Recommended Start/Finish
Lower or Upper Slaughter P.
Location
Just off the A429 between Bourton and Stow.
Link to other walks in this Guide
30 minute walk to St Lawrence's Church, Bourton on the Water.

FEATURES OF INTEREST...

Eyford Park. The path runs near the entrance to this C18 parkland, with early C20 house, and formal gardens. It is here that John Milton is reputed to have written his Magnum Opus, Paradise Lost. It is closed to visitors.

Lower Slaughter. Some visitors (usually Americans) to this village can't believe people actually live in these cottages – They believe it to be a film set! It is thus, one of the most popular villages in the Cotswolds, for little bridges cross the Eye Stream that runs beside the row of golden cottages. The much-painted C19 redbrick Corn Mill (see below) stands on the western edge of the village.

The Old Mill, Lower Slaughter. This iconic and much photographed C19 corn mill was lovingly restored into a small museum and became the life-blood of the village.

Now under new ownership with an uncertain future.

Upper Slaughter. This village lies a couple of miles upstream from its neighbour. It has an impressive old Manor House visible from the road, and once lived in by the Slaughter family. Around the corner, the old Post Office with a beautiful kitchen garden. But, keep going, for along the lane past the church the road ascends to provide a splendid view of a ford and stream hidden beneath lush vegetation.

WHERE TO EAT, DRINK, STAY... AND, BE MERRY

The Slaughters Manor House. A perfectly proportioned C17 Cotswold manor endowed with a walled garden and a unique, two-storey C15 dovecote. The hotel has spacious, comfortable rooms, furnished with antiques and Old Masters. 01451 820456 slaughtersmanor.co.uk

Lords of the Manor, Upper Slaughter. A luxurious, long-established Country House Hotel with C17 origins set in eight acres of parkland. Always a favourite destination for US visitors and those seeking to celebrate a "Special Occasion". Child and dog friendly. The former home of the Reverend F E B Witts, Rector of this parish who wrote his famous chronicle of the C18, The Diary of a Cotswold Parson. Serves afternoon tea to non-residents. 01451 820243 lordsofthemanor.com

The Slaughters Country Inn, Lower Slaughter. This C17 inn has undergone many guises; Eton cramming school, country house hotel and now a swanky inn standing in four acres of beautiful grounds beside the River Eye. The bar is a comfy, cosy bolt-hole to rest up and sooth your aching limbs and sore shins after a slog on the hills. 01451 822143 theslaughtersinn.co.uk

Lower Slaughter Summer Dusk

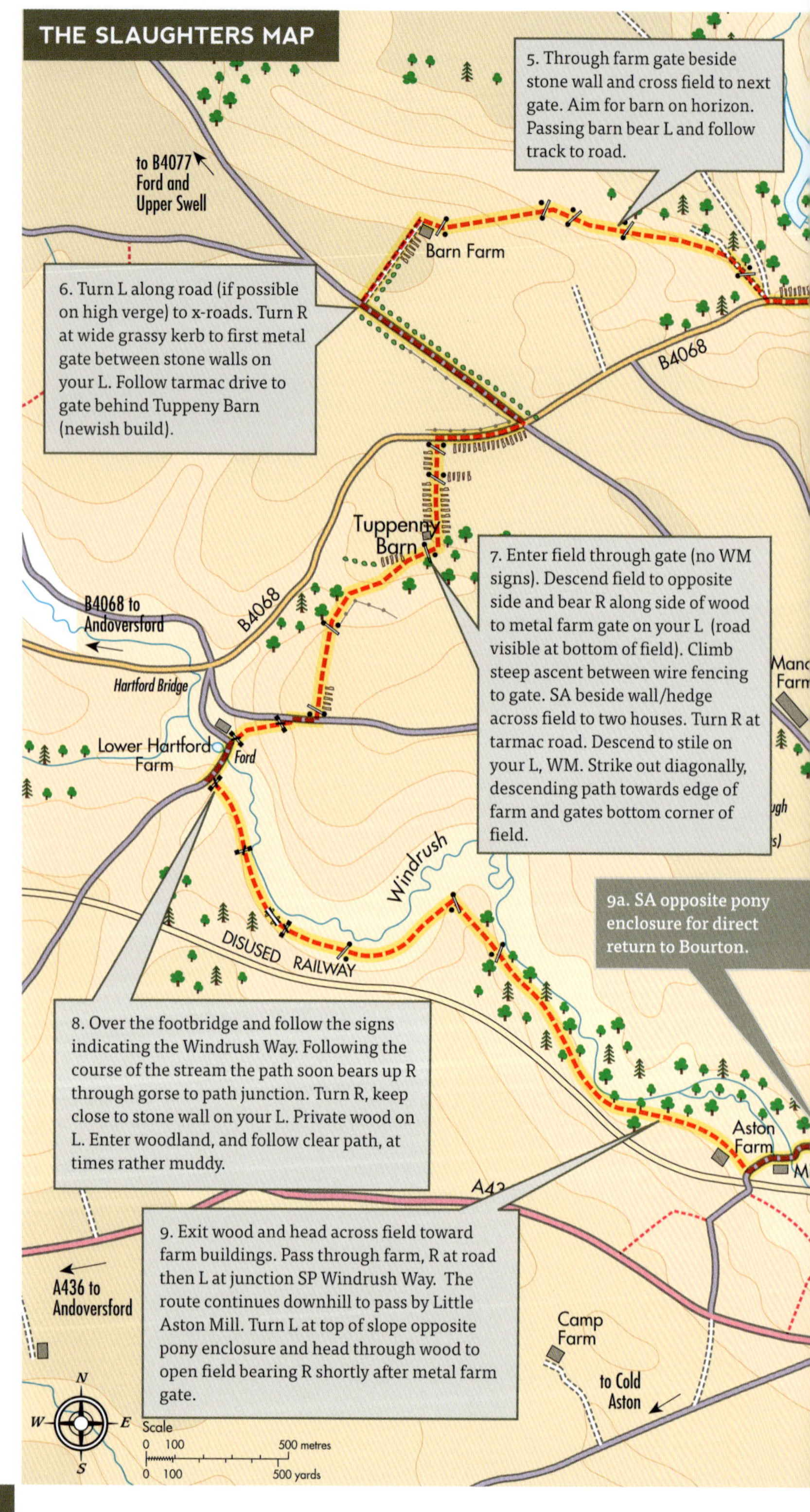

THE SLAUGHTERS MAP

5. Through farm gate beside stone wall and cross field to next gate. Aim for barn on horizon. Passing barn bear L and follow track to road.

to B4077 Ford and Upper Swell

Barn Farm

B4068

6. Turn L along road (if possible on high verge) to x-roads. Turn R at wide grassy kerb to first metal gate between stone walls on your L. Follow tarmac drive to gate behind Tuppeny Barn (newish build).

Tuppeny Barn

B4068 to Andoversford

B4068

Hartford Bridge

Lower Hartford Farm

Ford

7. Enter field through gate (no WM signs). Descend field to opposite side and bear R along side of wood to metal farm gate on your L (road visible at bottom of field). Climb steep ascent between wire fencing to gate. SA beside wall/hedge across field to two houses. Turn R at tarmac road. Descend to stile on your L, WM. Strike out diagonally, descending path towards edge of farm and gates bottom corner of field.

Manor Farm

Windrush

9a. SA opposite pony enclosure for direct return to Bourton.

DISUSED RAILWAY

8. Over the footbridge and follow the signs indicating the Windrush Way. Following the course of the stream the path soon bears up R through gorse to path junction. Turn R, keep close to stone wall on your L. Private wood on L. Enter woodland, and follow clear path, at times rather muddy.

Aston Farm

A42

9. Exit wood and head across field toward farm buildings. Pass through farm, R at road then L at junction SP Windrush Way. The route continues downhill to pass by Little Aston Mill. Turn L at top of slope opposite pony enclosure and head through wood to open field bearing R shortly after metal farm gate.

Camp Farm

A436 to Andoversford

to Cold Aston

N
W   E
S

Scale
0   100   500 metres
0   100   500 yards

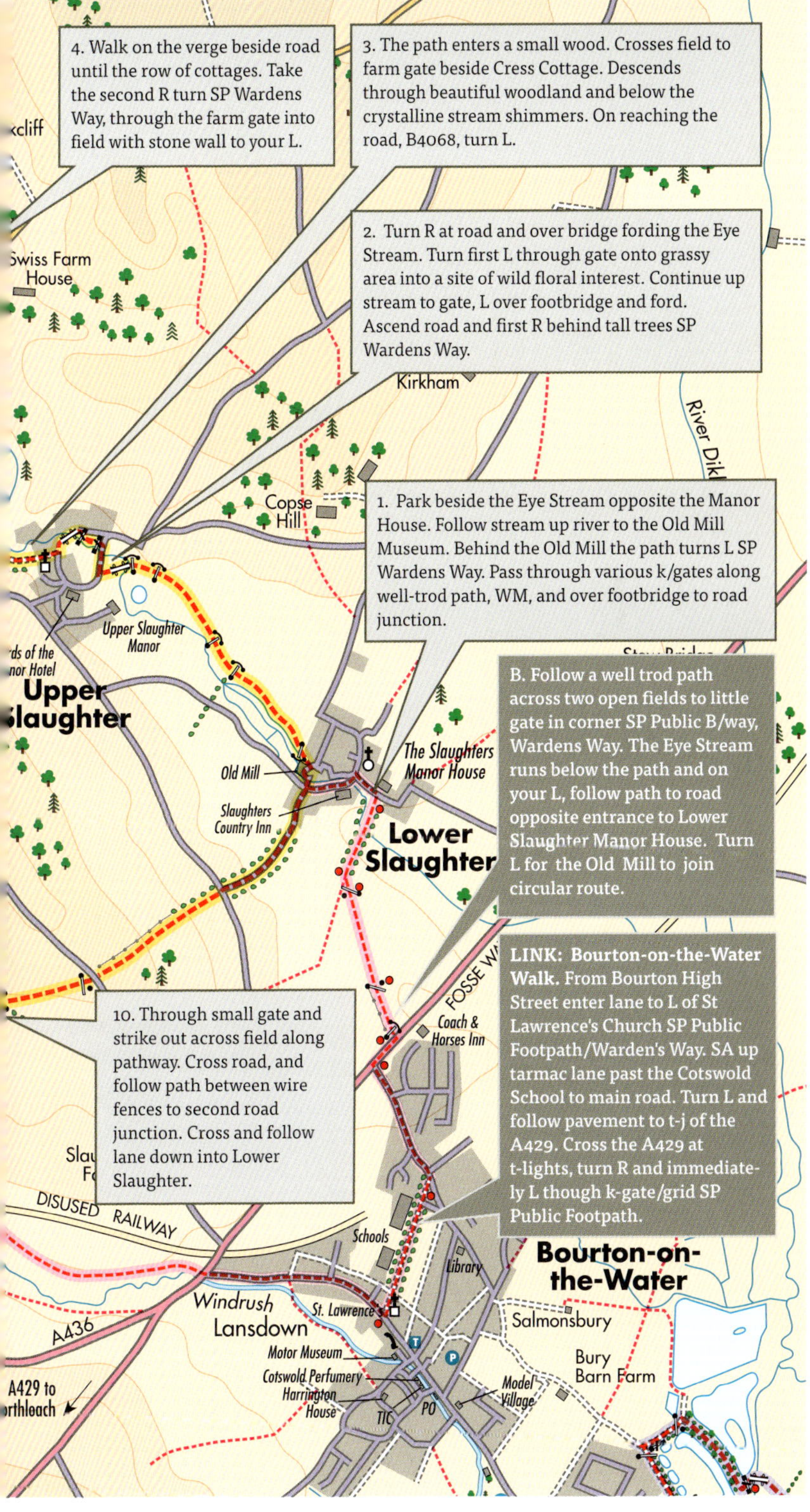

4. Walk on the verge beside road until the row of cottages. Take the second R turn SP Wardens Way, through the farm gate into field with stone wall to your L.

3. The path enters a small wood. Crosses field to farm gate beside Cress Cottage. Descends through beautiful woodland and below the crystalline stream shimmers. On reaching the road, B4068, turn L.

2. Turn R at road and over bridge fording the Eye Stream. Turn first L through gate onto grassy area into a site of wild floral interest. Continue up stream to gate, L over footbridge and ford. Ascend road and first R behind tall trees SP Wardens Way.

1. Park beside the Eye Stream opposite the Manor House. Follow stream up river to the Old Mill Museum. Behind the Old Mill the path turns L SP Wardens Way. Pass through various k/gates along well-trod path, WM, and over footbridge to road junction.

B. Follow a well trod path across two open fields to little gate in corner SP Public B/way, Wardens Way. The Eye Stream runs below the path and on your L, follow path to road opposite entrance to Lower Slaughter Manor House. Turn L for the Old Mill to join circular route.

LINK: Bourton-on-the-Water Walk. From Bourton High Street enter lane to L of St Lawrence's Church SP Public Footpath/Warden's Way. SA up tarmac lane past the Cotswold School to main road. Turn L and follow pavement to t-j of the A429. Cross the A429 at t-lights, turn R and immediately L though k-gate/grid SP Public Footpath.

10. Through small gate and strike out across field along pathway. Cross road, and follow path between wire fences to second road junction. Cross and follow lane down into Lower Slaughter.

Swiss Farm House
kcliff
Kirkham
Copse Hill
River Dik
ds of the nor Hotel
Upper Slaughter
Upper Slaughter Manor
Old Mill
Slaughters Country Inn
The Slaughters Manor House
Lower Slaughter
FOSSE WAY
Coach & Horses Inn
Slau Fo
DISUSED RAILWAY
Windrush
Lansdown
St. Lawrence's
Schools
Library
Bourton-on-the-Water
Salmonsbury
Bury Barn Farm
A436
Motor Museum
Cotswold Perfumery
Harrington House
A429 to rthleach
TIC
PO
Model Village

First wander around Bourton and look beyond the crowds at the magnificent buildings and the graceful bridges spanning the River Windrush. And, pack your binoculars as the walk passes havens of birdlife. The early route circumnavigates the lakes and can be muddy but soon climbs up to the pretty and isolated village of Little Rissington with its quaint church and golden cottages, before returning to Bourton with fine views over Bourton Vale.

Distance
3.5 miles/5.6km.

Minimum Time
2 hours.

Grade/Level of Difficulty
Easy.

Terrain/Paths
Grass, farm tracks, muddy field up to Little Rissington (Wellington Boots advised).

Landscape
Lakes and pastured farmland.

Dogs
To be kept under control through farmland but generally quite good for dogs.

Public Toilets
Bourton High Street.

Parking (P)
Next to Birdland, or in lay-by on the Rissington Road.

Recommended Start/Finish
From lay-by on the Rissington Road.

Location
On the A429 between Northleach and Stow-on-the-Wold.

Link to other walks in this Guide
30-minute walk to Lower Slaughter from St Lawrence's Church.

 Little Rissington Church

FEATURES OF INTEREST...

Bourton on the Water. One of the most popular beauty spots in the Cotswolds, but one that invites mixed opinions and is best visited out of season. It can be charming on a quiet, frostbitten morning when only the postman is out and about, but is best avoided on a busy bank holiday. You must, however, look beyond the crowds and wander the little streets for there are some beautiful houses to admire. The River Windrush flows through the many gardens, beside tree-lined lawns and is spanned by low, graceful bridges built in the mid C18. The village is built above Salmonsbury Camp, a Roman settlement. There are numerous attractions within Bourton including Birdland Park & Gardens, the Cotswold Motoring Museum and the Model Village.

The Lakes. Flooded gravel pits from the 1960s and 70s. Now utilised as an angling lake. There is a great abundance of wildlife; plants, insects and birds.

Little Rissington. Tiny Cotswold village with C12 church that is home to a moving memorial to RAF servicemen. An RAF airbase was located nearby in World War II.

Oxfordshire Way. A long distance footpath from Bourton-on-the-Water to Henley-on-Thames, linking the Cotswolds with the Chilterns. Follows the ancient tracks of the county through meadows and woods, along quiet river valleys and over windy escarpments through many a delightful village. Waymarked.

Salmonsbury Camp. The Romans' second legion of 5,000 soldiers was encamped here and built Lansdown Bridge to ford the Windrush on the Fosse Way.

Windrush Valley. A slow, trickling stream in summer, with a tendency to flood in winter. The river snakes its way through quiet golden villages to create the idyllic Cotswold scene.

WHERE TO EAT & DRINK...

Bakery On The Water, Sherborne Street. An established business for 89-years run by the 4th generation, and now 9-years in Bourton. An artisan bakery serving a simple breakfast (no fry ups), homemade cakes and bread - all made on the premises. 01451 822748
bakeryonthewater.co.uk

WHERE TO STAY...

Harrington House. A centre for walking holidays, guided walks, yoga, cycle touring, pen and wash, complete with drying room. One of the finest houses in Bourton embellished with Palladian facade, Cotswold stone roof, all surrounded by a domed belvedere. 29 bedrooms. 020 39748865
hfholidays.co.uk

The Old New Inn. Originally a Queen Anne coaching inn that now provides traditional comfort within 9-luxurious bedrooms. Home to the Model Village. 01451 820467
theoldnewinn.co.uk

WHERE TO STAY JUST OFF THE MAP...

Clapton Manor B&B, Clapton-on-the-Hill. Stunning Grade II listed Tudor house with a beautiful garden created by your host - a garden designer and historian serving fabulous organic breakfasts. 01451 810202
claptonmanor.co.uk

The Plough Inn B&B, Cold Aston. A fine country pub offering the full gamut: home-cooked fresh food, real ales, craft beers, great wines, flagstone floors, original beams and a roaring fire. Plus, 3 luxurious double-bedrooms with bathroom. All offered with gracious hospitality. 01451 822602
coldastonplough.com

The Wildings Campsite, Lankett Lane. A quiet location offering solitude within a family farm: iPods, bell tents, yurts - just bring your own bedding/sleeping bags. A Cook House is available with cooking facilities, and more comforts. 01451 518869
thewildingscampsite.co.uk

In addition to the above, Bourton has an ever expanding surplus of tearooms, fish and chip shops and tourist pubs.

Bridge at Dawn, Bourton

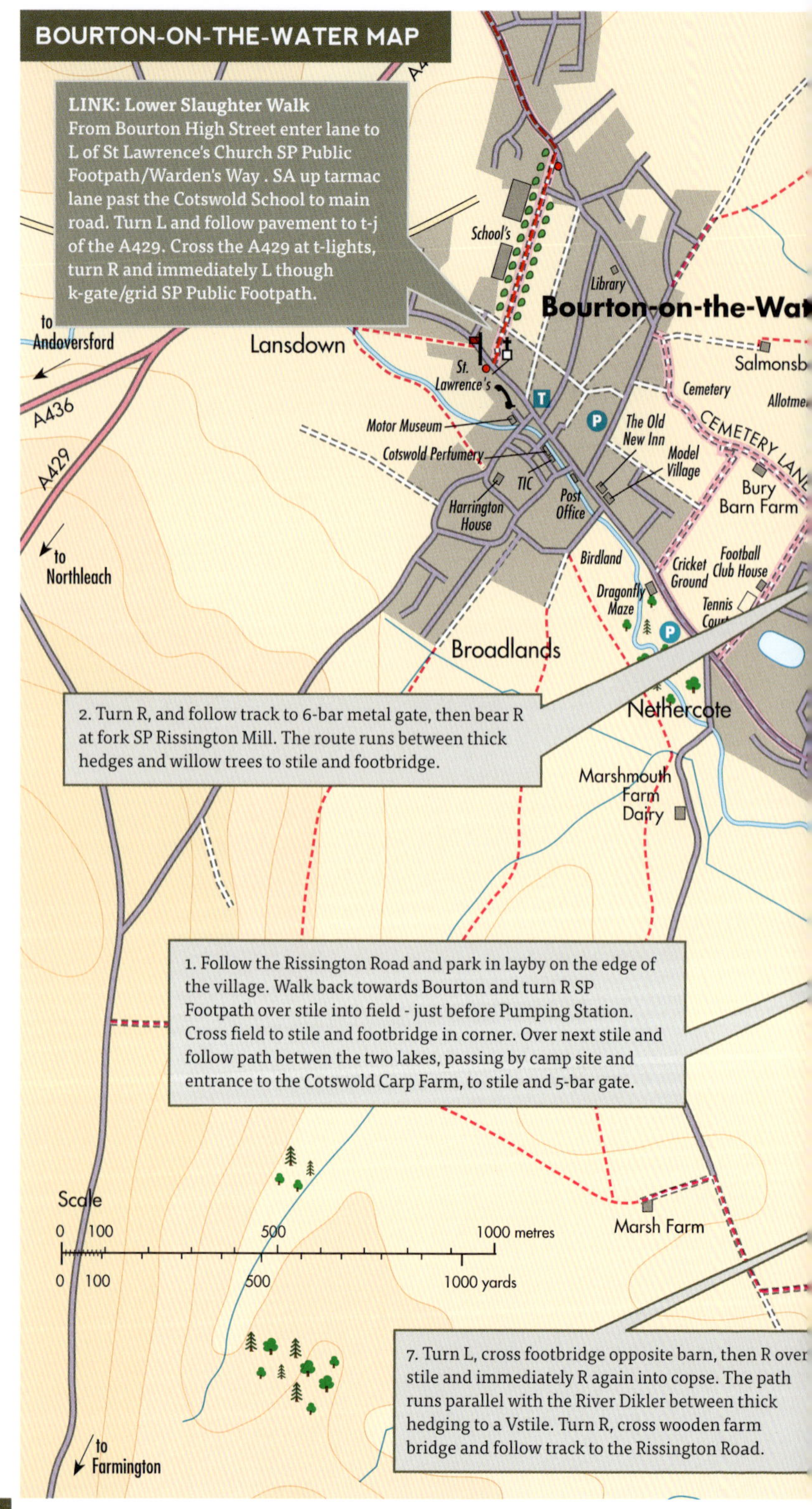

BOURTON-ON-THE-WATER MAP
LINK: Lower Slaughter Walk
From Bourton High Street enter lane to L of St Lawrence's Church SP Public Footpath/Warden's Way . SA up tarmac lane past the Cotswold School to main road. Turn L and follow pavement to t-j of the A429. Cross the A429 at t-lights, turn R and immediately L though k-gate/grid SP Public Footpath.
to Andoversford
A436
A429
to Northleach
Lansdown
School's
Library
Bourton-on-the-Water
Salmonsb
St. Lawrence's
Cemetery
Allotme
CEMETERY LANE
Motor Museum
Cotswold Perfumery
The Old New Inn
Model Village
Bury Barn Farm
TIC
Post Office
Harrington House
Birdland
Cricket Ground
Football Club House
Dragonfly Maze
Tennis Cour
Broadlands
Nethercote
2. Turn R, and follow track to 6-bar metal gate, then bear R at fork SP Rissington Mill. The route runs between thick hedges and willow trees to stile and footbridge.
Marshmouth Farm Dairy
1. Follow the Rissington Road and park in layby on the edge of the village. Walk back towards Bourton and turn R SP Footpath over stile into field - just before Pumping Station. Cross field to stile and footbridge in corner. Over next stile and follow path betwen the two lakes, passing by camp site and entrance to the Cotswold Carp Farm, to stile and 5-bar gate.
Scale
0 100 500 1000 metres
0 100 500 1000 yards
Marsh Farm
to Farmington
7. Turn L, cross footbridge opposite barn, then R over stile and immediately R again into copse. The path runs parallel with the River Dikler between thick hedging to a Vstile. Turn R, cross wooden farm bridge and follow track to the Rissington Road.

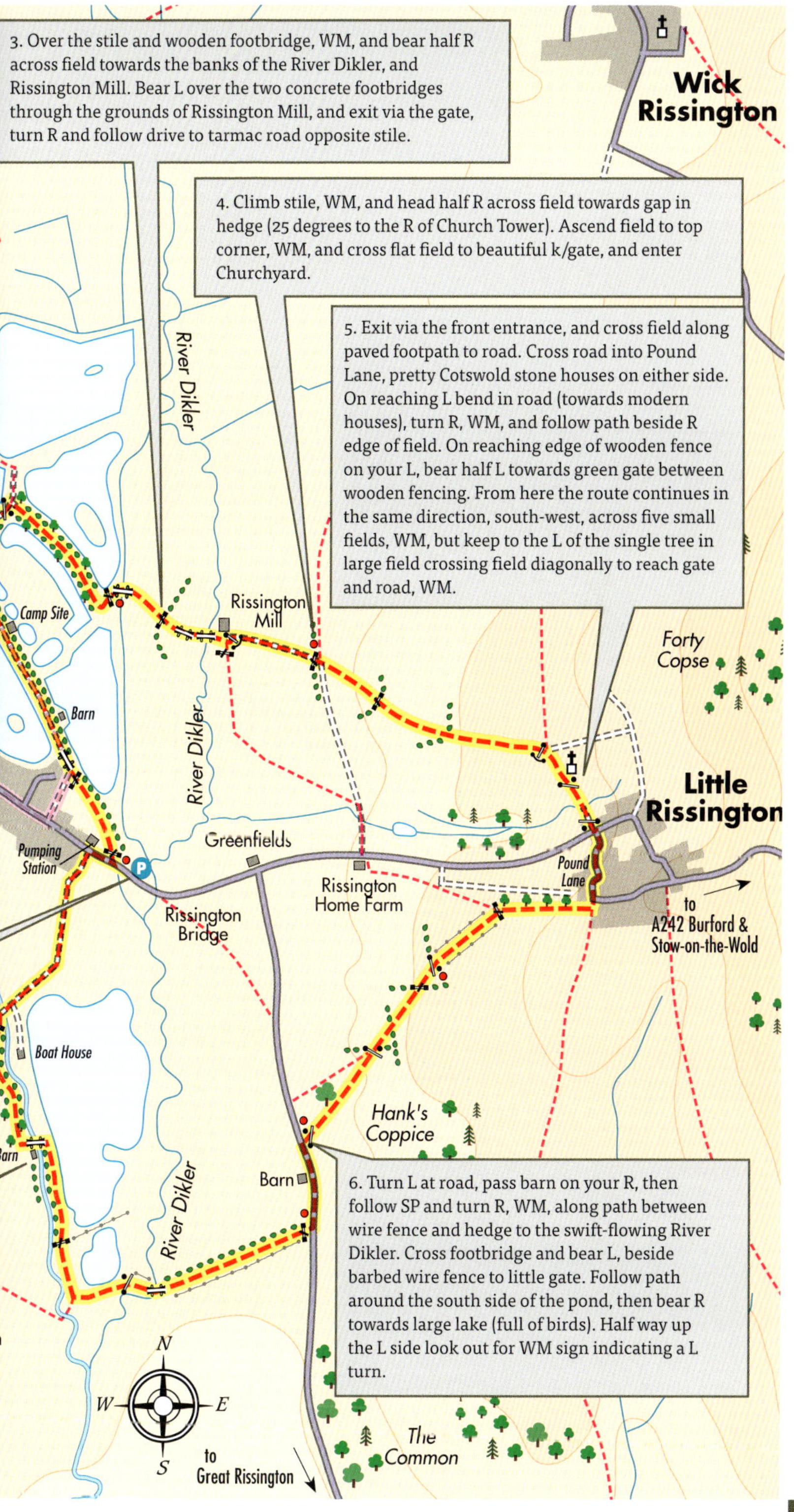

3. Over the stile and wooden footbridge, WM, and bear half R across field towards the banks of the River Dikler, and Rissington Mill. Bear L over the two concrete footbridges through the grounds of Rissington Mill, and exit via the gate, turn R and follow drive to tarmac road opposite stile.

4. Climb stile, WM, and head half R across field towards gap in hedge (25 degrees to the R of Church Tower). Ascend field to top corner, WM, and cross flat field to beautiful k/gate, and enter Churchyard.

5. Exit via the front entrance, and cross field along paved footpath to road. Cross road into Pound Lane, pretty Cotswold stone houses on either side. On reaching L bend in road (towards modern houses), turn R, WM, and follow path beside R edge of field. On reaching edge of wooden fence on your L, bear half L towards green gate between wooden fencing. From here the route continues in the same direction, south-west, across five small fields, WM, but keep to the L of the single tree in large field crossing field diagonally to reach gate and road, WM.

6. Turn L at road, pass barn on your R, then follow SP and turn R, WM, along path between wire fence and hedge to the swift-flowing River Dikler. Cross footbridge and bear L, beside barbed wire fence to little gate. Follow path around the south side of the pond, then bear R towards large lake (full of birds). Half way up the L side look out for WM sign indicating a L turn.

Wick Rissington
River Dikler
Camp Site
Barn
Rissington Mill
River Dikler
Forty Copse
Little Rissington
Pumping Station
P
Greenfields
Pound Lane
Rissington Bridge
Rissington Home Farm
to A242 Burford & Stow-on-the-Wold
Boat House
Hank's Coppice
Barn
Barn
River Dikler
N
W
E
S
to Great Rissington
The Common

THE VALUE & SURVIVAL OF HOSPITALITY

The Covid-19 Pandemic has been likened to a tsunami; b&bs, cafés, camp sites, hotels, inns/pubs, restaurants and self-catering businesses have been closed, some swept away for ever. Those with a will and an opportunity have sold take-away meals to ease their cash flow, and the Government has kept many businesses alive through the Furlough Scheme. But, this has all been for the short-term. The self-employed entrepreneur who has placed all their savings into their business will not wish to take on more debt and risk. A number of restaurateurs with a number of establishments have reduced them to one, or closed them for good. It is a hard game.

Indeed, the doyen, the original that created the genre of the English Country House Hotel, the Sharrow Bay in Cumbria went into administration. Covid-19 may not have been wholly responsible for its demise. Had it not addressed the new markets so steadfastly pursued by the likes of Barnsley House, The Painswick, Lords of the Manor? Today, these hotels need something extra, whether it be a brilliant chef or various hedonistic pleasures. They also need strong leadership, a passion and a vocation to serve. Others are hanging on by their fingertips in the hope that these months of Staycation will restore their livelihoods and we wish them every success and good luck.

It has not been an easy task to up-date this book. When we set out in February to up-date the Listings, what would we find? Who had closed down (with finality) and who was preparing to open for the season? Our policy has always been highly subjective. We like good manners, comfort, discretion, style and professional expertise. We like quirky personalities and value-for-money. We rarely include multiples. It is the Independent, free-spirited host/hostesses we are drawn to. So, we include the full gamut; the posh, country house hotel, the lively Inn With Rooms, the wacky rustic camp site…the delicious deli and coffee shop. It is a wide range. Those that do open again will require your patience and good faith. Many will have lost staff and will have had to train the new. Their financial frailties will have been tested, but one hopes they will find new vigour to welcome you! In the article below an idyllic hostelry (Inn With Rooms/Small Hotel) is described. Many generations of the same family have run this business. They provide comfort, good manners, wholesome food, a refuge from this crazy world. They have no debt, no bank manager giving them grief. They have independence from a brewery. They are chilled. How many like them do you know in the UK?

AN EXTRACT FROM A WALKING MAN'S JOURNAL

Winter. For five months I had been tramping across Europe following paths, ancient tracks, canal and riverside paths. Where I could, I bought the local maps but very often I would just set my compass in a south-easterly bearing. Now I had reached a mountain range, and to cross a tricky col had decided to follow the old Pilgrim's path. I had heard it was way-marked and I needed an easy route down the mountain. Thing is, I missed it. A storm had come in. I had become disorientated and followed a parallel path that led me down into a valley where I had found refuge in a deserted barn.

For two or three days the storm raged. A helter-skelter of snow, hail and wind. I dined on packets of minestrone soup, chunks of brown bread, raisins, chorizo sausage and dark chocolate (always, chocolate in reserve).

On Saturday morning the day shone brightly. But, somehow I lost the path again, and found myself sliding down a rough track beside a torrent. Hopskipping over boulder to boulder, wet, cold, bedraggled, I slowly got off the mountain. By mid-afternoon I was pretty well beaten up and worried about where I could find refuge. A church bell woke me from my reverie. Through the mist I spied a mountain village. Entering the village a group were standing idly at the church's gate. Did they know of a local inn I could stay at? Oh yes. The inn was in that direction. I couldn't miss it.

I smelt the wood smoke before I saw it. A solid stone built building with large chimney stacks at either end. Lights ablaze inside. The Inn stood on its own. A couple of vehicles were parked to the side, behind wood neatly stacked.

I entered through a heavy wooden door. A large, hairy bearded man stood inside slicing thin pieces of meat. Above him hanging from the ceiling were hams and sausages. On seeing me he stopped, quickly came around the bar and took my pack off me.

"Yes, we have been waiting for you. We spied you on the mountain this morning and wondered when you would arrive…come in, come in, settle yourself down over there by

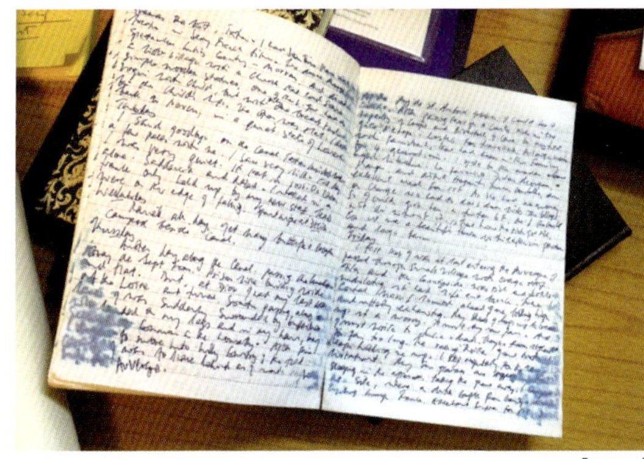

Journal

The meal is all a hazy memory. I remember a thick broth followed by thinly sliced cold meats and cheeses, followed by a casserole....and pints of warm ale. I have no idea why but they all appeared very interested in my adventures and asked me endless questions. It was all very exhausting and I can't remember being taken to bed. It was a raucous and friendly evening...

I stayed for two more nights and earned my keep by helping Andrea chop wood, load his trailer and stack them around the Inn. Now that was quite a skill. It so happened the Inn had been in Francesca's family for six generations. For me it was a home from home. Their hospitality and kindness was natural and sincere, the food, simple country fare, and the decor resounded in history and comfort. One word, snug, describes the Inn. Of course, like all who stayed I fell in love with Francesca and Andrea and their children, and Wolfie. I was to return many times until the earthquake destroyed much of the village. Luckily, the Inn survived and by then the children had grown and left home, and their parents had leased the building whilst they sort new adventures in the City.

the fire and I'll bring you some water - you must be dehydrated - No worries, a room has been prepared for you." I slumped into a threadbare armchair beside the blazing fire and looked about me; low beams, wooden panels and oil paintings of hunting scenes, mountains and torrential rivers. Animals heads; foxes, badgers, deer stood out on plinths....a long, bruegellesque table was set ready for a busy repast.

I fell asleep.

I dreamt I was standing beneath a waterfall, my face burnished by cool running water.... "Wake up, wake up." I looked into the brown eyes of a massive hairy beast who was licking my face. A wolf hound. The hound was pulled away and two little girls stood in front of me. Behind them stood one of the most beautiful women I had ever seen. "Hello, don't mind Wolfie. It's her way of saying welcome. I am Francesca and this is Flora and Isabella. I have drawn you a bath and there are clean clothes, I hope not too large for you, Andrea's, and if you don't mind taking these off upstairs we can get them into the wash." I noticed my boots had been pulled off me and my bare feet were being nibbled by Wolfie. My boots had been cleaned and

polished and were sitting beside the fire. Laughter and the noise of people having a good time were somewhere in the distance.

While I was taking all this in Francesca continued: "We have been expecting you. A shepherd friend sighted you early this morning and warned us of your imminent arrival. You are to be our guest. No arguments. You remind us of Andrea who like you lost his way ten years ago and arrived unannounced and has never left..."

I'm not surprised I thought. Lucky man. She continued. "Today is our Saint's Day. You saw the Choir entering the church for St Teresa's Mass. And, here they are this evening for a celebratory supper and you are to be their special guest. So no worries, enjoy your bath and come down in your own time."

Postcards

This is an easy, relaxing stroll away from the hustle and bustle of Burford. First, there is a slight ascent across open fields providing fine views of the surrounding countryside. Then, the route goes past conserved woodland to meander amidst lush green meadows beside the crystal clear waters of the River Windrush.

Distance
5.5 miles/8.8km.

Minimum Time
2.5 hours.

Grade/Level of Difficulty
Easy.

Terrain/Paths
Grass, meadowland, farm tracks.

Landscape
Rolling pastureland, meadows in river valley.

Dogs
Popular dog walking spot along the river. Some livestock, however, mostly arable pastures. Dogs to be kept under control around livestock.

Public Toilets
Burford High Street.

Parking (P)
Behind church, across bridge.

Recommended Start/Finish
Burford High Street.

Location
On the A40 midway between Oxford and Cheltenham, or on the A361 eleven miles north of Lechlade.

River Windrush in flood, Widford

FEATURES OF INTEREST...

Burford. The first major Cotswold town you come to, if travelling from the East, and what an introduction. The wide High Street with its classical gables atop some gracious houses, slopes down to the dreamy, River Windrush. Once an important coach and wool centre bursting with activity.

A history of civil rights and religious tolerance prevailed here with the Burford Levellers. On 17 May 1649, three soldiers were executed in Burford Churchyard on the orders of Oliver Cromwell. These three had sought to undermine the authority of Cromwell whom they considered to be a dictator rather than a liberator. This event is celebrated every year with song, dance and speeches. Today, there are many splendid inns, coffee shops (too many to mention) ideal for a pre-walk breakfast; The Priory, Lynwood Café, Huffkins and Mrs Bumble for take-away sandwiches/ lunch boxes.

Fulbrook. An attractive village of Cotswold stone with a quaint church and the Carpenter's

Arms. For those with the constitution it demands you could be forgiven for thinking this walk may very well turn into a pub crawl.

River Windrush. Seen at the beginning and end of this walk. The river can be a slow trickling stream in summer with a tendency to flood in winter. A very 'English' ambiance pervades its banks and meadows.

St John the Baptist's Church. One of the great Cotswold churches built in the C15 with proceeds earned by the local wool merchants. Hence the term 'Wool' church. It has a spacious interior more akin to a small cathedral. The porch and spire c.1450 are outstanding, as are the sculptured table tombs in the churchyard. Inside, don't miss the intricate medieval stained glass and the monuments (painted figures). Open daily 9-5 except during services. For refreshments visit the Warwick Hall & Café, a spectacular new build with outdoor seating beside the Windrush. warwickhallburford.org

Swinbrook. Former home of the Mitford Family. Beautiful church with famous Fettiplace monuments. The Swan Inn is a pretty pub beside the River Windrush and worth a detour if you have the time. Turn L at Widford towards St Oswald's church (built on the site of a Roman villa) and cross fields for Swinbrook.

Tolsey Museum, High Street. Burford's social and industrial history: charters, dolls house, objects of any rural trades.

WHERE TO EAT, DRINK & (OR) SLEEP...

Greyhounds B&B, 19 Sheep Street. Stylish, exceptional, luxurious, relaxing, immaculate, knockout - adjectives that one does not use lightly. Michael Taubenheim has created a refuge of delight and wonder in a historic build. Formerly home to the Countryman Magazine, before that built for a wool merchant in the C15.
01993 822780
greyhoundsburford.com

Mrs Bumbles, 31 Lower High Street. A Lancashire lass who knows and loves her food. This is where I go for a sandwich or picnic fare. Its a deli. Try her sumptuous scotch eggs, cheeses. Open daily 8.30-5.30. 01993 822209
bumblesofburford.co.uk

The Priory, 35 High Street. Opens every day for breakfast, lunch, cream teas and early suppers. Child friendly. B&B. Open daily. 01993 823249
prioryrestaurantburford.co.uk

Highway Inn, 117 High Street. A choice of nine cosy bedrooms furnished in a mix of antique and modern styles. The Highway Inn has plenty of character and prides itself on offering an informal and individual experience akin to visiting friends in the country. Simple food made using local and seasonal produce.
01993 823661
thehighwayinn.co.uk

Lamb Inn, Sheep Street. Your typical olde English hostelry: flagstone floors, low ceilings, nooks and crannies galore, fine ales, luxurious bedrooms and intimate lounges. Restaurant.
01993 823155
cotswold-inns-hotels.co.uk/
the-lamb-inn

Manfred Schotten Antiques B&B, High Street. Manfred and his wife Gabi are legends in the world of antiques, sports antiques and memorabilia, as well as classic and vintage motor cycles, living here the past 40-years. Their top floor houses a luxurious double bedroom with bathroom. Staying here is an experience that will live with you forever.
01993 822302
sportantiques.co.uk

The Angel, 14 Witney Street. My local spies inform me this Inn serves the finest food in town. A stylish brasserie in a C16 coaching inn with log fires providing mouth-watering fare: Mediterranean dishes and enormous breakfasts prepared for the adventurous traveller. B&B. 01993 822714
theangelatburford.co.uk

Wobbly Windows, Burford

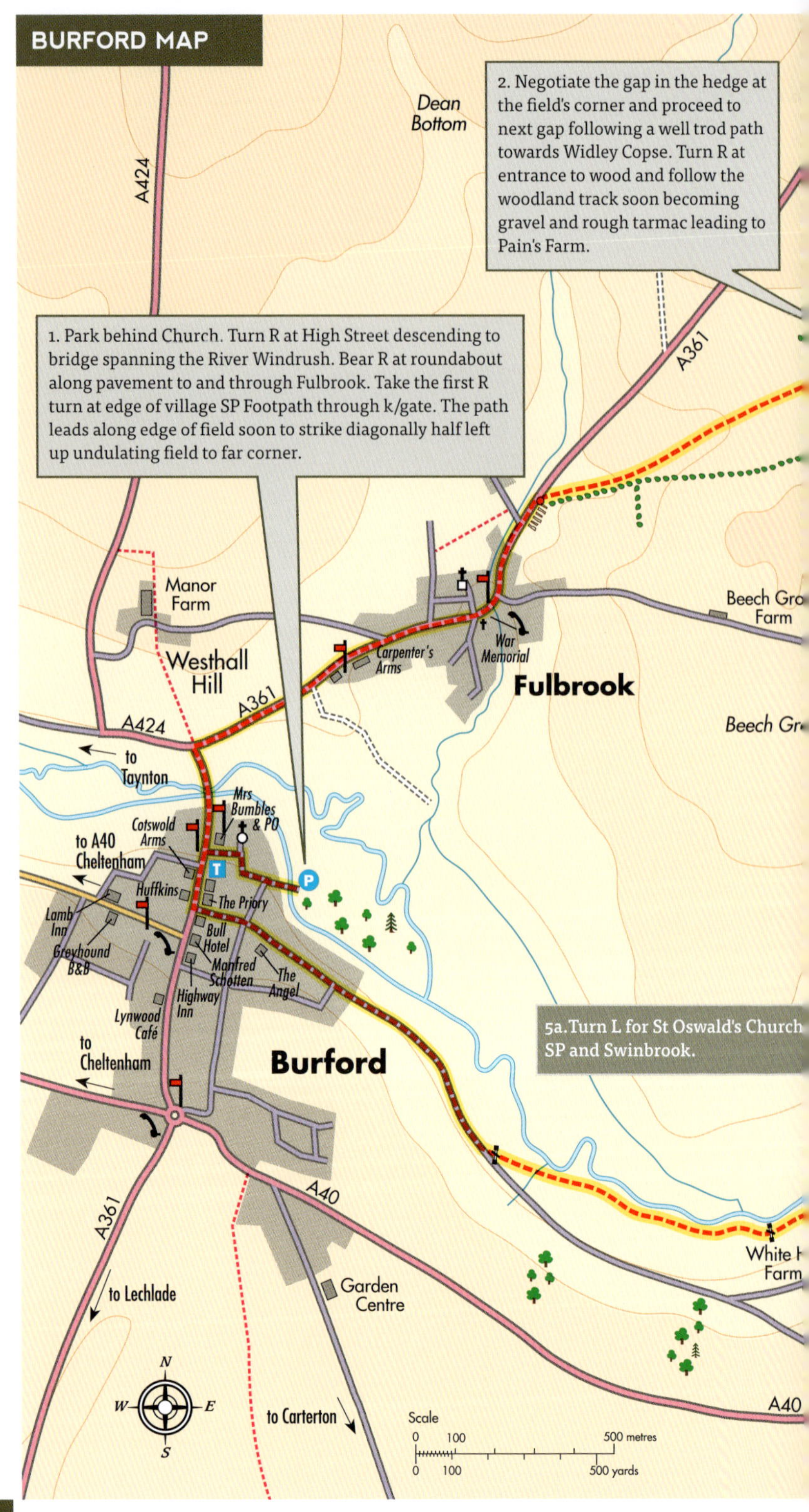

BURFORD MAP

2. Negotiate the gap in the hedge at the field's corner and proceed to next gap following a well trod path towards Widley Copse. Turn R at entrance to wood and follow the woodland track soon becoming gravel and rough tarmac leading to Pain's Farm.

Dean Bottom

A361

1. Park behind Church. Turn R at High Street descending to bridge spanning the River Windrush. Bear R at roundabout along pavement to and through Fulbrook. Take the first R turn at edge of village SP Footpath through k/gate. The path leads along edge of field soon to strike diagonally half left up undulating field to far corner.

A424

Manor Farm

Beech Gro Farm

Westhall Hill

A361

Carpenter's Arms

War Memorial

Fulbrook

Beech Gr

A424

to Taynton

Mrs Bumbles & PO

Cotswold Arms

to A40 Cheltenham

T

P

Huffkins

The Priory

Lamb Inn

Bull Hotel

Greyhound B&B

Manfred Schotten

The Angel

Highway Inn

Lynwood Café

to Cheltenham

Burford

5a. Turn L for St Oswald's Church SP and Swinbrook.

A361

A40

Garden Centre

to Lechlade

White Farm

A40

N
W E
S

to Carterton

Scale
0   100   500 metres
0   100   500 yards

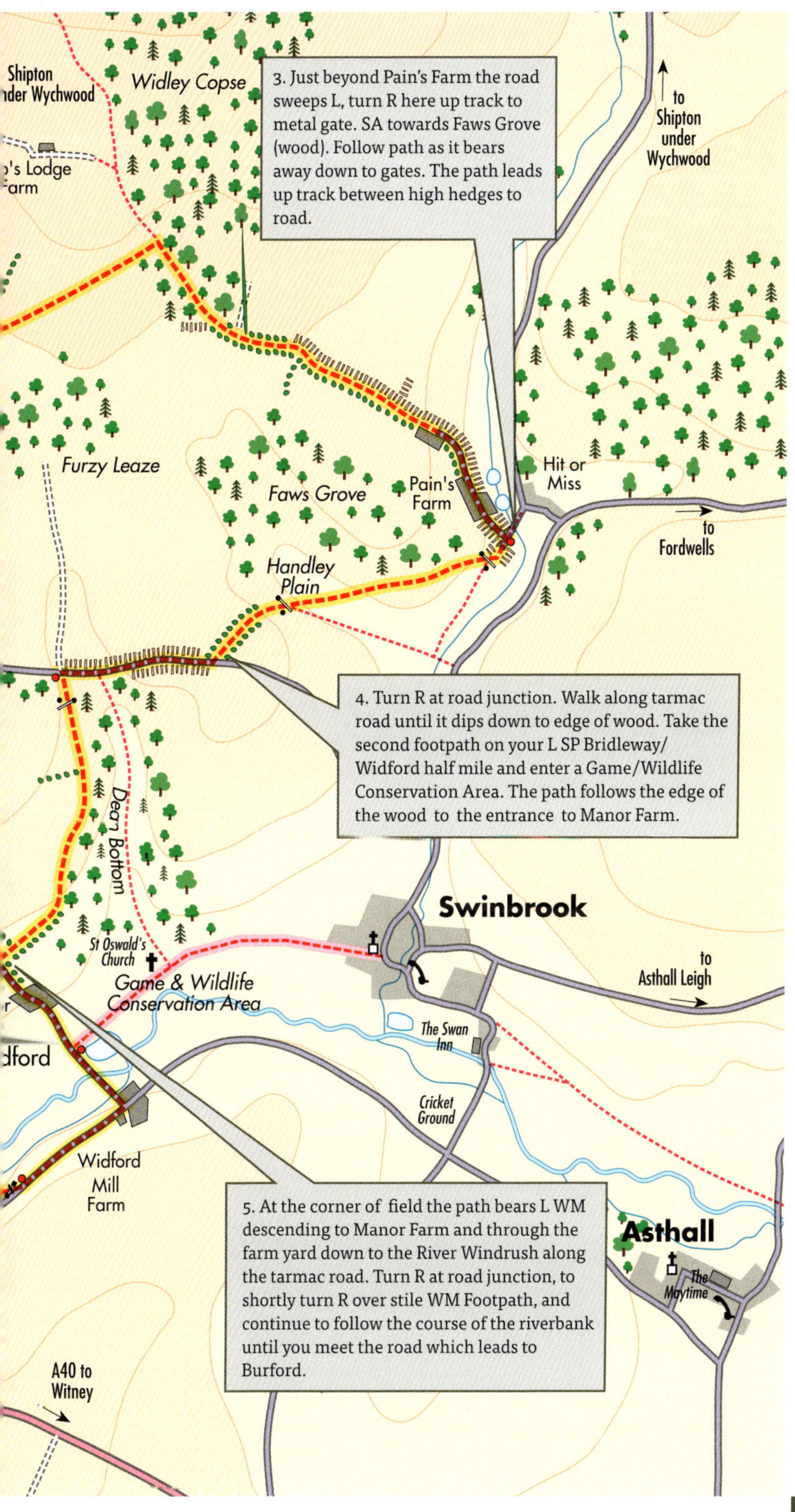

Shipton under Wychwood
Widley Copse
's Lodge Farm
Furzy Leaze
Faws Grove
Pain's Farm
Handley Plain
Hit or Miss
to Shipton under Wychwood
to Fordwells
Dean Bottom
St Oswald's Church
Game & Wildlife Conservation Area
dford
Widford Mill Farm
A40 to Witney
Swinbrook
The Swan Inn
Cricket Ground
to Asthall Leigh
Asthall
The Maytime
3. Just beyond Pain's Farm the road sweeps L, turn R here up track to metal gate. SA towards Faws Grove (wood). Follow path as it bears away down to gates. The path leads up track between high hedges to road.
4. Turn R at road junction. Walk along tarmac road until it dips down to edge of wood. Take the second footpath on your L SP Bridleway/ Widford half mile and enter a Game/Wildlife Conservation Area. The path follows the edge of the wood to the entrance to Manor Farm.
5. At the corner of field the path bears L WM descending to Manor Farm and through the farm yard down to the River Windrush along the tarmac road. Turn R at road junction, to shortly turn R over stile WM Footpath, and continue to follow the course of the riverbank until you meet the road which leads to Burford.

The walk starts among stone cottages in the pretty village before following the river valley. At this point it can be muddy so stout footwear is recommended. After crossing the River Windrush, the path ascends through woodland. A short stretch of hedged paths and pavement leads into Crawley before returning to Minster Lovell via fields.

Distance

3.75 miles/6km.

Minimum Time

1.5 hours.

Grade/Level of Difficulty

Easy.

Terrain/Paths

Muddy paths, grass.

Landscape

River valley, woodland.

Dogs

Keep under control across farmland - beware livestock. Can run free in woods.

Public Toilets None.

Parking (P)

By Churchyard, Minster Lovell.

Recommended Start/Finish

Minster Lovell.

Location

Just off the A40, between Burford and Witney.

FEATURES OF INTEREST...

Crawley. Tiny Oxfordshire village with Cotswold stone cottages, War Memorial and an old cloth Mill converted into separate industrial units.

Minster Lovell. Arguably one of the most attractive villages in the Windrush Valley. There is a fine C15 bridge leading to a street of pretty cottages and on to the C15 Church which rests beside the ancient Hall. The large open space beside the bridge is the Cricket Ground and popular picnic spot.

Minster Lovell Hall (EH). A picturesque C15 ruin beside the River Windrush. Reputed to be the haunted seat of the Lovell family who were associates of Richard III. There is evidence of medieval tracery. Associated with the rhyme *Mistletoe Bough*. Open daily in daylight hours. english-heritage.org.uk

St Kenelm's Church, Minster Lovell. The church is originally Norman of cruciform design which creates a most impressive space of Renaissance proportions. Perpendicular tower. C15 stained glass. Carvings. Restored in 1870. Splendid tomb. The path into the Hall runs to the left side of the church.

Witney. This is a town of hustle and bustle with a good share of attractive limestone buildings. Note the C17 Butter Cross with gabled roof, clock turret and sundial, the Town Hall with room overhanging a piazza and across Church Green the unusually handsome spire to the Parish Church, visible from far and wide. Local history ably recorded at Cogges Manor Farm Museum.

WHERE TO EAT, DRINK... SLEEP

Hill Grove Farm B&B, Crawley Dry Lane. 300-acre (mainly) arable working farm with cattle and free range poultry. Good farmhouse breakfast. Guests can use the garden and sunroom. Children welcome. No dogs. 01993 703120

The Lamb Inn, Crawley. A stylish country pub and restaurant serving top-nosh for hungry walkers, and a useful halfway stopping off point. Sebastian Snow the chef has gained a worthy reputation for providing good food. Children welcome. 01993 708792 lambpub.co.uk

Old Swan & Minster Mill, School Hill. Two buildings on the banks of the River Windrush: a C19 Mill and the C17 Old Swan Inn, with origins going back to the C14 has been transformed into a boutique-style hotel dedicated towards weekend breaks, family events (weddings) and the corporate. Windrush Spa. Trout fishing. Children and dogs welcome. 01993 862512 oldswan.co.uk

River Windrush, Crawley

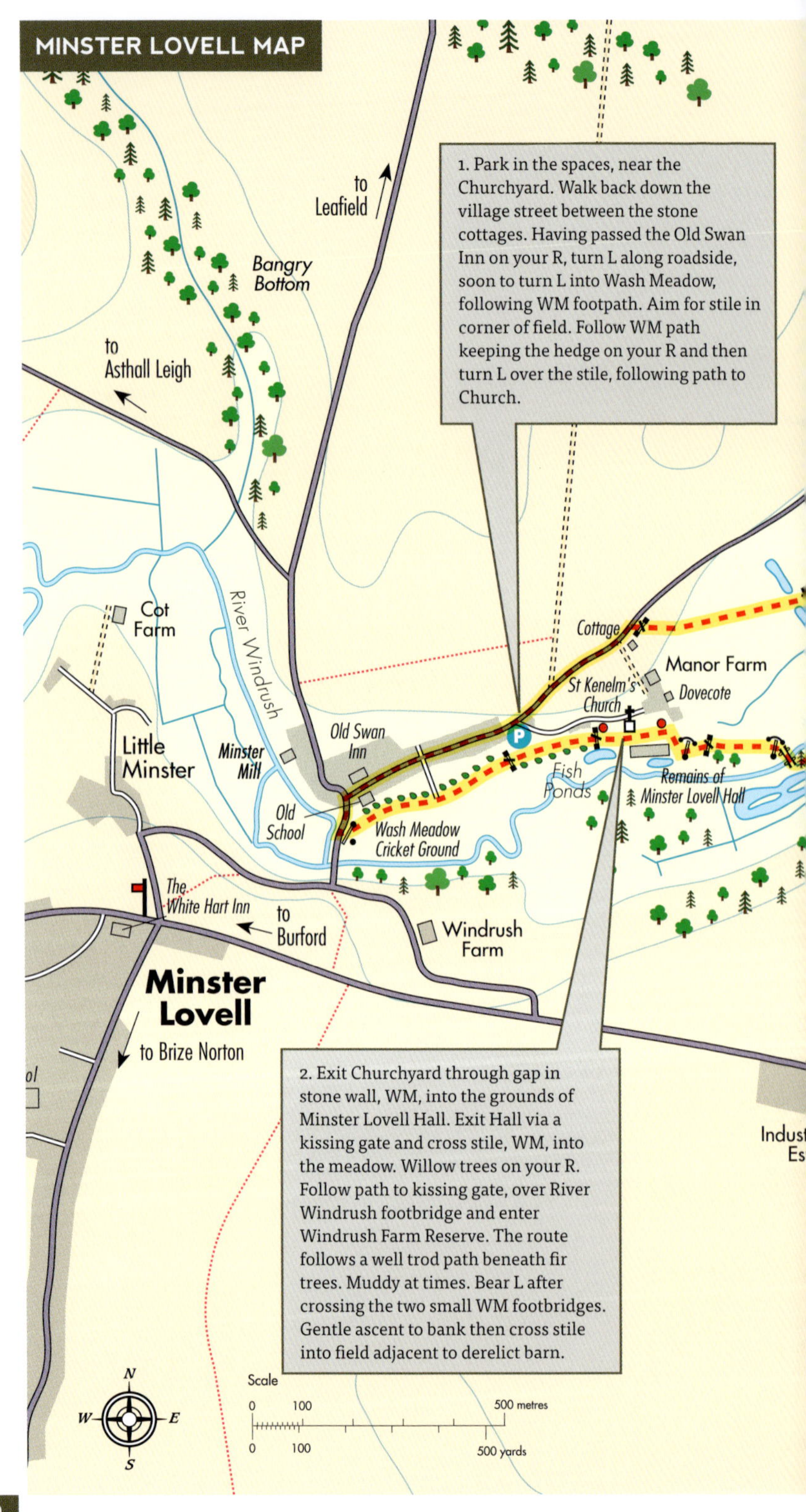

1. Park in the spaces, near the Churchyard. Walk back down the village street between the stone cottages. Having passed the Old Swan Inn on your R, turn L along roadside, soon to turn L into Wash Meadow, following WM footpath. Aim for stile in corner of field. Follow WM path keeping the hedge on your R and then turn L over the stile, following path to Church.

2. Exit Churchyard through gap in stone wall, WM, into the grounds of Minster Lovell Hall. Exit Hall via a kissing gate and cross stile, WM, into the meadow. Willow trees on your R. Follow path to kissing gate, over River Windrush footbridge and enter Windrush Farm Reserve. The route follows a well trod path beneath fir trees. Muddy at times. Bear L after crossing the two small WM footbridges. Gentle ascent to bank then cross stile into field adjacent to derelict barn.

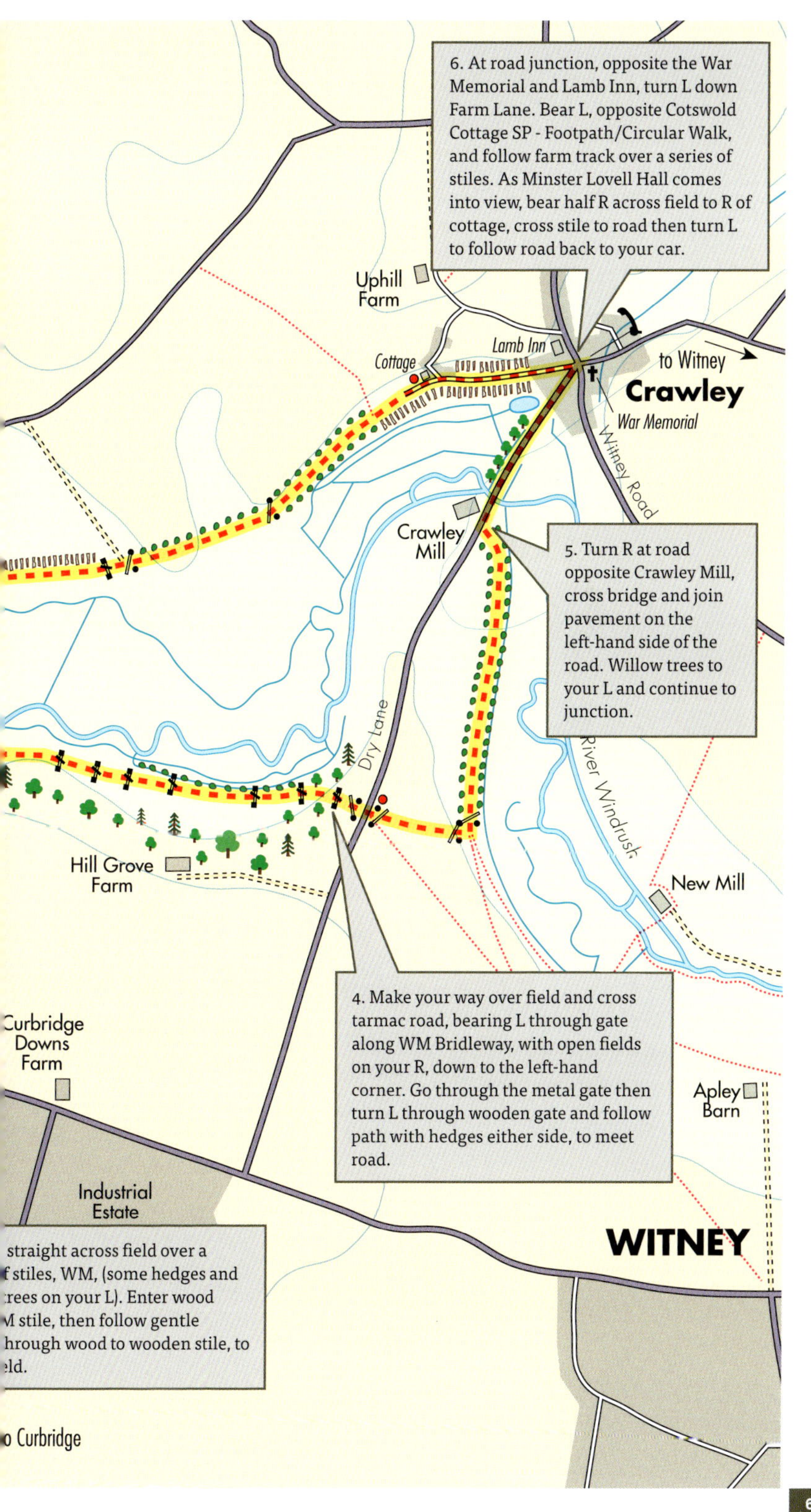

6. At road junction, opposite the War Memorial and Lamb Inn, turn L down Farm Lane. Bear L, opposite Cotswold Cottage SP - Footpath/Circular Walk, and follow farm track over a series of stiles. As Minster Lovell Hall comes into view, bear half R across field to R of cottage, cross stile to road then turn L to follow road back to your car.

5. Turn R at road opposite Crawley Mill, cross bridge and join pavement on the left-hand side of the road. Willow trees to your L and continue to junction.

4. Make your way over field and cross tarmac road, bearing L through gate along WM Bridleway, with open fields on your R, down to the left-hand corner. Go through the metal gate then turn L through wooden gate and follow path with hedges either side, to meet road.

straight across field over a f stiles, WM, (some hedges and rees on your L). Enter wood M stile, then follow gentle hrough wood to wooden stile, to eld.

o Curbridge

Uphill Farm
Cottage
Lamb Inn
to Witney
Crawley
War Memorial
Witney Road
Crawley Mill
Dry Lane
River Windrush
New Mill
Hill Grove Farm
Curbridge Downs Farm
Apley Barn
Industrial Estate
WITNEY

The first, short walk takes you around the village past idyllic cottage gardens surmounted by thatched or roof tiles and down to an overgrown spinney. The second walk circumnavigates the Great Park, a C19 Arboretum planted by John Claudius Loudon. Bring your book on trees!

Distance
Walk 1: 1.5 miles/2.4km.
Walk 2: 2.5 miles/4km.

Minimum Time
Walk 1: 1 hour.
Walk 2: 1.5 hours.

Grade/Level of Difficulty
Easy.

Terrain/Paths
Tracks, mud, grass.

Landscape
Arable fields, woodland.

Dogs
To be kept under control at all times.

Public Toilets
None.

Parking (P)
Great Tew village car park.

Recommended Start/Finish
From P or in village.

Location
Situated between Banbury and Chipping Norton just off the A361 on the B4022 leading to Enstone and the A44.

FEATURES OF INTEREST...

Cornbury Music Festival, Great Tew Park. Now establishing itself as a slightly cheaper and more personal, alternative to Glastonbury. Three days in early July with a full line up of stars.

Great Tew. A sensationally beautiful village lined with ironstone cottages covered in thatch and stone tiles. Many fell into disrepair but have undergone renovation. The village was designed by the Scottish architect, John Claudius Loudon. Venue for the Cornbury Music Festival In July.

Great Tew Park. Planted by Loudon in the early C19. The Park has the appearance of an Arboretum.

St Michael's Church. Norman church with C13, C14 and C17 additions. Fine Tympanum and doorway. Early C14 stone monuments of a Knight and his Lady in the North aisle. Memorial to Lucius Cary (Lord Falkland). A mass of daffodils in Spring.

Great Tew

WHERE TO EAT, DRINK... SLEEP

Falkland Arms. Named after Lord Falkland who lived here, and who died fighting for Charles I at the Battle of Newbury. A traditional pub with flagstone floors, oak beams, inglenook fireplace, mugs and bric-a-brac hanging from the ceiling, and Wadworth ales to refresh your vitals. Beer Garden. B&B with 6-bedrooms. No dogs or children U-16. Cottage to let. 01608 683653 falklandarms.co.uk

Soho Farmhouse. An exclusive members club and hotel originally founded for the creative industries but now accepts all comers with deep pockets. All is set in 100 acres of Oxfordshire countryside; Boathouse, Electric Barn Cinema, The Woodshed, Cowshed Spa and Cabins. You may even have the misfortune to spy the Beckhams. 01608 691000 sohohouse.com

Quince & Clover, The Old Post Office. Herewith a stylish café serving breakfast, brunch and lunch, and their home-made ice creams. Open daily except Tu from 8.30 to 4pm. 01608 683225 quinceandclover.co.uk

JUST OFF THE MAP...

White Horse Inn, Duns Tew. A beautiful and elegant C17 Inn with quality accommodation. À La Carte menu and bar snacks. 01869 340272 dunstewwhitehorse.co.uk

St Michael's Church

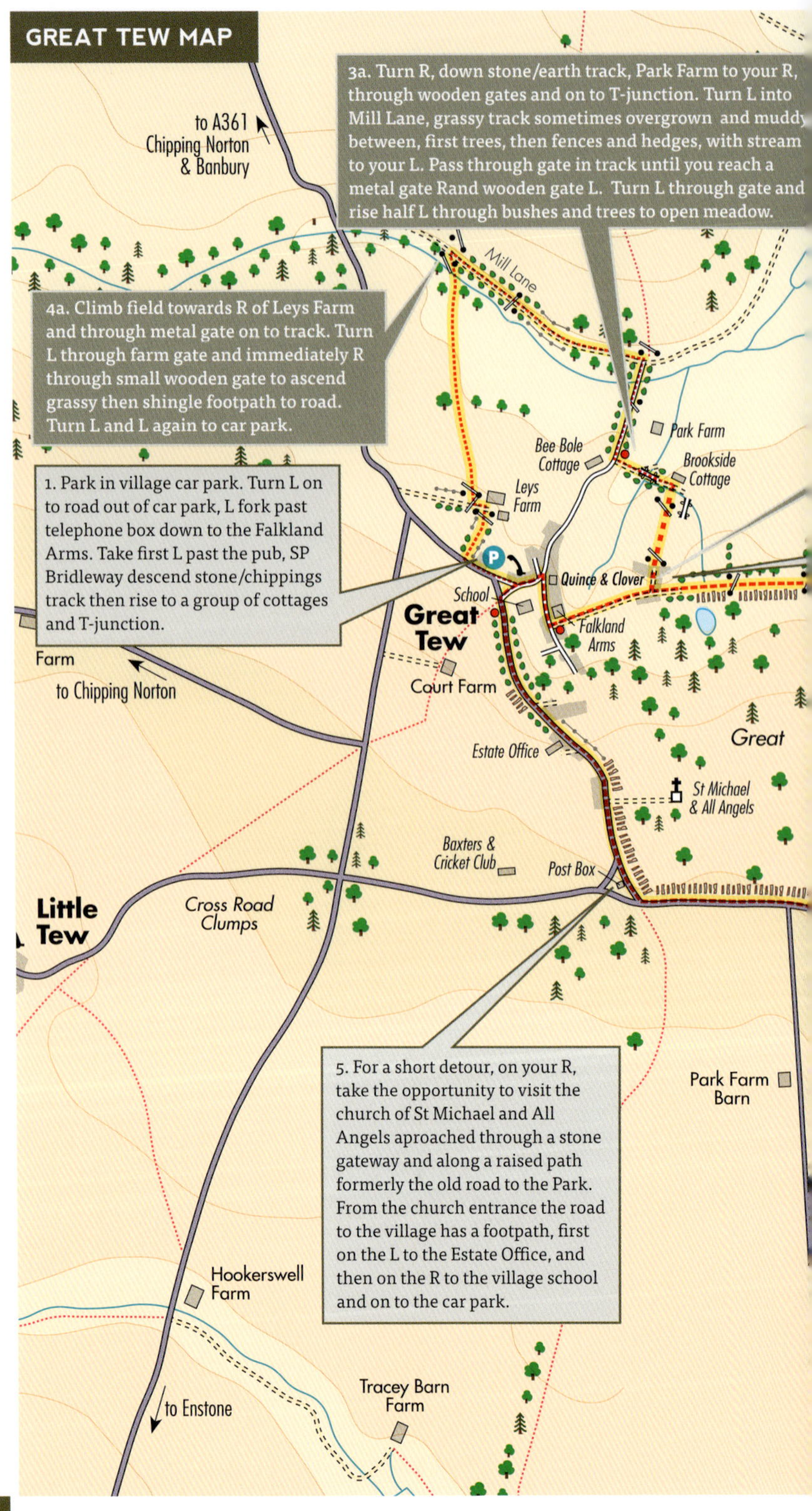

3a. Turn R, down stone/earth track, Park Farm to your R, through wooden gates and on to T-junction. Turn L into Mill Lane, grassy track sometimes overgrown and muddy between, first trees, then fences and hedges, with stream to your L. Pass through gate in track until you reach a metal gate Rand wooden gate L. Turn L through gate and rise half L through bushes and trees to open meadow.
4a. Climb field towards R of Leys Farm and through metal gate on to track. Turn L through farm gate and immediately R through small wooden gate to ascend grassy then shingle footpath to road. Turn L and L again to car park.
1. Park in village car park. Turn L on to road out of car park, L fork past telephone box down to the Falkland Arms. Take first L past the pub, SP Bridleway descend stone/chippings track then rise to a group of cottages and T-junction.
5. For a short detour, on your R, take the opportunity to visit the church of St Michael and All Angels aproached through a stone gateway and along a raised path formerly the old road to the Park. From the church entrance the road to the village has a footpath, first on the L to the Estate Office, and then on the R to the village school and on to the car park.
to A361
Chipping Norton
& Banbury
Mill Lane
Park Farm
Bee Bole
Cottage
Brookside
Cottage
Leys
Farm
Quince & Clover
School
Great
Tew
Falkland
Arms
Farm
to Chipping Norton
Court Farm
Estate Office
Great
St Michael
& All Angels
Baxters &
Cricket Club
Post Box
Little
Tew
Cross Road
Clumps
Park Farm
Barn
Hookerswell
Farm
to Enstone
Tracey Barn
Farm

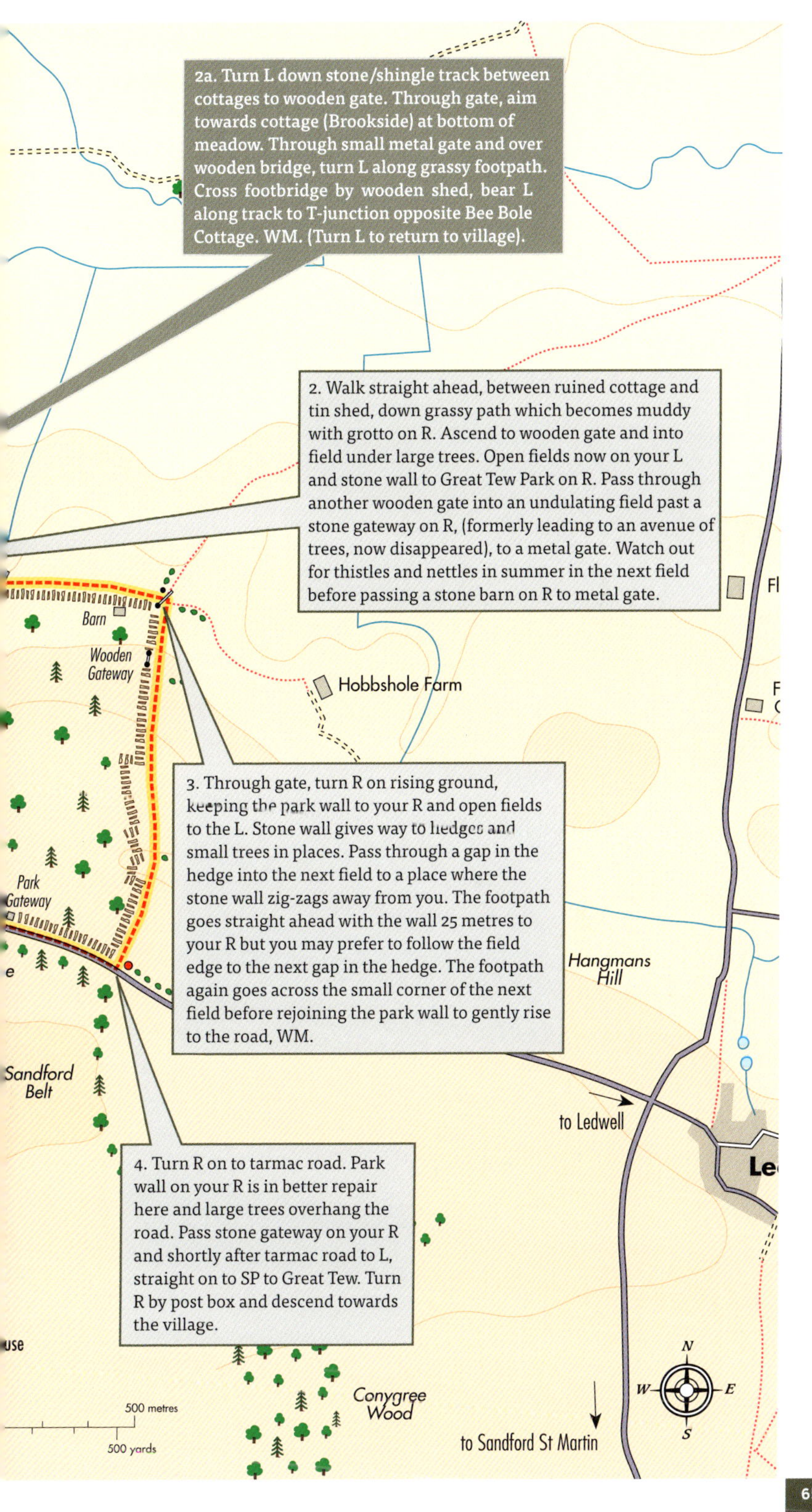

2a. Turn L down stone/shingle track between cottages to wooden gate. Through gate, aim towards cottage (Brookside) at bottom of meadow. Through small metal gate and over wooden bridge, turn L along grassy footpath. Cross footbridge by wooden shed, bear L along track to T-junction opposite Bee Bole Cottage. WM. (Turn L to return to village).

2. Walk straight ahead, between ruined cottage and tin shed, down grassy path which becomes muddy with grotto on R. Ascend to wooden gate and into field under large trees. Open fields now on your L and stone wall to Great Tew Park on R. Pass through another wooden gate into an undulating field past a stone gateway on R, (formerly leading to an avenue of trees, now disappeared), to a metal gate. Watch out for thistles and nettles in summer in the next field before passing a stone barn on R to metal gate.

3. Through gate, turn R on rising ground, keeping the park wall to your R and open fields to the L. Stone wall gives way to hedges and small trees in places. Pass through a gap in the hedge into the next field to a place where the stone wall zig-zags away from you. The footpath goes straight ahead with the wall 25 metres to your R but you may prefer to follow the field edge to the next gap in the hedge. The footpath again goes across the small corner of the next field before rejoining the park wall to gently rise to the road, WM.

4. Turn R on to tarmac road. Park wall on your R is in better repair here and large trees overhang the road. Pass stone gateway on your R and shortly after tarmac road to L, straight on to SP to Great Tew. Turn R by post box and descend towards the village.

Barn
Wooden Gateway
Park Gateway
Sandford Belt
Hobbshole Farm
Hangmans Hill
to Ledwell
Conygree Wood
to Sandford St Martin
500 metres
500 yards
N
W E
S

This walk starts from a traditional country inn noted for its rustic ales and set in one of a pair of exquisite Cotswold villages situated on opposing banks of the River Leach. The route enters the Hatherop Estate and heads towards the upper reaches of the River Leach which in summer disappears underground, and crosses rolling sheep pastures beside stone walls - the quintessential Cotswold landscape.

Distance
4.5 miles/7.2km.
Minimum Time
2 hours.
Grade/Level of Difficulty
Easy.
Terrain/Paths
Tarmac, grassland, mud.
Landscape
Dry river valley, rolling sheep pastures.
Dogs
To be kept under control - beware livestock.

Public Toilets
None.
Parking (P)
Opposite Victoria Inn.
Recommended Start/Finish
Eastleach Turville.
Location
In between Burford, Lechlade and Fairford with access via the A417, and from the A361, turning opposite Filkins.

FEATURES OF INTEREST...

Eastleach Turville & Eastleach Martin (Bouthrop). Twin villages on opposite banks of the river Leach connected by the ancient clapper bridge (Keble's Bridge). The two churches were probably built by two different Lords of the Manor. In Spring, a profusion of daffodils grow along the riverbank from Keble's Bridge. Many of the cottages were built for estate workers on Sir Thomas Bazleigh's Estate, Hatherop. There is a Children's Playground if the kids still have some energy at the end of the walk.

Keble's Bridge. Most probably built by the Keble family whose descendant, John Keble, was curate here in 1815. He founded the Oxford Movement, and is known for his volume of religious verse 'The Christian Year'.

St Andrew's Church, Eastleach Turville. Hidden beneath the trees this tiny church has a more interesting interior than its neighbour.

The Victoria Inn, Eastleach

C14 saddleback tower of Transitional and Early English period style. Norman doorway c.1130 with carved Tympanum of Christ.

St Michael & St Martin Church, Eastleach Martin. Founded by Richard Fitzpons, one of William the Conqueror's knights. C14 north transept. Decorated windows. Memorable exterior design and position beside the river. Closed for services in 1982.

Macaroni Downs. This is quite a sight. These rolling sheep pastures were once the location for Regency derring-do, gambling and horse racing. Today, it is the sheep who liven the location with their munching...you may also spot the odd mountain biker.

WHERE TO EAT, DRINK... RELAX

The Victoria Inn, Eastleach. A traditional country pub since 1856 that has been sensitively restored without losing its character. Superb pub-grub and Arkells ales combine to make your stay a pleasure in keeping with the beauty of its surroundings. Large beer garden suitable for muddy walkers and dogs. Opens W-Su 11am to 11pm. 01367 850277 thevictoriainneastleach.co.uk

Macaroni Downs, Eastleach

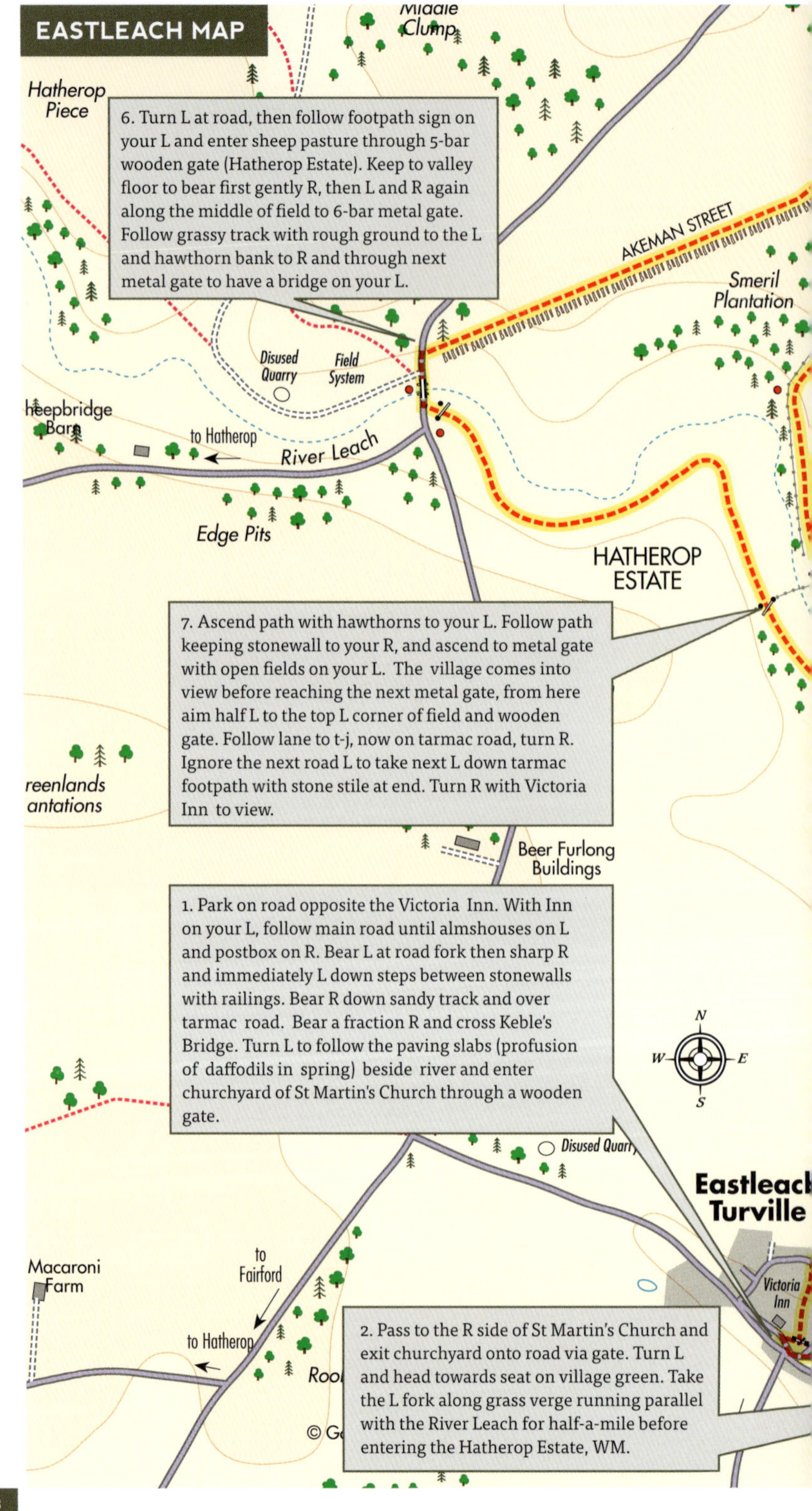

6. Turn L at road, then follow footpath sign on your L and enter sheep pasture through 5-bar wooden gate (Hatherop Estate). Keep to valley floor to bear first gently R, then L and R again along the middle of field to 6-bar metal gate. Follow grassy track with rough ground to the L and hawthorn bank to R and through next metal gate to have a bridge on your L.

7. Ascend path with hawthorns to your L. Follow path keeping stonewall to your R, and ascend to metal gate with open fields on your L. The village comes into view before reaching the next metal gate, from here aim half L to the top L corner of field and wooden gate. Follow lane to t-j, now on tarmac road, turn R. Ignore the next road L to take next L down tarmac footpath with stone stile at end. Turn R with Victoria Inn to view.

1. Park on road opposite the Victoria Inn. With Inn on your L, follow main road until almshouses on L and postbox on R. Bear L at road fork then sharp R and immediately L down steps between stonewalls with railings. Bear R down sandy track and over tarmac road. Bear a fraction R and cross Keble's Bridge. Turn L to follow the paving slabs (profusion of daffodils in spring) beside river and enter churchyard of St Martin's Church through a wooden gate.

2. Pass to the R side of St Martin's Church and exit churchyard onto road via gate. Turn L and head towards seat on village green. Take the L fork along grass verge running parallel with the River Leach for half-a-mile before entering the Hatherop Estate, WM.

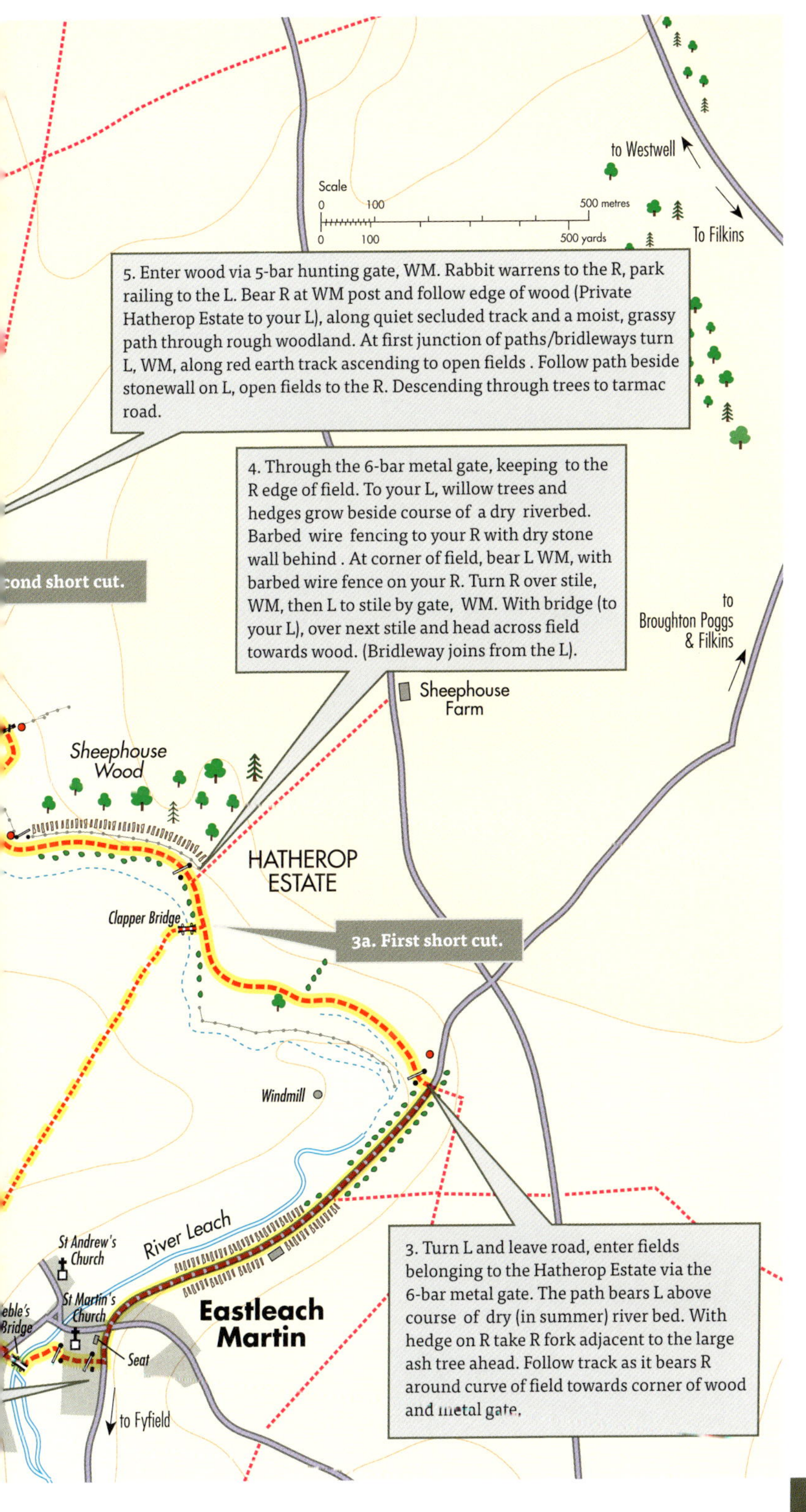

Scale
0   100   500 metres
0   100   500 yards

to Westwell
To Filkins

5. Enter wood via 5-bar hunting gate, WM. Rabbit warrens to the R, park railing to the L. Bear R at WM post and follow edge of wood (Private Hatherop Estate to your L), along quiet secluded track and a moist, grassy path through rough woodland. At first junction of paths/bridleways turn L, WM, along red earth track ascending to open fields . Follow path beside stonewall on L, open fields to the R. Descending through trees to tarmac road.

4. Through the 6-bar metal gate, keeping to the R edge of field. To your L, willow trees and hedges grow beside course of a dry riverbed. Barbed wire fencing to your R with dry stone wall behind . At corner of field, bear L WM, with barbed wire fence on your R. Turn R over stile, WM, then L to stile by gate, WM. With bridge (to your L), over next stile and head across field towards wood. (Bridleway joins from the L).

ond short cut.

to Broughton Poggs & Filkins

Sheephouse Farm

Sheephouse Wood

HATHEROP ESTATE

Clapper Bridge

3a. First short cut.

Windmill

St Andrew's Church

River Leach

eble's Bridge

St Martin's Church

Eastleach Martin

Seat

to Fyfield

3. Turn L and leave road, enter fields belonging to the Hatherop Estate via the 6-bar metal gate. The path bears L above course of dry (in summer) river bed. With hedge on R take R fork adjacent to the large ash tree ahead. Follow track as it bears R around curve of field towards corner of wood and metal gate.

One of the most popular walks in the Cotswolds. It's an easy walk along a pretty river valley connecting two enchanting villages. For those with tired legs or little time the map indicates a short cut. The route is undulating and provides views of rolling sheep pastures, an old Roman route - Akeman Street (barely visible), trout streams and rich water meadows. The view from amidst the trees down onto the village of Coln St Aldwyns is a delight.

Distance
5.75 miles/9.2km.
Minimum Time
2.5 hours.
Level of Difficulty
Easy.
Terrain/Paths
Farm tracks (muddy in winter), woodland, grass.
Landscape
Rolling farmland, sheep pastures, river valley.

Dogs
To be kept under control at all times. Sheep pastures along riverside.
Public Toilets
Bibury, opposite river.
Parking (P)
Bibury.
Recommended Start/Finish
Bibury or Coln St Aldwyns.
Location
Bibury is between Cirencester and Burford on the B4425.

 Towards Akeman Street, Bibury Walk

FEATURES OF INTEREST...

Arlington Row (NT). These iconic cottages were originally monastic wool barns. However, in the C17 they were converted into weavers' homes. Now domestic dwellings, they overlook Rack Isle, a four-acre water meadow where cloth was once hung out to dry. Today, it's an open wetland meadow and wildfowl reserve.

Arlington Mill. A beautiful, historic C17 watermill beside the River Coln. Formerly a countryside museum, but sadly all the artefacts were sold off and is now a luxurious holiday let.

Bibury. William Morris, the eminent Victorian poet, designer and artist lived nearby at Kelmscott and considered Bibury 'the most beautiful village in England', and few would argue with him. On the downside, it attracts the crowds and is a stop-off point for coach tours. On the up side, it is a honey-pot village made up of rose-covered cottages set behind idyllic kitchen gardens, and all overlook the sleepy River Coln inhabited by swans, trout and duckling. During the C17 Bibury was notorious as a buccaneering centre for gambling and horse racing.

Bibury Trout Farm. This working trout farm lies in a beautiful setting beside the River Coln. You can feed the fish, or try your hand at fly fishing in the Beginner's Fishery. There are fresh and prepared trout on sale, as well as plants and shrubs. Gift shop. Café. Open daily. 01285 740215 biburytroutfarm.co.uk

Coln St Aldwyns. Designated as one of the 10 most desirable villages in England. Coln is a lovingly-cared for village of Cotswold stone set amidst a lush river valley. It is a place full of rustic charm, and features many of the most picturesque properties in the Cotswolds, ranging from thatched Tudor cottages to Virginia creeper-clad Cotswold stone houses.

St Mary's Church, Bibury. If you seek a refuge from the hurly-burly of Bibury's tourists then walk along the banks of the River Coln and you'll soon find the entrance to this pretty church. With evidence of Saxon remains, Norman font and superb sculptured table tombs.

LIGHT BITES...COFFEE... TEAS

Coln Stores & Post Office, Coln St Aldwyns. This community store welcomes walkers and cyclists, and will serve you coffee, teas, cold drinks, sandwiches, cakes and much more. 01285 750294 colnstores.co.uk

WHERE TO EAT, DRINK... SLEEP

The Catherine Wheel, Arlington. A C15 Inn with four en-suite bedrooms and pretty garden. The decor is very much Farrow-Grey-Boringdom. Food served from 12noon to 9pm. Sunday roasts. 01285 740250 catherinewheel-bibury.co.uk

The New Inn, Coln St Aldwyns. Charming C16 ivy-clad inn delivers a combination of hotel-pub-restaurant. Efficient service, affordable cuisine specialising in burgers and contemporary, classy bedrooms. 01285 750651 thenewinncoln.co.uk

The Swan Hotel. Few hotels have such a fabulous location - overlooking the River Coln, an idyllic trout stream. Swan Brasserie serves light meals and afternoon tea. Fishing rights. 22-luxurious bedrooms. Dogs and children welcome. 01285 740695 cotswold-inns-hotels.co.uk/ the-swan-hotel

Arlington Row

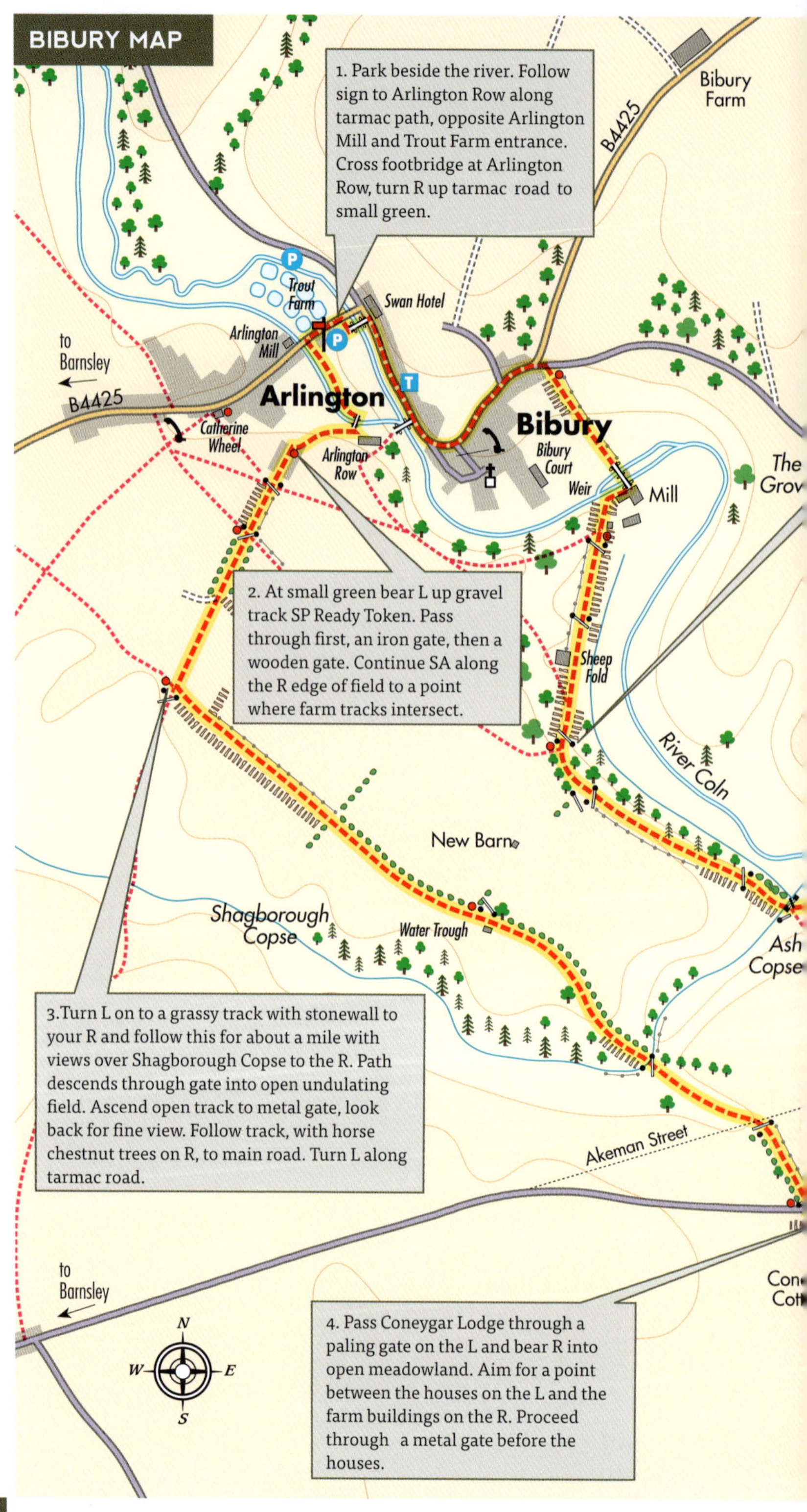

1. Park beside the river. Follow sign to Arlington Row along tarmac path, opposite Arlington Mill and Trout Farm entrance. Cross footbridge at Arlington Row, turn R up tarmac road to small green.
2. At small green bear L up gravel track SP Ready Token. Pass through first, an iron gate, then a wooden gate. Continue SA along the R edge of field to a point where farm tracks intersect.
3. Turn L on to a grassy track with stonewall to your R and follow this for about a mile with views over Shagborough Copse to the R. Path descends through gate into open undulating field. Ascend open track to metal gate, look back for fine view. Follow track, with horse chestnut trees on R, to main road. Turn L along tarmac road.
4. Pass Coneygar Lodge through a paling gate on the L and bear R into open meadowland. Aim for a point between the houses on the L and the farm buildings on the R. Proceed through a metal gate before the houses.
Bibury Farm
B4425
to Barnsley
B4425
Trout Farm
Swan Hotel
Arlington Mill
Arlington
Catherine Wheel
Arlington Row
Bibury
Bibury Court
Weir
Mill
The Grov
River Coln
Sheep Fold
New Barn
Shagborough Copse
Water Trough
Ash Copse
Akeman Street
to Barnsley
Con Cot
Coneygar Cott
N
W
E
S

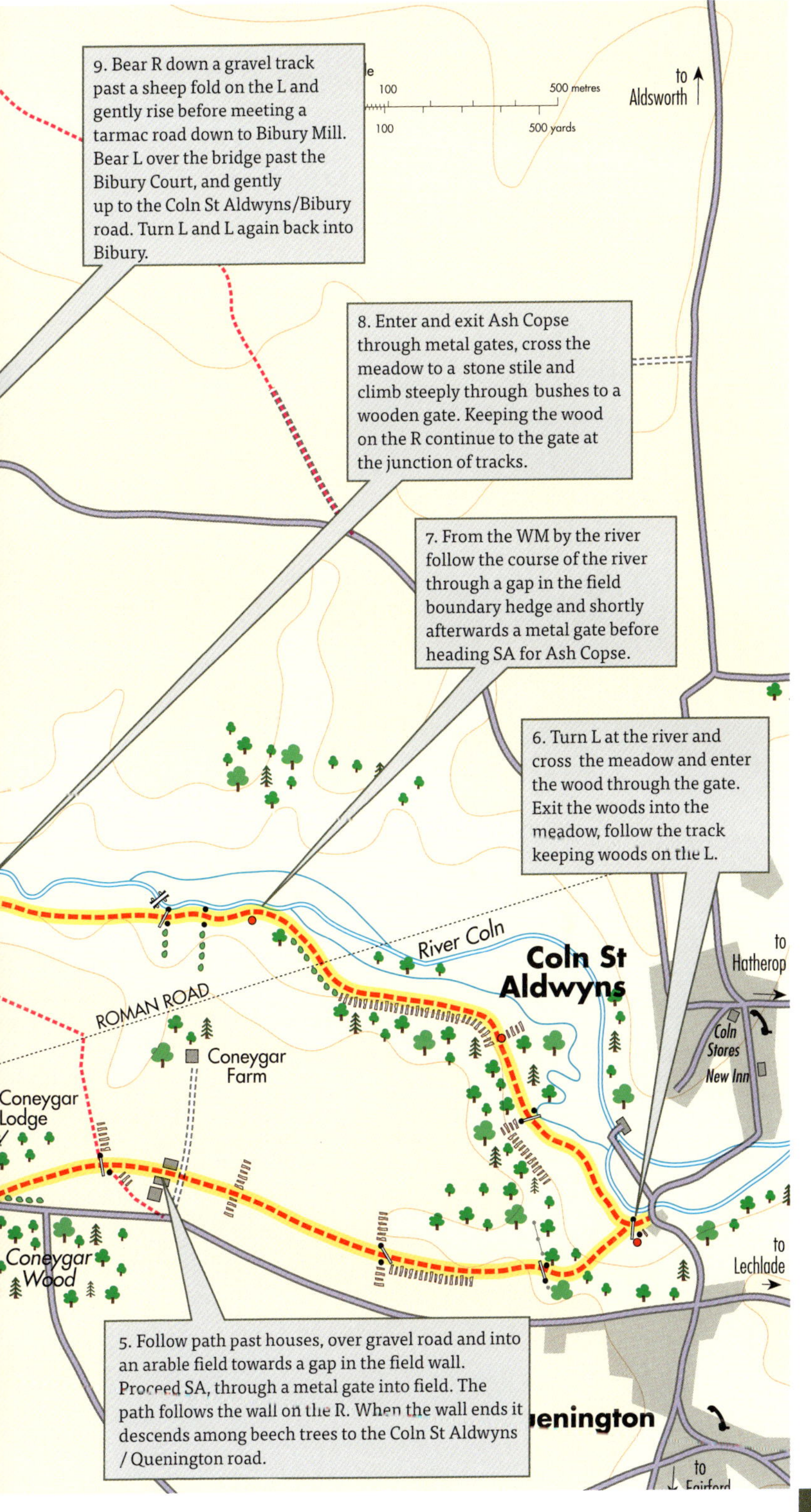

9. Bear R down a gravel track past a sheep fold on the L and gently rise before meeting a tarmac road down to Bibury Mill. Bear L over the bridge past the Bibury Court, and gently up to the Coln St Aldwyns/Bibury road. Turn L and L again back into Bibury.

100

500 metres

100

500 yards

to
Aldsworth

8. Enter and exit Ash Copse through metal gates, cross the meadow to a stone stile and climb steeply through bushes to a wooden gate. Keeping the wood on the R continue to the gate at the junction of tracks.

7. From the WM by the river follow the course of the river through a gap in the field boundary hedge and shortly afterwards a metal gate before heading SA for Ash Copse.

6. Turn L at the river and cross the meadow and enter the wood through the gate. Exit the woods into the meadow, follow the track keeping woods on the L.

River Coln

Coln St
Aldwyns

to
Hatherop

Coln
Stores

New Inn

ROMAN ROAD

Coneygar
Farm

Coneygar
Lodge

to
Lechlade

Coneygar
Wood

5. Follow path past houses, over gravel road and into an arable field towards a gap in the field wall. Proceed SA, through a metal gate into field. The path follows the wall on the R. When the wall ends it descends among beech trees to the Coln St Aldwyns / Quenington road.

enington

to
Fairford

This walk provides a kaleidoscope of sights, sounds and smells: Roman mosaics, the rattle of woodpeckers, woodland perfumes, cottage gardens, and rolling sheep pastures. It is mainly flat with a gradual climb to Camp Wood, then an easy descent across hunting country to Fossebridge. Finally, there is a stroll along the Chedworth valley, a short climb to the plateau overlooking the village for a mile, and a descent through the wood and back to the Roman Villa.

Distance
6.25 miles/10 km.

Minimum Time
3.5 hours.

Grade/Level of Difficulty
Easy.

Terrain/Paths
Woodland paths, farm tracks.

Landscape
Streams, woodland, farmland.

Dogs
Near Chedworth there are lots of farm fields and stiles where dogs are to be kept under control. Loop from parking through Chedworth Woods is good for dogs.

Public Toilets
None.

Parking (P)
In space 200 yards before the Roman Villa.

Recommended Start/Finish
Roman Villa.

Location
Chedworth is situated between Northleach and Cirencester, just off the A429.

 River Coln, Chedworth Woods

FEATURES OF INTEREST...

Chedworth. A long, extended village in a steep-sided valley made up of five hamlets: Chedworth, Calveshill, Bleakmoor, Pancakehill and Lower Chedworth. Rich in Cotswold stone, the old cottages intermingle with modern houses. The village has a spacious ambience with fine views up and down and across the valley.

Chedworth Roman Villa (NT). Discovered in 1864 by a local gamekeeper and later excavated between 1864 and 1866 revealing remains of a Romano-British villa containing mosaics, baths and hypocausts. Family trails. Museum. Open daily Mar to end-Nov, from 10am. 01242 890256 nationaltrust.org.uk

Chedworth Woods. A network of footpaths that criss-cross through tangled woodland close to the Roman Villa.

Coln Valley. Charming valley with the slow moving River Coln snaking its lazy way through the meadows and sheep pastures and through typically quaint Cotswold villages: Calcot, Coln Rogers, Coln St Dennis, Winson and Ablington. The Coln Valley is an example of the quintessential Cotswold river valley that meanders through green pastures, home to cattle and sheep, the moorhen and heron.

Fossebridge. Ancient coaching inn/watering hole on the Roman Fosse Way.

St Andrew's Church, Chedworth. 'Wool' church with Norman origins. C15 'wine glass' pulpit. Gargoyles.

St James the Great Church, Coln St Dennis. Picturesque. Massive Norman tower.

Stowell Park. Home of the Vestey family. Quaint Norman church with Doom painting. Gardens open under NGS scheme.

WHERE TO EAT, DRINK...SLEEP

Denfurlong Farm Caravan & Campsite. Owned by the same family for 5-generations. The Camp Site is basic, centred around a large field. Open Apr-Oct. 07707 181126 denfurlongfarm.co.uk

The Inn at Fossebridge. A former coaching inn conveniently positioned on the Fosseway. The Georgian hotel is set in pleasant, spacious grounds and provides comfortable rooms and pub-grub in the bar. 01285 720721 innatfossebridge.co.uk

Seven Tuns, Queen Street. This old pub, a favourite of the author has had a precarious existence, and thankfully it has been resurrected to somewhere near its former glory. Pub-grub, flagstone floors and three fires. Dog and child friendly. 01285 720630 seventuns.com

WHERE TO STAY JUST OFF THE MAP...

Far Peak Camping. A simple, rustic campsite centred smack in the middle of the Cotswolds, within walking distance of Northleach. Glamping: Domes, Shepherd Huts and Bell Tents. Bike hire and climbing tower. Café. 01285 700370 farpeakcamping.co.uk

Montreal House, Barnsley. An isolated and charming Cotswold stone house offering luxurious B&B. Five double bedrooms and four bathroom. All the comforts of home. 01285 707785 montrealhouse.co.uk

The Stump, Foss Cross. Once a traditional country inn with oak fireplaces, now a Baz & Fred operation converted into a pizza and cocktail dive. Sizeable garden with swanky bedrooms. 01285 720288 thestump.co.uk

The Wheatsheaf, Northleach. For those with deep pockets who yearn for some luxurious bedrooms, fine dining with a twist, one could do worse. 01451 539889 cotswoldwheatsheaf.com

Chedworth Woods at Dawn

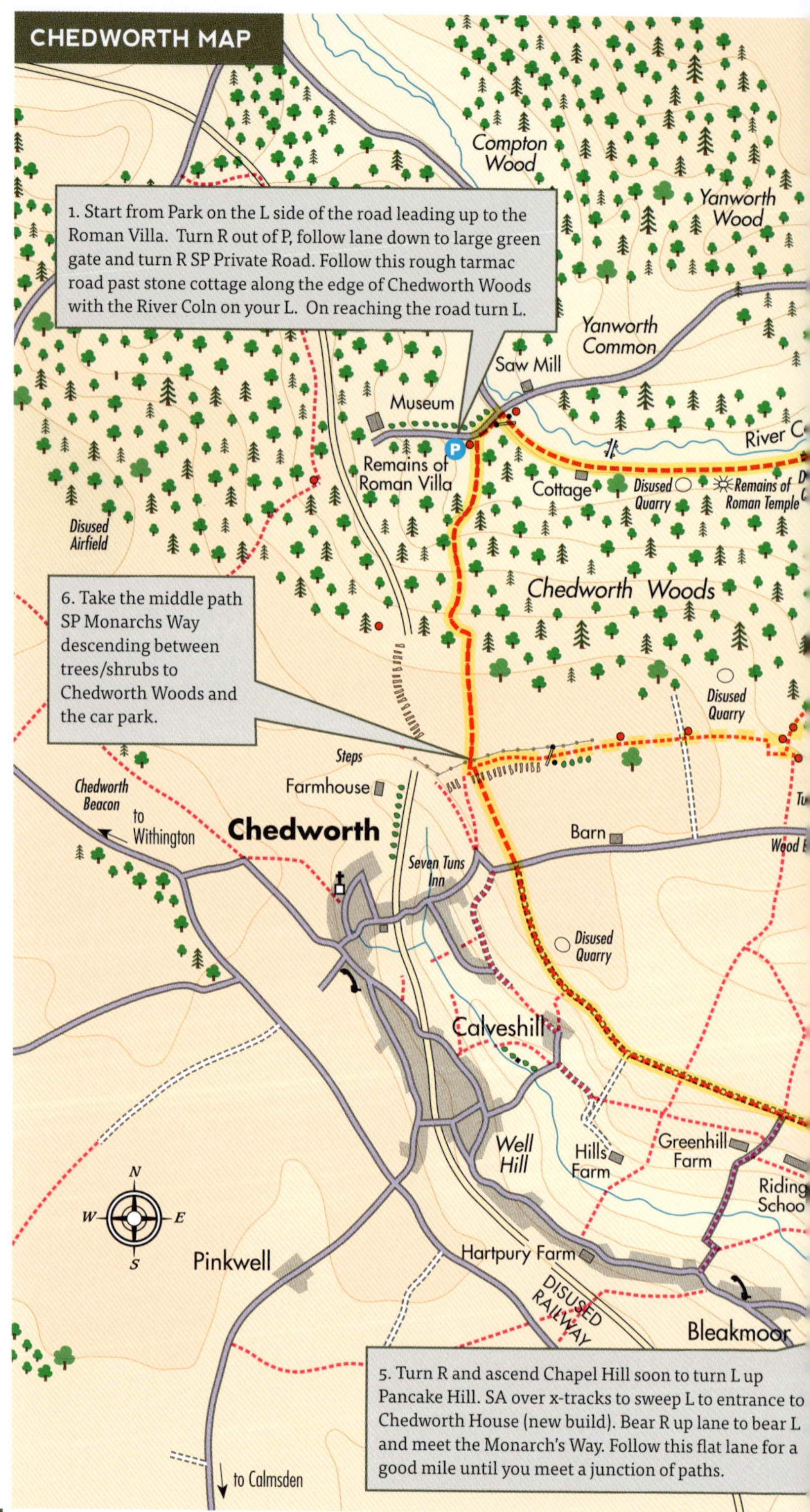

1. Start from Park on the L side of the road leading up to the Roman Villa. Turn R out of P, follow lane down to large green gate and turn R SP Private Road. Follow this rough tarmac road past stone cottage along the edge of Chedworth Woods with the River Coln on your L. On reaching the road turn L.

6. Take the middle path SP Monarchs Way descending between trees/shrubs to Chedworth Woods and the car park.

5. Turn R and ascend Chapel Hill soon to turn L up Pancake Hill. SA over x-tracks to sweep L to entrance to Chedworth House (new build). Bear R up lane to bear L and meet the Monarch's Way. Follow this flat lane for a good mile until you meet a junction of paths.

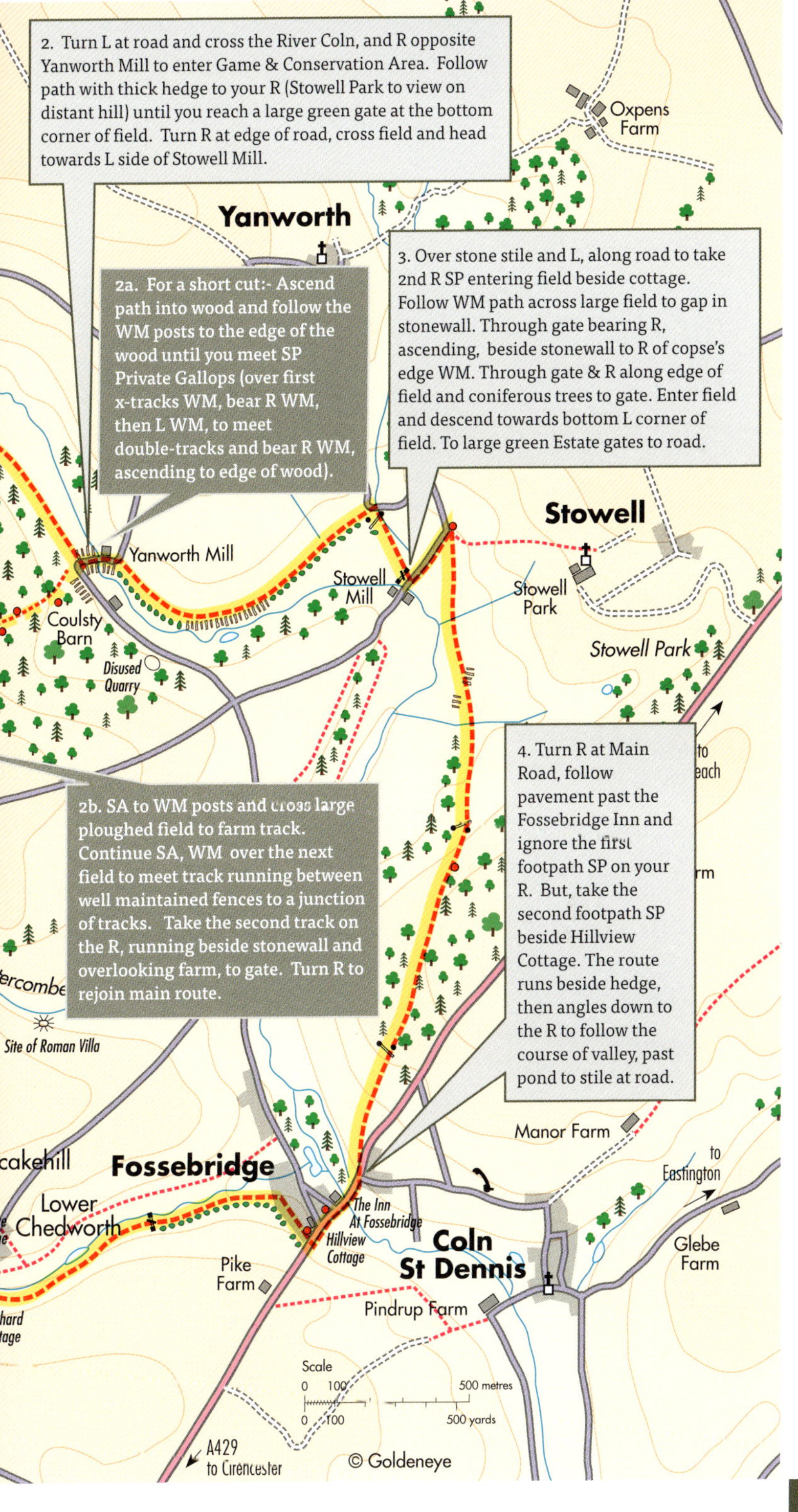

2. Turn L at road and cross the River Coln, and R opposite Yanworth Mill to enter Game & Conservation Area. Follow path with thick hedge to your R (Stowell Park to view on distant hill) until you reach a large green gate at the bottom corner of field. Turn R at edge of road, cross field and head towards L side of Stowell Mill.

Oxpens Farm

Yanworth

2a. For a short cut:- Ascend path into wood and follow the WM posts to the edge of the wood until you meet SP Private Gallops (over first x-tracks WM, bear R WM, then L WM, to meet double-tracks and bear R WM, ascending to edge of wood).

3. Over stone stile and L, along road to take 2nd R SP entering field beside cottage. Follow WM path across large field to gap in stonewall. Through gate bearing R, ascending, beside stonewall to R of copse's edge WM. Through gate & R along edge of field and coniferous trees to gate. Enter field and descend towards bottom L corner of field. To large green Estate gates to road.

Stowell

Yanworth Mill

Stowell Mill

Stowell Park

Stowell Park

Coulsty Barn

Disused Quarry

2b. SA to WM posts and cross large ploughed field to farm track. Continue SA, WM over the next field to meet track running between well maintained fences to a junction of tracks. Take the second track on the R, running beside stonewall and overlooking farm, to gate. Turn R to rejoin main route.

4. Turn R at Main Road, follow pavement past the Fossebridge Inn and ignore the first footpath SP on your R. But, take the second footpath SP beside Hillview Cottage. The route runs beside hedge, then angles down to the R to follow the course of valley, past pond to stile at road.

to each

rm

tercombe

Site of Roman Villa

Manor Farm

to Eastington

cakehill

Fossebridge

Lower Chedworth

The Inn At Fossebridge

Hillview Cottage

Coln St Dennis

Glebe Farm

Pike Farm

Pindrup Farm

chard ttage

Scale
0   100
0   100
500 metres
500 yards

A429 to Cirencester

© Goldeneye

The Edgeworth walk explores much of the rolling countryside of the Golden Valley, and its isolation provides solitude. The Misarden Park walk is designed for young families with pushchairs. One long descent, followed by three short climbs in rolling parkland and ancient woodland. The link between the two walks has one very steep descent in woodland and is a reminder of the wonder of Gloucestershire's trees.

Distance
Edgeworth: 2.5 miles/4km.
Misarden Park: 1.5 miles/2.4km.
Minimum Time
Edgeworth: 2.5 hours.
Misarden Park: 1.5 hours.
Grade/Level of Difficulty
Both Easy.
Terrain/Paths
Edgeworth: Grass, woodland track.
Misarden Park: Tarmac, grass track.
Landscape
Woodland, rolling pastureland.
Dogs
The Edgeworth walk has more woodland. Lots of sheep in Misarden Park - dogs to be kept under control.

Public Toilets
None.
Parking (P)
Edgeworth: Beside Village Hall.
Misarden Park: Beside School.
Recommended Start/Finish
From Car Parks as above.
Location
Edgeworth is close to Miserden, located near Birdlip, Cirencester and Stroud. The easiest access is either via the A419 from Cirencester (via Sapperton/Daneway), or from the East via the A417 through Duntisbourne Abbots.
Link between both these walks
Allow 45 minutes to join the Edgeworth section from Miserden.

Miserden Church

FEATURES OF INTEREST...

Edgeworth. Situated in an isolated position overlooking the River Frome, and the upper reaches of the Stroud valleys.

Edgeworth Manor. Formerly the home of Paul Hamlyn, book publisher and philanthropist.

The Garden at Miserden. The home of the Wills family, has shrubs, a traditional rose garden, mixed perennial borders, extensive yew topiary, magnolia Goulangeana and spring bulbs amidst a picturesque woodland setting. Rill and Summerhouse. The Elizabethan mansion has mullion windows and was extended by Waterhouses in the C19 and by Lutyens who added a new wing in 1920-21. Airbnb at Miserden Park Flat. The gardens are open in season Th-Su & BH Ms, 10-5. 01285 821303 miserden.org

Miserden Estate. Estate village overlooking the Golden Valley. John Barnes built many of the estate cottages in 1920. 01285 821303 miserden.org

St Andrew's Church, Miserden. Late Saxon in origin, with a Norman font and windows. Some C16 tombs in churchyard. Sadly much was destroyed by the amateur architect, the Reverend W H Lowder, in 1886. Note the War Memorial by Lutyens and the beech and yew trees.

St Mary's Church, Edgeworth. Early Saxon with some Norman additions: nave, chancel and south door. A restored C13 porch and C14 stained glass. Look for the cross in the churchyard with medieval base and mutilated head.

WHERE TO EAT & DRINK...

Carpenter's Arms, Miserden. This old inn retains its Inglenook fireplaces and original stone floors. The village is very popular with film crews. Beer garden. Dogs welcome. 01285 821283 thecarps-miserden.co.uk

The Garden Café, Miserden Estate. This café originated out of the old glasshouses in the kitchen garden serves great coffees and seasonal food. Host to new Pop Up Restaurant. Wheelchair access. Open in season W-Su 10-5. 01285 821303

Edgeworth Ewes

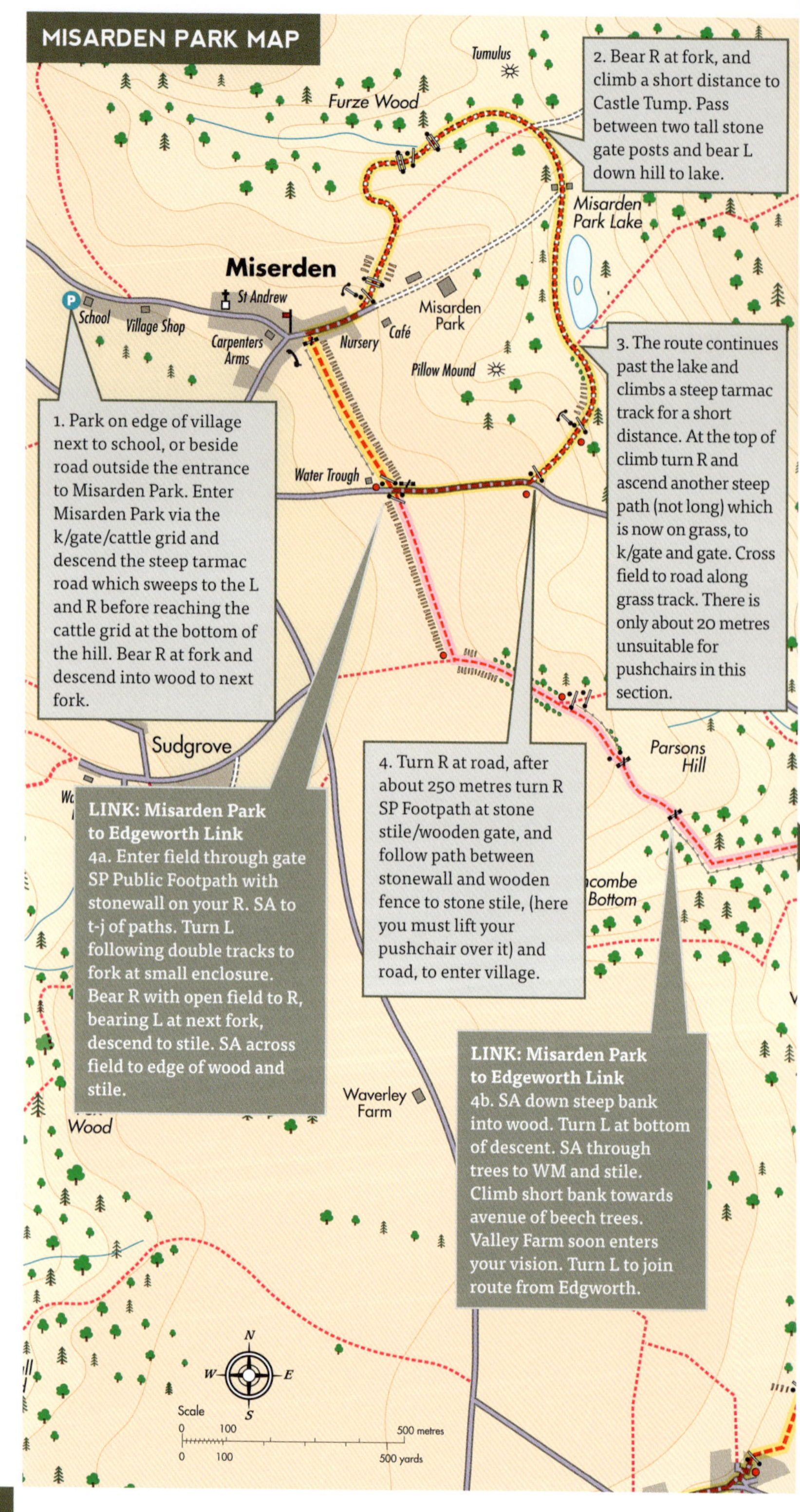

2. Bear R at fork, and climb a short distance to Castle Tump. Pass between two tall stone gate posts and bear L down hill to lake.

3. The route continues past the lake and climbs a steep tarmac track for a short distance. At the top of climb turn R and ascend another steep path (not long) which is now on grass, to k/gate and gate. Cross field to road along grass track. There is only about 20 metres unsuitable for pushchairs in this section.

1. Park on edge of village next to school, or beside road outside the entrance to Misarden Park. Enter Misarden Park via the k/gate/cattle grid and descend the steep tarmac road which sweeps to the L and R before reaching the cattle grid at the bottom of the hill. Bear R at fork and descend into wood to next fork.

4. Turn R at road, after about 250 metres turn R SP Footpath at stone stile/wooden gate, and follow path between stonewall and wooden fence to stone stile, (here you must lift your pushchair over it) and road, to enter village.

LINK: Misarden Park to Edgeworth Link
4a. Enter field through gate SP Public Footpath with stonewall on your R. SA to t-j of paths. Turn L following double tracks to fork at small enclosure. Bear R with open field to R, bearing L at next fork, descend to stile. SA across field to edge of wood and stile.

LINK: Misarden Park to Edgeworth Link
4b. SA down steep bank into wood. Turn L at bottom of descent. SA through trees to WM and stile. Climb short bank towards avenue of beech trees. Valley Farm soon enters your vision. Turn L to join route from Edgworth.

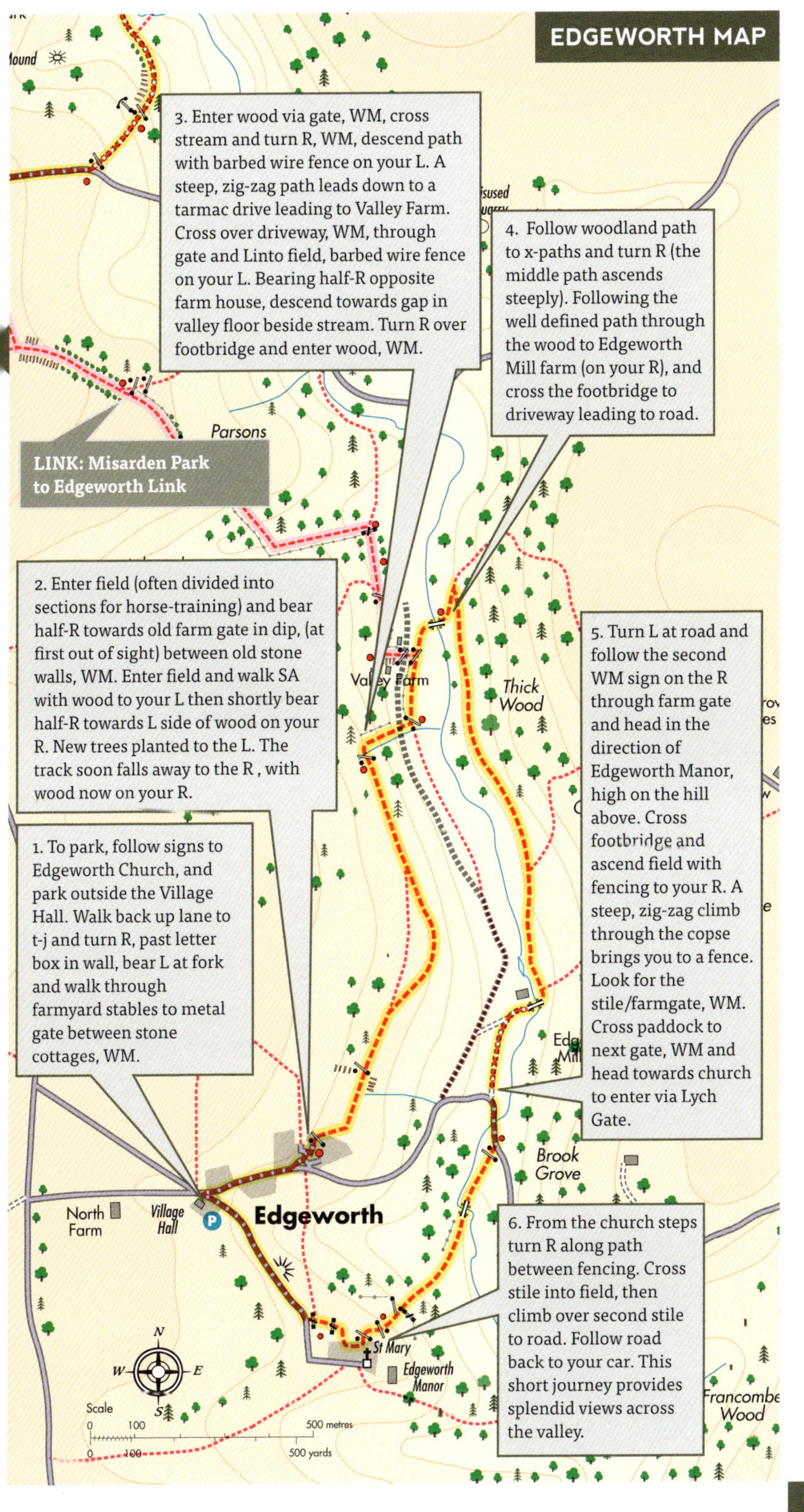

Mound

3. Enter wood via gate, WM, cross stream and turn R, WM, descend path with barbed wire fence on your L. A steep, zig-zag path leads down to a tarmac drive leading to Valley Farm. Cross over driveway, WM, through gate and Linto field, barbed wire fence on your L. Bearing half-R opposite farm house, descend towards gap in valley floor beside stream. Turn R over footbridge and enter wood, WM.

Disused Quarry

4. Follow woodland path to x-paths and turn R (the middle path ascends steeply). Following the well defined path through the wood to Edgeworth Mill farm (on your R), and cross the footbridge to driveway leading to road.

Parsons

LINK: Misarden Park to Edgeworth Link

2. Enter field (often divided into sections for horse-training) and bear half-R towards old farm gate in dip, (at first out of sight) between old stone walls, WM. Enter field and walk SA with wood to your L then shortly bear half-R towards L side of wood on your R. New trees planted to the L. The track soon falls away to the R , with wood now on your R.

Valley Farm

Thick Wood

5. Turn L at road and follow the second WM sign on the R through farm gate and head in the direction of Edgeworth Manor, high on the hill above. Cross footbridge and ascend field with fencing to your R. A steep, zig-zag climb through the copse brings you to a fence. Look for the stile/farmgate, WM. Cross paddock to next gate, WM and head towards church to enter via Lych Gate.

1. To park, follow signs to Edgeworth Church, and park outside the Village Hall. Walk back up lane to t-j and turn R, past letter box in wall, bear L at fork and walk through farmyard stables to metal gate between stone cottages, WM.

Edg Mill

Brook Grove

North Farm

Village Hall

Edgeworth

6. From the church steps turn R along path between fencing. Cross stile into field, then climb over second stile to road. Follow road back to your car. This short journey provides splendid views across the valley.

N
W   E
S

St Mary

Edgeworth Manor

Francombe Wood

Scale
0   100
500 metres
0   100
500 yards

   Uley Bury (on left), Downham Hill (centre) & Cam Long Down (on right) from Coaley Peak

This walk provides splendid views from Sapperton over the Golden Valley and woodlands below. Then it follows the Golden Valley beside the Thames and Severn Canal, passing by nature reserves, wild flowers, areas rich in industrial heritage and water courses set aside for freshwater habitats. There are a couple of steep climbs which will create a thirst to be slaked in one of the two pubs, en route.

Distance
4.25 miles/6.75km.

Minimum Time
2.5 hours.

Grade/Level of Difficulty
Easy/Moderate.

Terrain/Paths
Mud, canal path, woodland tracks.

Landscape
Woodland, pastureland.

Dogs
Mostly woodland where dogs can run free.

Public Toilets
None.

Parking (P)
Beside Sapperton church, or at the Daneway.

Recommended Start/Finish
As above.

Location
Just off the A419 between Stroud and Cirencester.

FEATURES OF INTEREST...

Daneway Banks Nature Reserve. Regeneration of freshwater habitats. Wildflowers abound, notably the 'Lilies of the Valley' and a colony of the large blue butterfly.

Daneway House. Small C14 Grade 1 manor with Jacobean ceilings. A workshop and showroom was set up here in 1902 by Ernest Gimson, and the Barnsley Brothersof the "Arts & Crafts Movement" rented from Lord Bathurst. Later, in 1948 the home of Octavia Hill, the architect. Restoration took place in the 1060s.

Daneway Portal. Entrance to the Sapperton Tunnel built in 1874-89. At the time the longest canal tunnel built for the Thames and Severn Canal which linked the Stroudwater to the Thames. The Cotswold Canal Trust are actively restoring it and thereby creating freshwater habitats.

Golden Valley. Runs from Sapperton to Chalford; Superb autumnal colours from the beech, ash and oak trees.

Pinbury Park. John Masefield, Poet Laureate rented it during World War II. Earlier the Bathursts lived here and entertained Queen Mary and Rudyard Kipling.

Sapperton. In a splendid position overlooking woodland and the Golden Valley. Home of the William Morris protégés, Ernest Gimson and Sydney and Ernest Barnsley of the Cotswold Arts and Crafts Movement, creators of beautiful furniture who also built their own cottages in the village. Their fame rose after completing restorative work at nearby Pinbury Park. Ernest Gimson died young at 59 and is buried in the churchyard. The area is rich in industrial heritage, woodland and circular walks. Charles I stayed at Sapperton House on 13 July, 1644.

Siccaridge Wood Nature Reserve. Rich in wildlife, this ancient woodland has been managed as a coppice-with-standards system. There are wood anemones, common dormouse, the rare mountain bullion snail, the rare wildflower: angular solomon's seal.

St Kenelm's Church. Of Norman origins with elaborately carved oak panels supplied from the Manor House. Exquisite kneelers. Effigy of a C16 Knight. Monument to Sir Henry Poole, and wife.

WHERE TO EAT & DRINK...SLEEP...

The Bell at Sapperton. A popular dining pub with the chattering classes given to natural stonewalls, polished flagstone floors, and in winter, welcome log fires provide a comfortable ambience. Local beers. Al fresco in summer. Recipient of one of the late Adrian Gill's hilarious reviews. New - luxurious bedrooms! 01285 760298 bellsapperton.co.uk

The Daneway. Traditional country pub that has had a complete makeover. Gone is the rusticity, hail the dining pub-grub Inn! Wadworth ales a bonus. 100m from the pub is a basic camping field in a tranquil wooded valley, open all year. Toilet and washing facilities beside the pub. 01285 760297 thedaneway.pub

Sapperton Church Wood Carvings

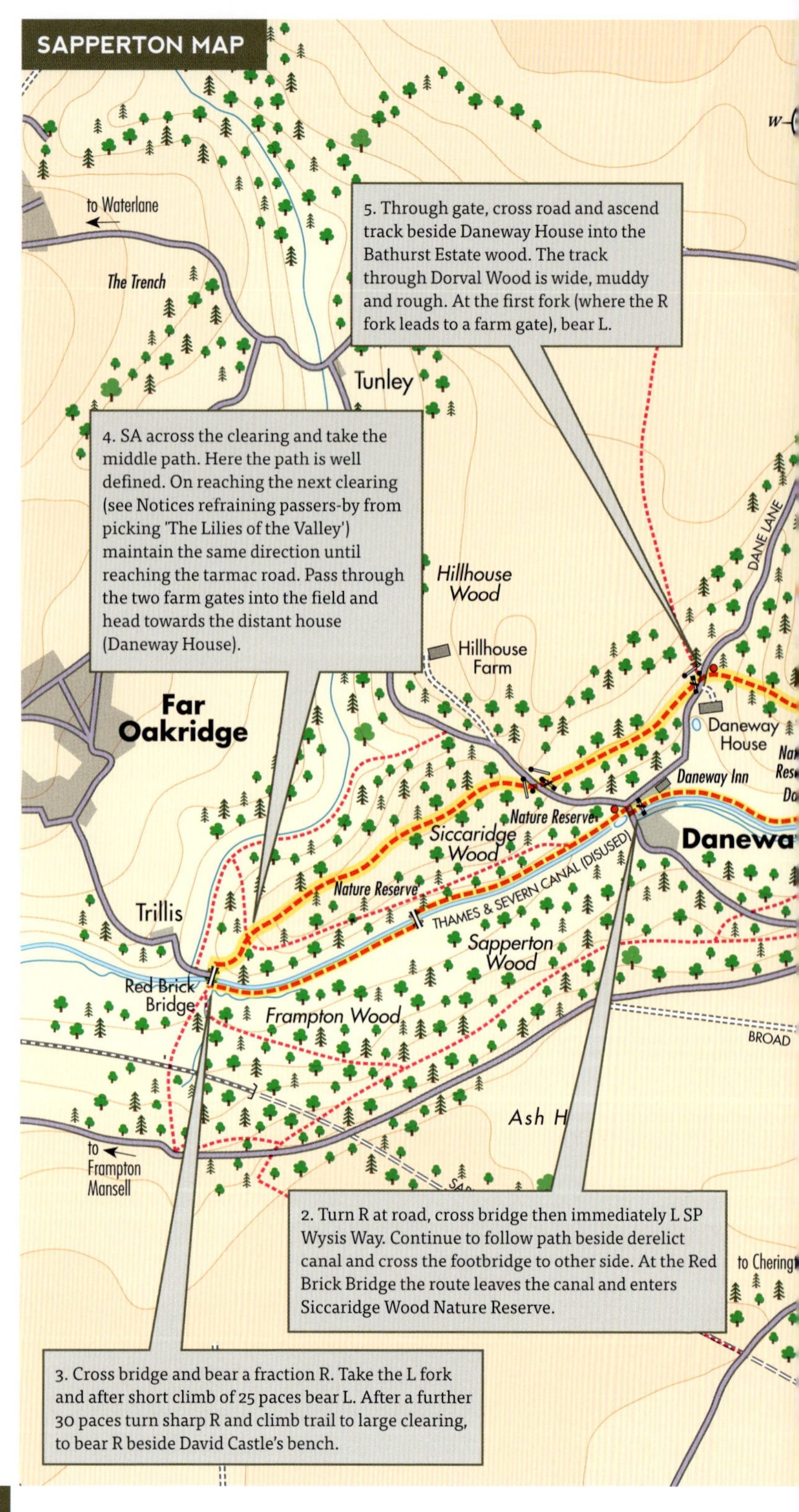

to Waterlane
The Trench
Tunley
5. Through gate, cross road and ascend track beside Daneway House into the Bathurst Estate wood. The track through Dorval Wood is wide, muddy and rough. At the first fork (where the R fork leads to a farm gate), bear L.
4. SA across the clearing and take the middle path. Here the path is well defined. On reaching the next clearing (see Notices refraining passers-by from picking 'The Lilies of the Valley') maintain the same direction until reaching the tarmac road. Pass through the two farm gates into the field and head towards the distant house (Daneway House).
Hillhouse Wood
DANE LANE
Far Oakridge
Hillhouse Farm
Daneway House
Nat
Res
Da
Daneway Inn
Nature Reserve
Siccaridge Wood
Danewa
Trillis
Nature Reserve
THAMES & SEVERN CANAL (DISUSED)
Sapperton Wood
Red Brick Bridge
Frampton Wood
BROAD
Ash H
to Frampton Mansell
2. Turn R at road, cross bridge then immediately L SP Wysis Way. Continue to follow path beside derelict canal and cross the footbridge to other side. At the Red Brick Bridge the route leaves the canal and enters Siccaridge Wood Nature Reserve.
to Chering
3. Cross bridge and bear a fraction R. Take the L fork and after short climb of 25 paces bear L. After a further 30 paces turn sharp R and climb trail to large clearing, to bear R beside David Castle's bench.

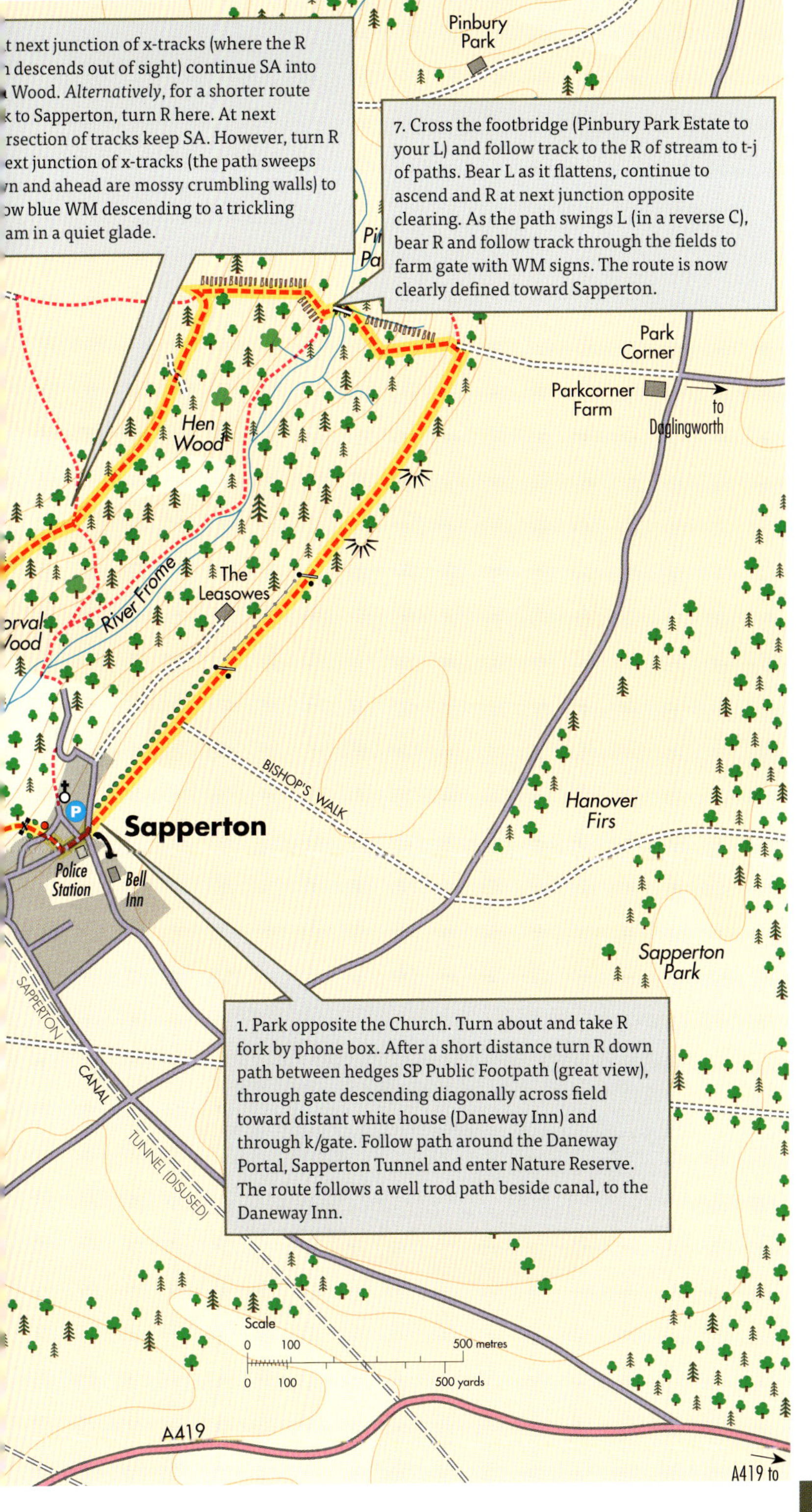

Pinbury Park

.t next junction of x-tracks (where the R
n descends out of sight) continue SA into
Wood. *Alternatively*, for a shorter route
k to Sapperton, turn R here. At next
rsection of tracks keep SA. However, turn R
ext junction of x-tracks (the path sweeps
n and ahead are mossy crumbling walls) to
w blue WM descending to a trickling
am in a quiet glade.

7. Cross the footbridge (Pinbury Park Estate to
your L) and follow track to the R of stream to t-j
of paths. Bear L as it flattens, continue to
ascend and R at next junction opposite
clearing. As the path swings L (in a reverse C),
bear R and follow track through the fields to
farm gate with WM signs. The route is now
clearly defined toward Sapperton.

Park
Corner

Parkcorner
Farm

to
Daglingworth

Hen
Wood

The
Leasowes

River Frome

orval
Wood

BISHOP'S WALK

Hanover
Firs

Sapperton

Police
Station

Bell
Inn

Sapperton
Park

SAPPERTON CANAL

TUNNEL (DISUSED)

1. Park opposite the Church. Turn about and take R
fork by phone box. After a short distance turn R down
path between hedges SP Public Footpath (great view),
through gate descending diagonally across field
toward distant white house (Daneway Inn) and
through k/gate. Follow path around the Daneway
Portal, Sapperton Tunnel and enter Nature Reserve.
The route follows a well trod path beside canal, to the
Daneway Inn.

Scale

0   100

0   100

500 metres

500 yards

A419

A419 to

This could be described as a tree walk (or pub crawl), for the walk passes close to three popular inns. However, it also joins two delightful Cotswold villages affording wonderful views across a Cotswold landscape. Especially delightful are the trees in Saltridge Wood and the wildlife and flowers in the Nature Reserve. Best in early summer and autumn.

Distance
6 miles/9km.
Minimum Time
2.5 hours.
Grade/Level of Difficulty
Easy/Moderate.
Terrain/Paths
Woodland tracks, mud.
Landscape
Woodland, rolling pastureland, limestone villages.
Dogs
Keep under control in villages and on farm track/tarmac road. Lots of woodland where dogs can run free.

Public Toilets
None.
Parking (P)
Buckholt Wood, Cranham.
Recommended Start/Finish
Cranham.
Location
Cranham and Sheepscombe are just off the B4070 between Stroud and Birdlip.
Link to other walks in this Guide
Short, 15 minute link to the Painswick-Slad Valley Walk via driveway to Down Barn Farm.

FEATURES OF INTEREST...

Cranham. This village has a mixed bag of architectural styles. It is not noted for its great aesthetics but divided by the Common and surrounded by beautiful woodlands to the north and south. Pretty church, popular pub and Cranham Feast in August.

Cranham Woods. Nature Reserve with a tangled web of pathways. The approach from Birdlip in early summer with the new foliage is memorable.

Saltridge Wood. Nature Reserve with paths that afford superb views down the valley towards Painswick.

Sheepscombe. A straggling village surrounded by beautiful woodland, rolling pastures and green hills. The view down the valley looking towards Painswick church is a beauty. It is the ancestral home of Laurie Lee whose parents moved to Slad. He maintained a connection with the village by purchasing the field for the cricket club, so named Laurie Lee Field. A network of footpaths leads through woodland to Painswick, Cranham and Slad.

WHERE TO EAT, DRINK... RELAX

Black Horse Inn, Cranham. A popular pub with walkers. The food is nourishing and good value and the real ales go down a treat. Unpretentious and cosy. Once, a family favourite with the Frickers, especially their sausages and cauliflower cheese! Opens at midday. 01452 812217

Butcher's Arms, Sheepscombe. The Butcher's

Butcher's Arms

Arms has an unlikely national claim to fame - the much photographed carved sign of a butcher sipping a pint of beer with a pig tethered to his leg. 'Pie and a Pint' meal deal. Solid pub-grub on offer. 01452 812113 butchers-arms.co.uk

Fostons Ash, Slad Road. Close to the mid-point of this walk is this newly renovated Inn named after a former Turnpike Keeper. 01452 863262 fostonsash.co.uk

Sheepscombe Vale, Glos

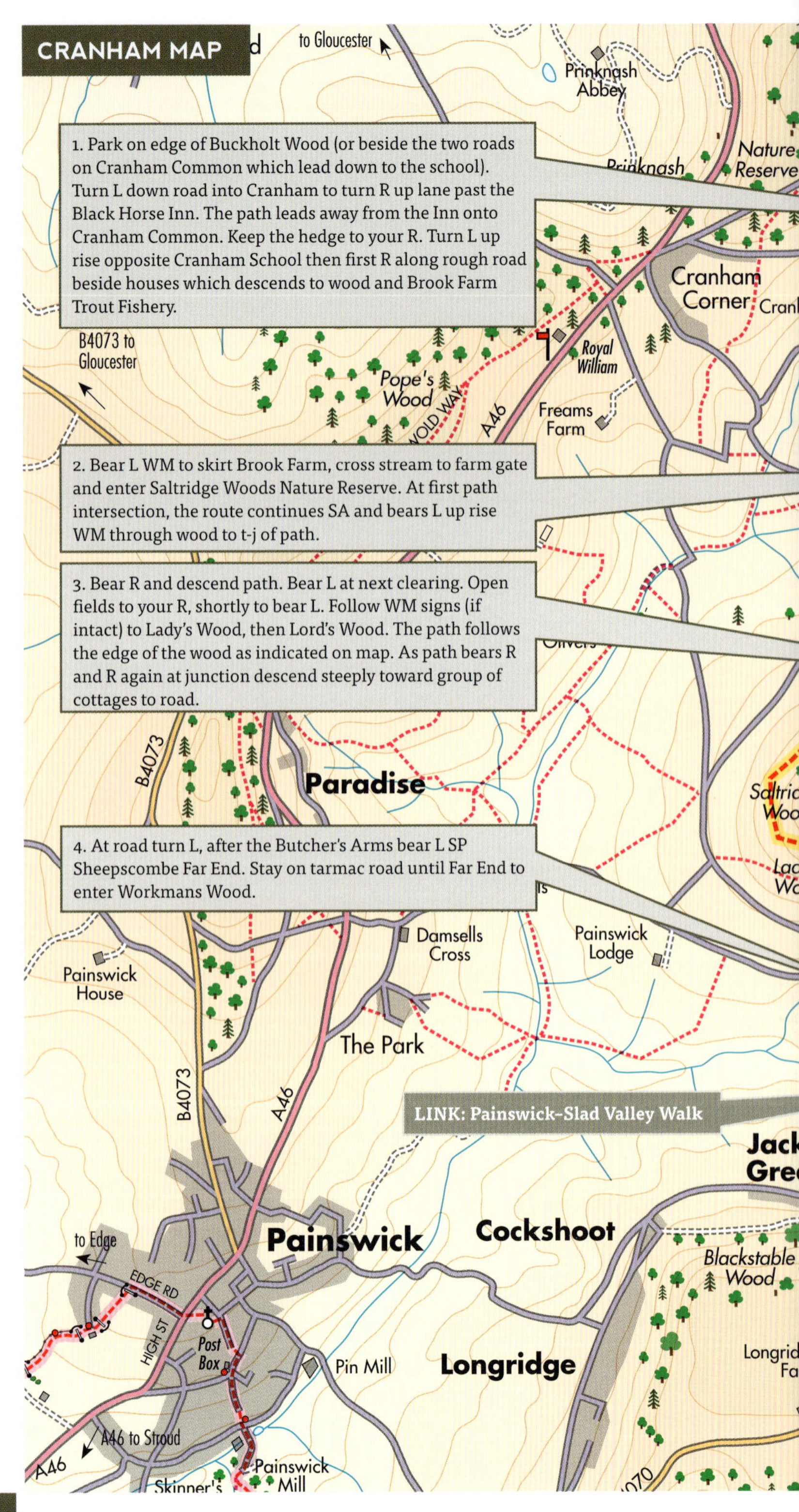

to Gloucester
Prinknash Abbey
Prinknash
Nature Reserve
1. Park on edge of Buckholt Wood (or beside the two roads on Cranham Common which lead down to the school). Turn L down road into Cranham to turn R up lane past the Black Horse Inn. The path leads away from the Inn onto Cranham Common. Keep the hedge to your R. Turn L up rise opposite Cranham School then first R along rough road beside houses which descends to wood and Brook Farm Trout Fishery.
Cranham Corner
Cran
B4073 to Gloucester
Pope's Wood
COTSWOLD WAY
A46
Royal William
Freams Farm
2. Bear L WM to skirt Brook Farm, cross stream to farm gate and enter Saltridge Woods Nature Reserve. At first path intersection, the route continues SA and bears L up rise WM through wood to t-j of path.
3. Bear R and descend path. Bear L at next clearing. Open fields to your R, shortly to bear L. Follow WM signs (if intact) to Lady's Wood, then Lord's Wood. The path follows the edge of the wood as indicated on map. As path bears R and R again at junction descend steeply toward group of cottages to road.
Olivers
Saltric Woo
B4073
Paradise
Lad Wo
4. At road turn L, after the Butcher's Arms bear L SP Sheepscombe Far End. Stay on tarmac road until Far End to enter Workmans Wood.
Damsells Cross
Painswick Lodge
Painswick House
The Park
LINK: Painswick–Slad Valley Walk
B4073
A46
Jack Gree
to Edge
EDGE RD
Painswick
Cockshoot
Blackstable Wood
HIGH ST
Post Box
Pin Mill
Longridge
Longri Fa
A46 to Stroud
A46
Painswick Mill
Skinner's

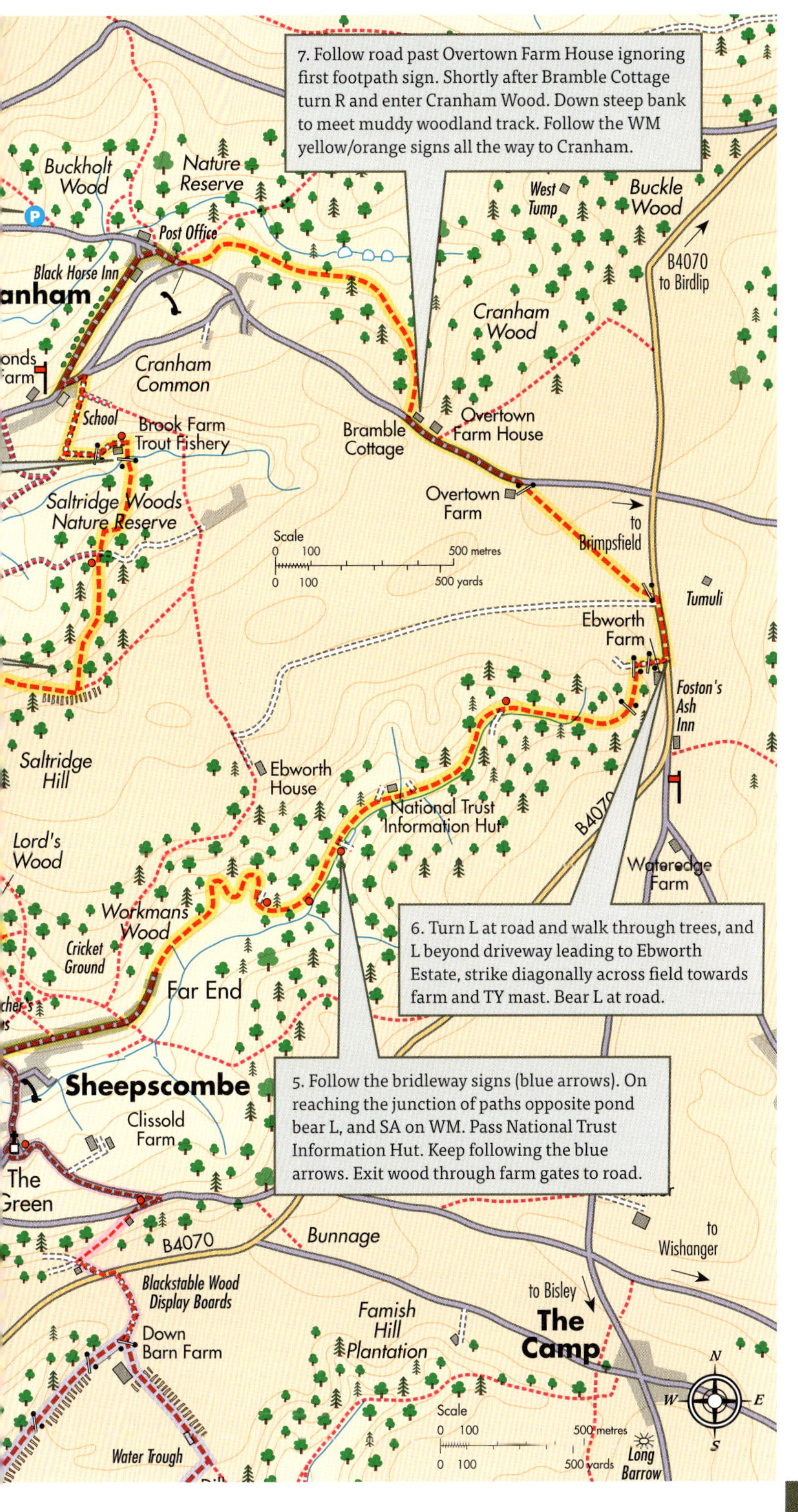

7. Follow road past Overtown Farm House ignoring first footpath sign. Shortly after Bramble Cottage turn R and enter Cranham Wood. Down steep bank to meet muddy woodland track. Follow the WM yellow/orange signs all the way to Cranham.

6. Turn L at road and walk through trees, and L beyond driveway leading to Ebworth Estate, strike diagonally across field towards farm and TY mast. Bear L at road.

5. Follow the bridleway signs (blue arrows). On reaching the junction of paths opposite pond bear L, and SA on WM. Pass National Trust Information Hut. Keep following the blue arrows. Exit wood through farm gates to road.

Buckholt Wood
Nature Reserve
West Tump
Buckle Wood
Post Office
B4070 to Birdlip
Black Horse Inn
anham
Cranham Wood
Cranham Common
Bramble Cottage
Overtown Farm House
School
Brook Farm Trout Fishery
Overtown Farm
onds arm
to Brimpsfield
Saltridge Woods Nature Reserve
Tumuli
Ebworth Farm
Foston's Ash Inn
Scale
0   100   500 metres
0   100   500 yards
Saltridge Hill
Ebworth House
National Trust Information Hut
B4070
Lord's Wood
Wateredge Farm
Workmans Wood
Cricket Ground
Far End
cher's s
Sheepscombe
Clissold Farm
The Green
Bunnage
to Wishanger
B4070
Blackstable Wood Display Boards
Famish Hill Plantation
to Bisley
The Camp
Down Barn Farm
N
W   E
S
Water Trough
Scale
0   100   500 metres
0   100   500 yards
Long Barrow

This is the most strenuous of the walks in this book, and yet, is perhaps the most rewarding. Certainly, you will have earned your pint in the Woolpack! The route takes you up and down Cotswold combes and provides breathtaking views of a very English landscape that so inspired the local boy, Laurie Lee, author of the classic 'Cider with Rosie'.

Distance
7.5 miles/11km.
Minimum Time
4 hours.
Grade/Level of Difficulty
Moderate/Strenuous.
Terrain/Paths
Mud, tracks, grass.
Landscape
Woodland, undulating pastureland.
Dogs
Keep under control around livestock. Lots of woodland where dogs can run free but will be on and off the lead a lot.

Public Toilets
Painswick.
Parking (P)
Painswick or Bulls Cross.
Recommended Start/Finish
Painswick or Bulls Cross.
Location
Painswick lies between Stroud and Cheltenham on the A46. Slad is situated on the B4070 between Stroud and Birdlip.
Link to other walks in this Guide
To Haresfield Beacon or Cranham to Sheepscombe Walk via the Cotswold Way.

FEATURES OF INTEREST...

Catswood. Lovely woodland paths provide superb views across the valley.

Dillay Valley. A hidden Cotswold combe with magical qualities.

Laurie Lee 1914-1997 (& Wildlife Way). Poet, musician and traveller who was brought up in this valley, and who spent half his time here (the rest in Chelsea). His most famous book *Cider with Rosie* captures an England long forgotten. If you have recently read it you will recognise the valleys and woods. Gloucestershire Wildlife Trust have created a waymarked walk that includes part of our walk. It is signposted with poetry posts and imagery. It is 2-miles shorter than our route. We have not illustrated this route for fear of confusing you. If you have 2-days to spare it may well be worth trying both of them. We welcome feedback.

Painswick. Its local description as 'The Queen of the Cotswolds' is fully justified. The houses and cottages are built from a grey, almost white limestone, in marked contrast to Broadway and Chipping Campden, and some of the buildings have an almost Palladian. Yet, statuesque quality about them. Look out for the Court House and The

Badger Post

Painswick (hotel). Wander down the pretty side streets and visit the churchyard famous for the legendary 99 yew trees. The 100th yew tree has been planted, time and again, but has never survived. Painswick is one of the gems of the southern Cotswolds and is a worthy base from which to explore this region. It is also connected to a network of footpaths including the Cotswold Way so you can arrive by car or taxi and then just walk for the rest of your stay.

Rococo Garden. A beautiful C18 Rococo garden in 6-acres dating from a period of flamboyant and romantic garden design nestles in a hidden Cotswold valley. Be sure you visit in February for the display of magical snowdrops. Nursery. Open daily mid-Jan to Sept 10.30-5. New Nursery, restaurant and Gift Shop. 01452 813204 rococogarden.org.uk

Slad. One of the Stroud villages where cloth was spun in the little cottages before it all moved to South Riding, Yorkshire. Hundreds flock here to walk in the shadow of Laurie Lee's Cider With Rosie and to sample the brew still available in the Woolpack. You may wish to make your way to Bulls Cross, the hanging place and now the start point for many walks. Laurie Lee lies buried in the churchyard opposite the Woolpack. Surrounded by green pastures and ancient woodland.

St Mary's Church, Painswick. It is the soaring spire that will first captivate you, then, as you enter, it will be the line of yew trees, and as you wander around the churchyard, the tombs or monuments carved with their intricate figures. But

do look up and admire the gold clock. The spire has been struck by lightning on many occasions including 1763 and 1883. The 100th yew tree always withers away.

WHERE TO EAT, DRINK... RELAX

St Michaels Bistro/ Restaurant & B&B, Victoria Street. This is where I stop for coffee and brunch when in Painswick. Overlooking the Churchyard the location is a delight and in summer you can sit outside watching the passersby. Bistro open Tu-Su from 10 am. 01452 203306, B&B 01452 812712 stmichaelsbistro.co.uk

Woolpack Inn, Slad. Traditional Cotswold pub with exceptional food, simply cooked and home to a cup of Rosie's cider, and the spirit of Laurie Lee. Newspapers, views, cricketers... A good halfway stopping point on the walk. 01452 813429 thewoolpackslad.com

WHERE TO STAY IN PAINSWICK...

The Painswick, Kemps Lane. Palladian-style Cotswold rectory transformed, again, but this time (thankfully) back into a comfortable and stylish country house hotel. There is chic hedonism aplenty, contemporary furnishings and lavishing of mouth-watering fare. It's a Treat! 01452 813688 thepainswick.co.uk

St Anne's B&B, Gloucester Street. A listed C18 former wool merchant's house with a relaxed family atmosphere. Within easy walking distance of pubs and restaurants. 01452 812879 st-annes-painswick.co.uk

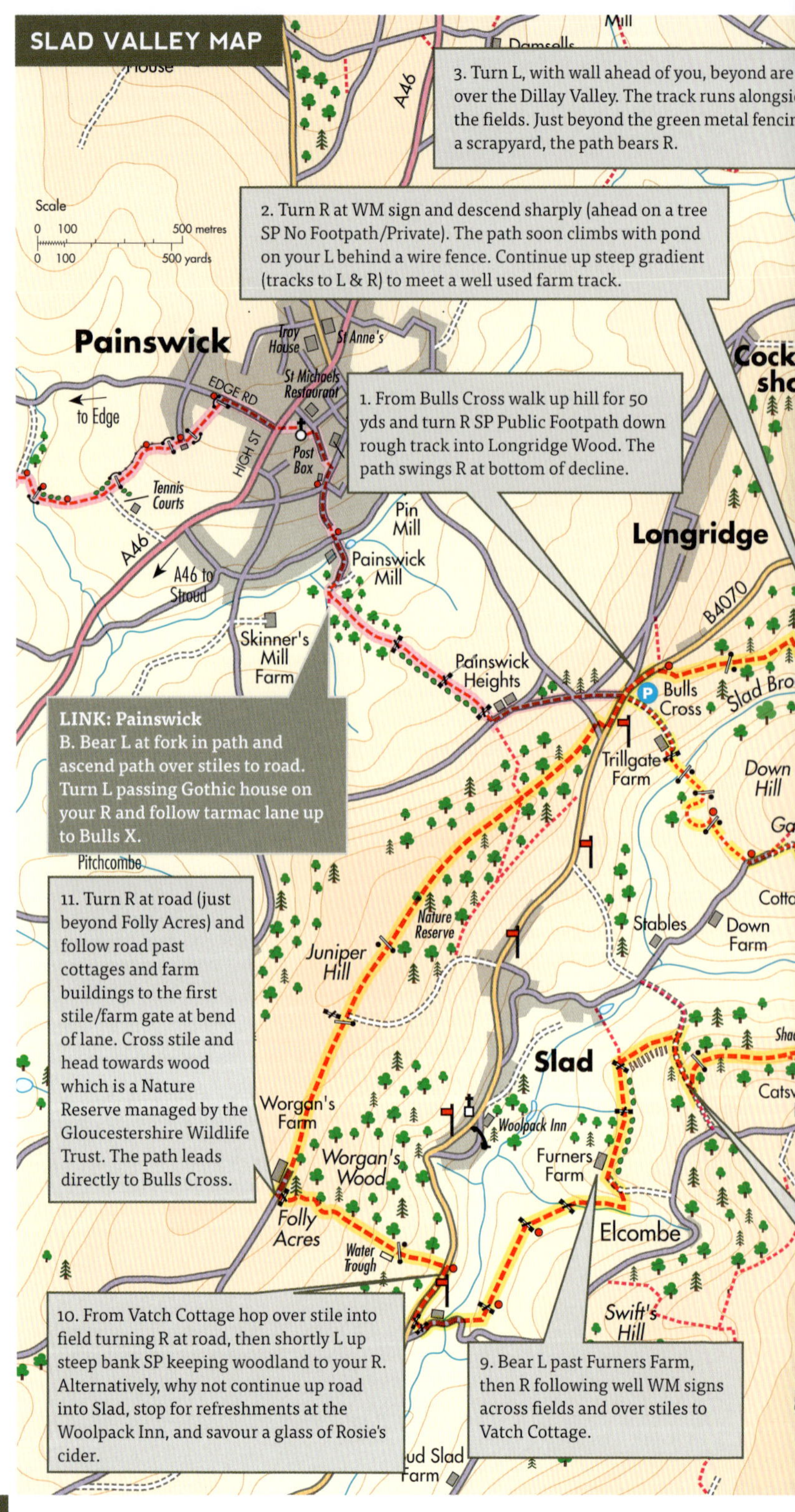

3. Turn L, with wall ahead of you, beyond are over the Dillay Valley. The track runs alongsi the fields. Just beyond the green metal fencin a scrapyard, the path bears R.

2. Turn R at WM sign and descend sharply (ahead on a tree SP No Footpath/Private). The path soon climbs with pond on your L behind a wire fence. Continue up steep gradient (tracks to L & R) to meet a well used farm track.

1. From Bulls Cross walk up hill for 50 yds and turn R SP Public Footpath down rough track into Longridge Wood. The path swings R at bottom of decline.

LINK: Painswick
B. Bear L at fork in path and ascend path over stiles to road. Turn L passing Gothic house on your R and follow tarmac lane up to Bulls X.

11. Turn R at road (just beyond Folly Acres) and follow road past cottages and farm buildings to the first stile/farm gate at bend of lane. Cross stile and head towards wood which is a Nature Reserve managed by the Gloucestershire Wildlife Trust. The path leads directly to Bulls Cross.

10. From Vatch Cottage hop over stile into field turning R at road, then shortly L up steep bank SP keeping woodland to your R. Alternatively, why not continue up road into Slad, stop for refreshments at the Woolpack Inn, and savour a glass of Rosie's cider.

9. Bear L past Furners Farm, then R following well WM signs across fields and over stiles to Vatch Cottage.

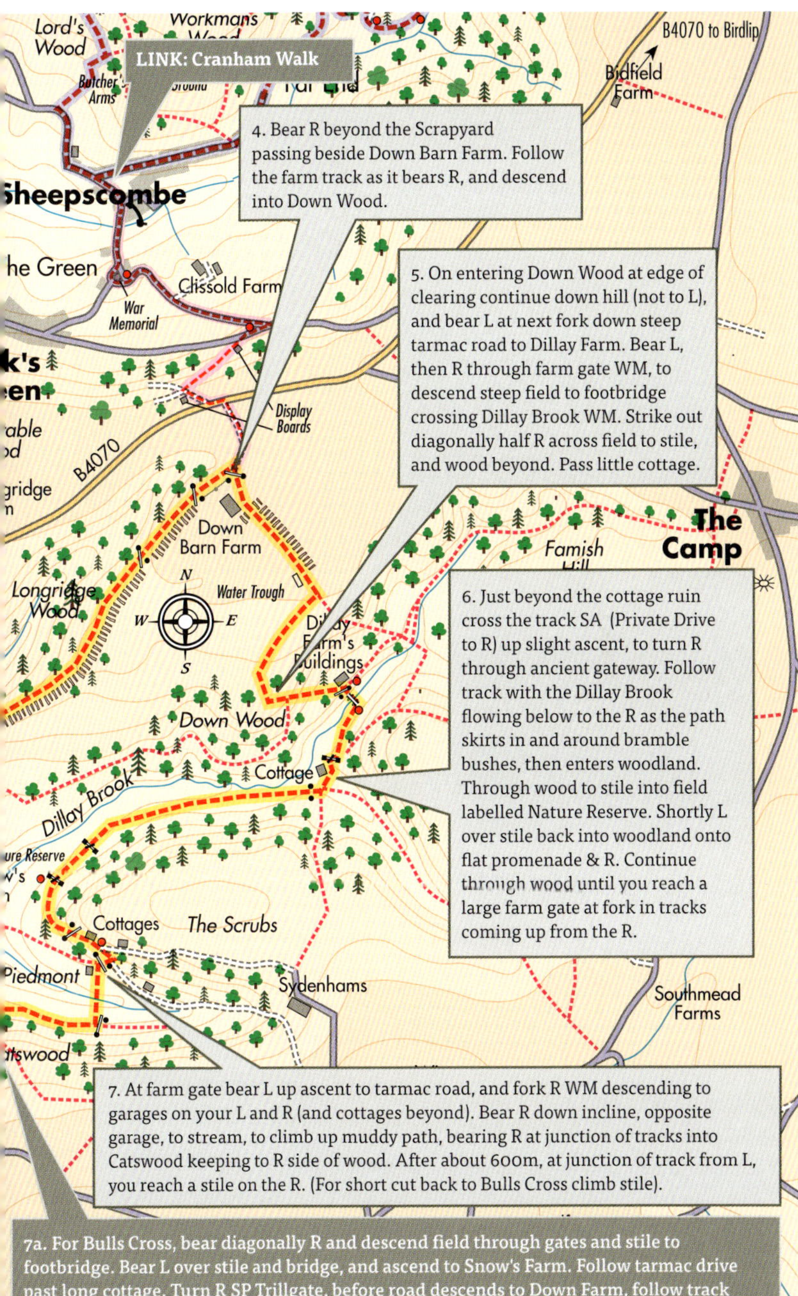

Lord's Wood
Workmans Wood
B4070 to Birdlip
LINK: Cranham Walk
Butcher's Arms
Bidfield Farm
Sheepscombe
he Green
Clissold Farm
War Memorial
k's en
able d
gridge n
B4070
Display Boards
Longridge Wood
Down Barn Farm
N
W   E
S
Water Trough
Dillay Farm's Buildings
Down Wood
Cottage
Dillay Brook
ure Reserve
v's
Cottages   The Scrubs
Piedmont
Sydenhams
tswood
Famish Hill
The Camp
Southmead Farms

4. Bear R beyond the Scrapyard passing beside Down Barn Farm. Follow the farm track as it bears R, and descend into Down Wood.

5. On entering Down Wood at edge of clearing continue down hill (not to L), and bear L at next fork down steep tarmac road to Dillay Farm. Bear L, then R through farm gate WM, to descend steep field to footbridge crossing Dillay Brook WM. Strike out diagonally half R across field to stile, and wood beyond. Pass little cottage.

6. Just beyond the cottage ruin cross the track SA (Private Drive to R) up slight ascent, to turn R through ancient gateway. Follow track with the Dillay Brook flowing below to the R as the path skirts in and around bramble bushes, then enters woodland. Through wood to stile into field labelled Nature Reserve. Shortly L over stile back into woodland onto flat promenade & R. Continue through wood until you reach a large farm gate at fork in tracks coming up from the R.

7. At farm gate bear L up ascent to tarmac road, and fork R WM descending to garages on your L and R (and cottages beyond). Bear R down incline, opposite garage, to stream, to climb up muddy path, bearing R at junction of tracks into Catswood keeping to R side of wood. After about 600m, at junction of track from L, you reach a stile on the R. (For short cut back to Bulls Cross climb stile).

7a. For Bulls Cross, bear diagonally R and descend field through gates and stile to footbridge. Bear L over stile and bridge, and ascend to Snow's Farm. Follow tarmac drive past long cottage. Turn R SP Trillgate, before road descends to Down Farm, follow track beside edge of field bearing L at fork, then R through gate SP Bulls Cross. Down slippery slope to stream and ascend steep climb to stile and tarmac drive.

ate here! Shortly after the wood meets the open fields on your L, NB. the path takes a very URN, reversing back on itself, opposite a holly bush. To descend between steep banks either side glade. Turn L at first junction of paths. High trees above. The path has a field to L and high R, is easily followed across two stiles, fields and orchard to Furners Farm.

The route follows part of the Cotswold Way on the edge of the escarpment which affords spectacular views across the Vale of Gloucester, Severn Estuary and Wales. It then passes by an Iron Age fort and through some of Britain's most ancient woodland. The link to the Painswick-Slad walk allows for an interesting contrast.

Distance
5 miles/8km.

Minimum Time
3 hours.

Grade/Level of Difficulty
Easy/Moderate.

Terrain/Paths
Mud, tracks and grass.

Landscape
Woodland, Cotswold escarpment and pastures.

Dogs
Some livestock and farms where dogs must be kept under control. Lots of woodland where they can run free.

Public Toilets
None.

Parking (P)
Shortwood or Haresfield Beacon.

Recommended Start/Finish
Shortwood Car Park.

Location
East of Stroud with access via the B4008, off the A419.

Link to other walks in this Guide
To Painswick to Slad Valley Walk via the Cotswold Way.

FEATURES OF INTEREST...

Cromwell's Stone. Laid here to celebrate the Parliamentarians successful siege of Gloucester in 1643.

Edge. As its name suggests, a group of cottages overlook the Painswick Valley, on the edge of the escarpment. Pretty village green.

Haresfield Beacon. High open grassland at 700 feet that was a natural fort for Iron Age and Roman settlements. Provides panoramic views of the Severn Estuary, Forest of Dean and Vale of Gloucester.

Shortwood Topograph. Displays the visible landscape in relief and illustrates views.

Standish Wood. An area of ancient woodland recorded in 1297. The wood is delightful when the bluebells and primroses bloom in Spring.

WHERE TO EAT & DRINK...

Edgemoor Inn, Edge. This late C19 Inn is well known for its pretty panoramic views and has an extensive terrace overlooking the Painswick Valley & surrounding countryside. Tasty selection of food for lunch and supper, Sundays a treat.
01452 813576
edgemoorinn.co.uk

View from Haresfield Beacon

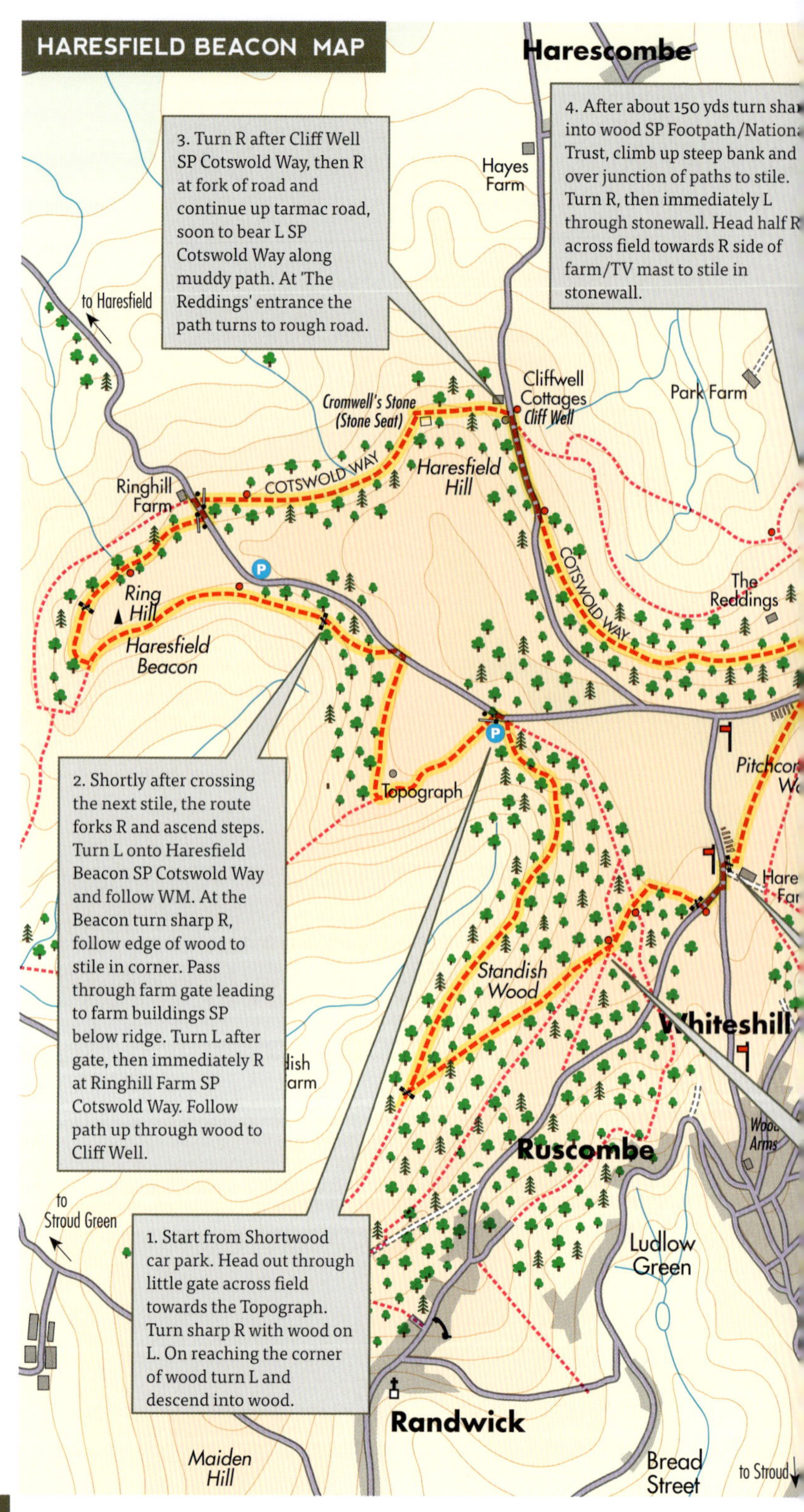
Harescombe
Hayes Farm
4. After about 150 yds turn sha... into wood SP Footpath/Nationa... Trust, climb up steep bank and over junction of paths to stile. Turn R, then immediately L through stonewall. Head half R across field towards R side of farm/TV mast to stile in stonewall.
Park Farm
Cliffwell Cottages
Cliff Well
3. Turn R after Cliff Well SP Cotswold Way, then R at fork of road and continue up tarmac road, soon to bear L SP Cotswold Way along muddy path. At 'The Reddings' entrance the path turns to rough road.
to Haresfield
Cromwell's Stone (Stone Seat)
Haresfield Hill
COTSWOLD WAY
Ringhill Farm
COTSWOLD WAY
The Reddings
Ring Hill
Haresfield Beacon
Topograph
Pitchco... W...
Hare Far...
2. Shortly after crossing the next stile, the route forks R and ascend steps. Turn L onto Haresfield Beacon SP Cotswold Way and follow WM. At the Beacon turn sharp R, follow edge of wood to stile in corner. Pass through farm gate leading to farm buildings SP below ridge. Turn L after gate, then immediately R at Ringhill Farm SP Cotswold Way. Follow path up through wood to Cliff Well.
Standish Wood
...dish ...arm
Whiteshill
Ruscombe
Woo... Arms
to Stroud Green
1. Start from Shortwood car park. Head out through little gate across field towards the Topograph. Turn sharp R with wood on L. On reaching the corner of wood turn L and descend into wood.
Ludlow Green
Randwick
Maiden Hill
Bread Street
to Stroud

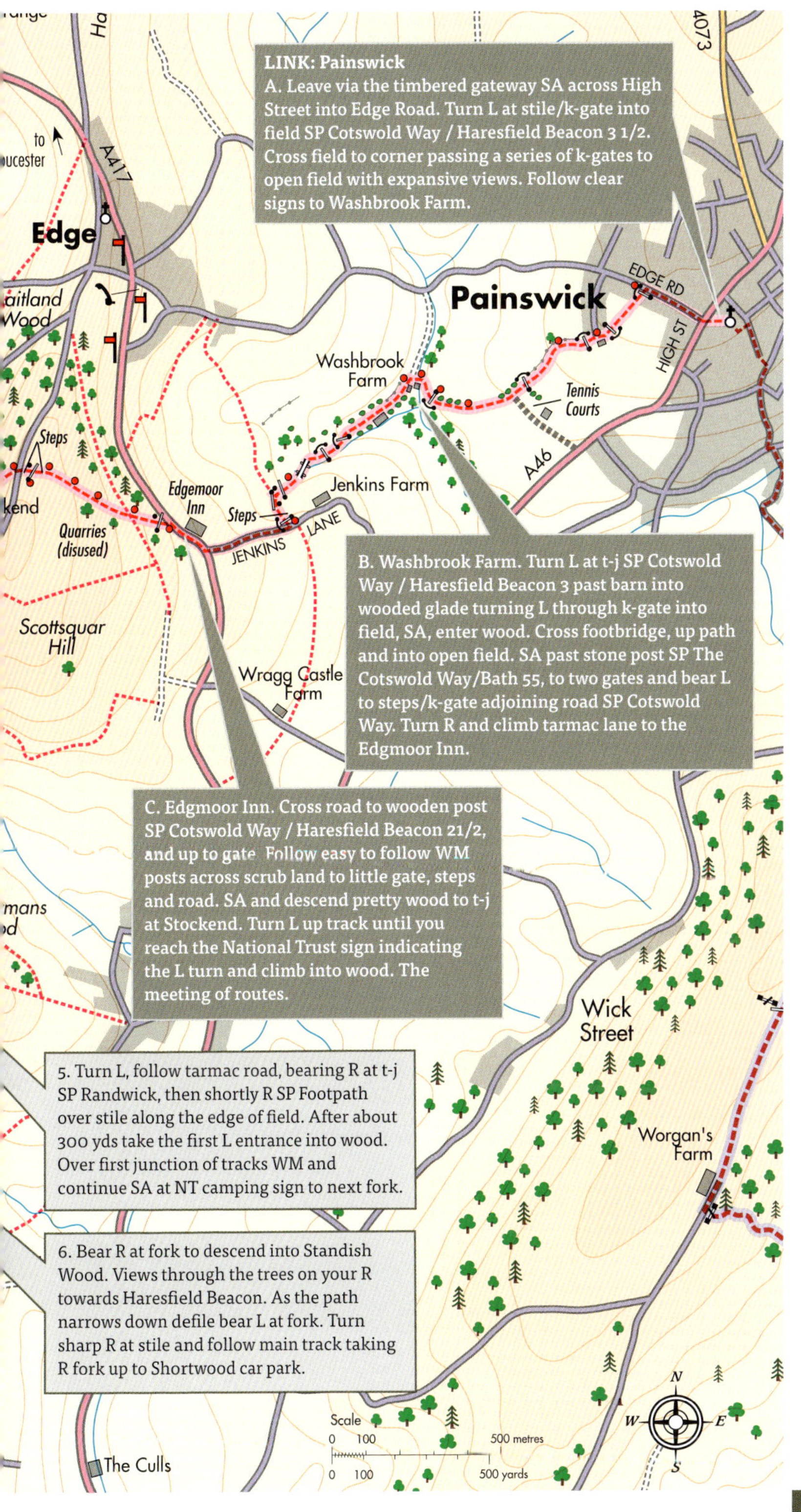

LINK: Painswick
A. Leave via the timbered gateway SA across High Street into Edge Road. Turn L at stile/k-gate into field SP Cotswold Way / Haresfield Beacon 3 1/2. Cross field to corner passing a series of k-gates to open field with expansive views. Follow clear signs to Washbrook Farm.

B. Washbrook Farm. Turn L at t-j SP Cotswold Way / Haresfield Beacon 3 past barn into wooded glade turning L through k-gate into field, SA, enter wood. Cross footbridge, up path and into open field. SA past stone post SP The Cotswold Way/Bath 55, to two gates and bear L to steps/k-gate adjoining road SP Cotswold Way. Turn R and climb tarmac lane to the Edgmoor Inn.

C. Edgmoor Inn. Cross road to wooden post SP Cotswold Way / Haresfield Beacon 21/2, and up to gate. Follow easy to follow WM posts across scrub land to little gate, steps and road. SA and descend pretty wood to t-j at Stockend. Turn L up track until you reach the National Trust sign indicating the L turn and climb into wood. The meeting of routes.

5. Turn L, follow tarmac road, bearing R at t-j SP Randwick, then shortly R SP Footpath over stile along the edge of field. After about 300 yds take the first L entrance into wood. Over first junction of tracks WM and continue SA at NT camping sign to next fork.

6. Bear R at fork to descend into Standish Wood. Views through the trees on your R towards Haresfield Beacon. As the path narrows down defile bear L at fork. Turn sharp R at stile and follow main track taking R fork up to Shortwood car park.

The first walk around the ramparts of Uley Bury, the Iron Age hill fort is easy-going and pushchair-friendly for young families. The views are spectacular. Thereafter, the route across Cam Long Down, along the Cotswold Way is equally spectacular with fine views towards the River Severn and Welsh Hills. Be prepared for a couple of stiff climbs.

Distance
Walk One: 1.25 miles/2km.
Walk Two: 4 miles/6.4km.
Minimum Time
Walk One: 1 hour.
Walk Two: 2.5 hours.
Grade/Level of Difficulty
Easy/Moderate.
Terrain/Paths
Grass, farm tracks, muddy fields.
Landscape
Outcrops of limestone hillocks, and the escarpment. Patchwork of fields.

Dogs
Uley Bury walk is popular with local dog walkers as there is not much livestock. The longer walk has more livestock – dogs to be kept under control at all times.
Public Toilets
None.
Parking (P)
Uley Bury.
Recommended Start/Finish
Uley Bury P.
Location
Uley is between Stroud and Dursley on the B4066.

FEATURES OF INTEREST...

Cam Long Down. A humpbacked ridge of oolitic limestone that once seen is never forgotten. From the top it's a good viewpoint touched by the Cotswold Way surrounded by beech woods and bracken.

Hetty Pegler's Tump (Uley Tumulus). Neolithic Long Barrow 120ft x 22ft, 4 chambers, 38 skeletons found in C19. Torch and Wellington boots needed.

St Giles' Church, Uley. In a spectacular position overlooking the valley. Noted for the Norman font, fine roof and stained glass.

Owlpen Manor. An iconic group of picturesque Cotswold buildings: Manor House, Tithe Barn, Church, Mill and Court House. Water Garden and terrace. The Tudor manor dates from 1150 to 1616 but the whole estate has 900-years of history. Holiday cottages for hire. Events & Parties. 01453 860261 owlpen.com

Prema, Uley. An independent rural arts centre with café showing new work by emerging artists and craftspersons in their converted Bethesda chapel. Open daily. Vestry Café W-Sa 9-4. 01453 860703 prema.org.uk

The Old Brewery, Uley. The mill owner Samuel Price built this brewery in 1833 to assuage his workers' thirst. It was restored in 1984 and has since won many awards for their Old Spot, Pigs Ear and Uley Bitter. It is not open to prying visitors, only the trade. You can sample their wares in the Old Crown Inn at the top of the village, or in various hostelries around the Cotswolds. 01453 860120 uleybrewery.com

Uley. A long, attractive village with some fine Georgian houses. Famous centre of cloth in the C17 and C18. In 1608 three Uley clothiers represented 29 local weavers of broadcloth, and also, the 13 weavers from Owlpen. Roman settlement.

Uley Bury Iron Age Hill Fort. This is the Cotswolds' most famous Iron Age site. The deep ramparts provide superb views across the Severn Vale, Welsh Hills, Dursley and Owlpen Woods. An enclosed area of about 32 acres used for arable crops.

WHERE TO EAT, DRINK, SLEEP...

The Old Crown Inn, Uley. C17 Inn on village green which has been refurbished. Homemade lunches and evening meals, as well as cream teas in the afternoons. Serves real ale from the local Uley brewery and Butcombe. B&B. If you wish to sup firkins of Gloucester Old Spot, then rest here awhile. 01453 860502 theoldcrownuley.co.uk

Eastern View of Cam Long Down

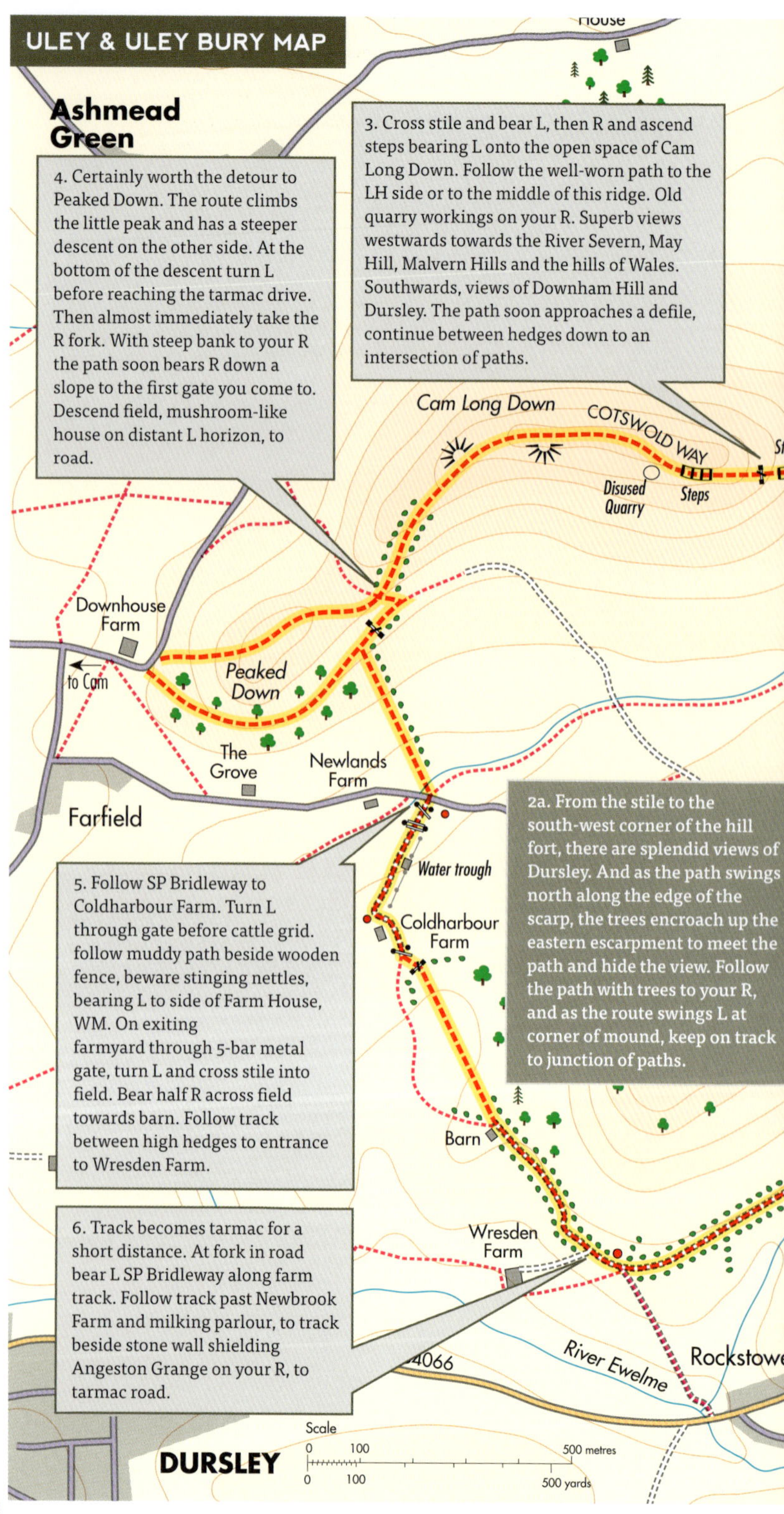

Ashmead
Green

4. Certainly worth the detour to Peaked Down. The route climbs the little peak and has a steeper descent on the other side. At the bottom of the descent turn L before reaching the tarmac drive. Then almost immediately take the R fork. With steep bank to your R the path soon bears R down a slope to the first gate you come to. Descend field, mushroom-like house on distant L horizon, to road.

3. Cross stile and bear L, then R and ascend steps bearing L onto the open space of Cam Long Down. Follow the well-worn path to the LH side or to the middle of this ridge. Old quarry workings on your R. Superb views westwards towards the River Severn, May Hill, Malvern Hills and the hills of Wales. Southwards, views of Downham Hill and Dursley. The path soon approaches a defile, continue between hedges down to an intersection of paths.

House

Cam Long Down
COTSWOLD WAY
Ste
Disused
Quarry
Steps

Downhouse
Farm

to Cam

Peaked
Down

The
Grove

Newlands
Farm

Farfield

Water trough

Coldharbour
Farm

2a. From the stile to the south-west corner of the hill fort, there are splendid views of Dursley. And as the path swings north along the edge of the scarp, the trees encroach up the eastern escarpment to meet the path and hide the view. Follow the path with trees to your R, and as the route swings L at corner of mound, keep on track to junction of paths.

5. Follow SP Bridleway to Coldharbour Farm. Turn L through gate before cattle grid. follow muddy path beside wooden fence, beware stinging nettles, bearing L to side of Farm House, WM. On exiting farmyard through 5-bar metal gate, turn L and cross stile into field. Bear half R across field towards barn. Follow track between high hedges to entrance to Wresden Farm.

Barn

6. Track becomes tarmac for a short distance. At fork in road bear L SP Bridleway along farm track. Follow track past Newbrook Farm and milking parlour, to track beside stone wall shielding Angeston Grange on your R, to tarmac road.

Wresden
Farm

River Ewelme
Rockstowe

A4066

DURSLEY

Scale
0   100   500 metres
0   100   500 yards

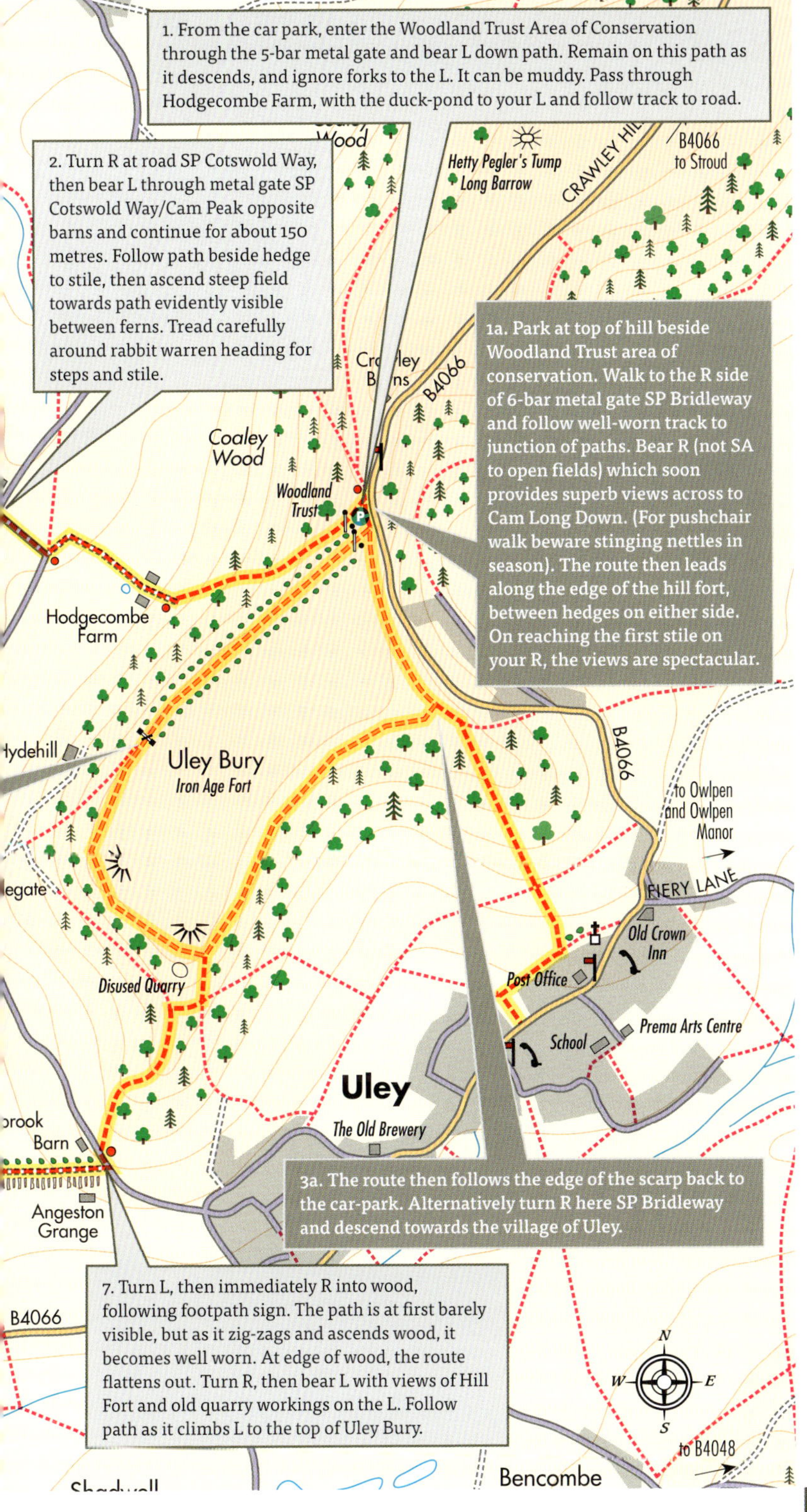

1. From the car park, enter the Woodland Trust Area of Conservation through the 5-bar metal gate and bear L down path. Remain on this path as it descends, and ignore forks to the L. It can be muddy. Pass through Hodgecombe Farm, with the duck-pond to your L and follow track to road.

2. Turn R at road SP Cotswold Way, then bear L through metal gate SP Cotswold Way/Cam Peak opposite barns and continue for about 150 metres. Follow path beside hedge to stile, then ascend steep field towards path evidently visible between ferns. Tread carefully around rabbit warren heading for steps and stile.

1a. Park at top of hill beside Woodland Trust area of conservation. Walk to the R side of 6-bar metal gate SP Bridleway and follow well-worn track to junction of paths. Bear R (not SA to open fields) which soon provides superb views across to Cam Long Down. (For pushchair walk beware stinging nettles in season). The route then leads along the edge of the hill fort, between hedges on either side. On reaching the first stile on your R, the views are spectacular.

3a. The route then follows the edge of the scarp back to the car-park. Alternatively turn R here SP Bridleway and descend towards the village of Uley.

7. Turn L, then immediately R into wood, following footpath sign. The path is at first barely visible, but as it zig-zags and ascends wood, it becomes well worn. At edge of wood, the route flattens out. Turn R, then bear L with views of Hill Fort and old quarry workings on the L. Follow path as it climbs L to the top of Uley Bury.

Hetty Pegler's Tump
Long Barrow
CRAWLEY HILL
B4066
to Stroud
Coaley Wood
Crawley Barns
B4066
Woodland Trust
Hodgecombe Farm
Hydehill
Uley Bury
Iron Age Fort
B4066
to Owlpen and Owlpen Manor
FIERY LANE
Old Crown Inn
Post Office
Prema Arts Centre
School
Disused Quarry
Uley
The Old Brewery
gate
brook Barn
Angeston Grange
B4066
N
W E
S
to B4048
Bencombe
Shadwell

Perhaps the remotest and most isolated of these walks. These deep combes are havens for wildlife and flowers, and are overlooked by sweeping sheep pastures. And yet, dotted along this remote area are gems of domestic architecture such as manor houses with their little churches. A picnic or supplies for the walk are recommended.

Distance
Walk One: 1.5 miles/2.4km.
Walk Two: 5 miles/8km.

Minimum Time
Walk One: 1 hour.
Walk Two: 2.5 hours.

Grade/Level of Difficulty
Easy.

Terrain/Paths
Woodland tracks, grass.

Landscape
Valleys, pastures and woodland.

Dogs
Keep under control - beware livestock in farm fields (& pheasants in season).

Public Toilets
None.

Parking (P)
Ozleworth.

Recommended Start/Finish
Ozleworth.

Location
Two miles east of Wotton-under-Edge. Best approached from the junction of the B4058 and A4135, Dursley-Tetbury road.

FEATURES OF INTEREST...

Boxwell Court. C15 origins, formerly owned by Gloucester Cathedral. Tudor doorway.

BT Tower. Built in 1965. 240 ft high at 750 ft above sea level.

Lasborough Manor. Built in 1630 for Sir Thomas Estcourt. Renaissance chimney pots. Enormous bay windows of three storeys. Estcourt heraldry.

Lasborough Park. C18 monuments and stained glass. Tudor gothic style, castellated with four towers.

Newark Park, Ozleworth (NT). Former Tudor hunting lodge with an eclectic art collection. Countryside walks. Plant sales. Garden open from 10, House from 11 daily. 01453 842644 nationaltrust.org.uk

Ozleworth Bottom. Wild, remote and beautiful. A deep combe with wild flowers, birdlife and ancient woodlands. A thriving valley in the C17 and C18s when 15 fulling mills (to cleanse and thicken cloth) operated within 5-miles.

Ozleworth Park. C18 house with spacious lawns and Rose Garden. Home to an affluent shoot - beware of activity in the winter pheasant season- dogs on lead, please!

St Bartholomew's Church, Newington Bagpath. Private church boarded up. Jacobean pulpit. West tower and chancel rebuilt in 1858.

St Mary's Church, Lasborough. Norman font and elaborate roof trusses. Rebuilt 1861-62.

St Mary the Virgin's Church, Boxwell. C13 origins. Massive stone bell-cot and grotesque corbels.

St Nicholas' Church, Ozleworth. Extremely rare C12 hexagonal tower. Norman remains. Rare weathercock. C13 font and Clutterbuck monument.

WHERE TO EAT... DRINK...STAY... JUST OFF THE MAP...

Black Horse Inn, North Nibley. Family-run country inn with restaurant and public bar, live music nights and reported ghostly sightings! B&B. Child and dog friendly. 01453 453895 blackhorsenorthnibley.co.uk

Calcot & Spa. This is a leisure complex combining a Country House Hotel & Spa. All the pampering you may well desire after a day in the combes and hills of Gloucestershire. Gumstool Inn next door for a glass of ale and pub-grub. 01666 890391 calcot.co

Royal Oak, Leighterton. Comfortable old Inn given to conversation, friendship and good food. All endeared by locally-sourced produce and a child friendly ambience make up the ingredients for this popular dining pub. Large garden. 01666 890250 royaloakleighterton.co.uk

Ozleworth Bottom in winter

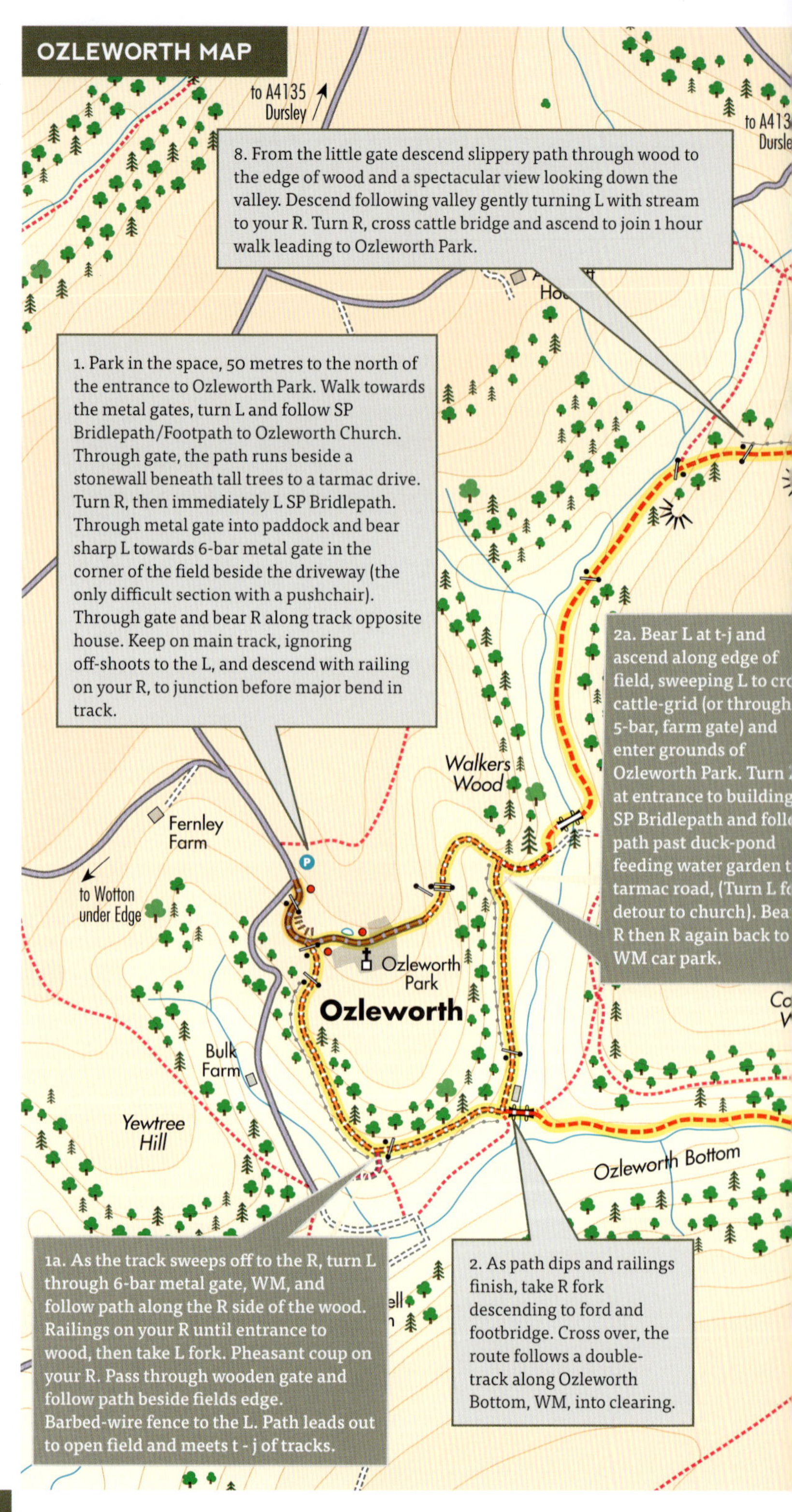

to A4135 Dursley

to A413 Dursle

8. From the little gate descend slippery path through wood to the edge of wood and a spectacular view looking down the valley. Descend following valley gently turning L with stream to your R. Turn R, cross cattle bridge and ascend to join 1 hour walk leading to Ozleworth Park.

1. Park in the space, 50 metres to the north of the entrance to Ozleworth Park. Walk towards the metal gates, turn L and follow SP Bridlepath/Footpath to Ozleworth Church. Through gate, the path runs beside a stonewall beneath tall trees to a tarmac drive. Turn R, then immediately L SP Bridlepath. Through metal gate into paddock and bear sharp L towards 6-bar metal gate in the corner of the field beside the driveway (the only difficult section with a pushchair). Through gate and bear R along track opposite house. Keep on main track, ignoring off-shoots to the L, and descend with railing on your R, to junction before major bend in track.

2a. Bear L at t-j and ascend along edge of field, sweeping L to cro cattle-grid (or through 5-bar, farm gate) and enter grounds of Ozleworth Park. Turn at entrance to building SP Bridlepath and foll path past duck-pond feeding water garden t tarmac road, (Turn L fo detour to church). Bea R then R again back to WM car park.

Walkers Wood

Fernley Farm

to Wotton under Edge

Ozleworth Park

Ozleworth

Bulk Farm

Yewtree Hill

Ozleworth Bottom

Co V

1a. As the track sweeps off to the R, turn L through 6-bar metal gate, WM, and follow path along the R side of the wood. Railings on your R until entrance to wood, then take L fork. Pheasant coup on your R. Pass through wooden gate and follow path beside fields edge. Barbed-wire fence to the L. Path leads out to open field and meets t - j of tracks.

2. As path dips and railings finish, take R fork descending to ford and footbridge. Cross over, the route follows a double-track along Ozleworth Bottom, WM, into clearing.

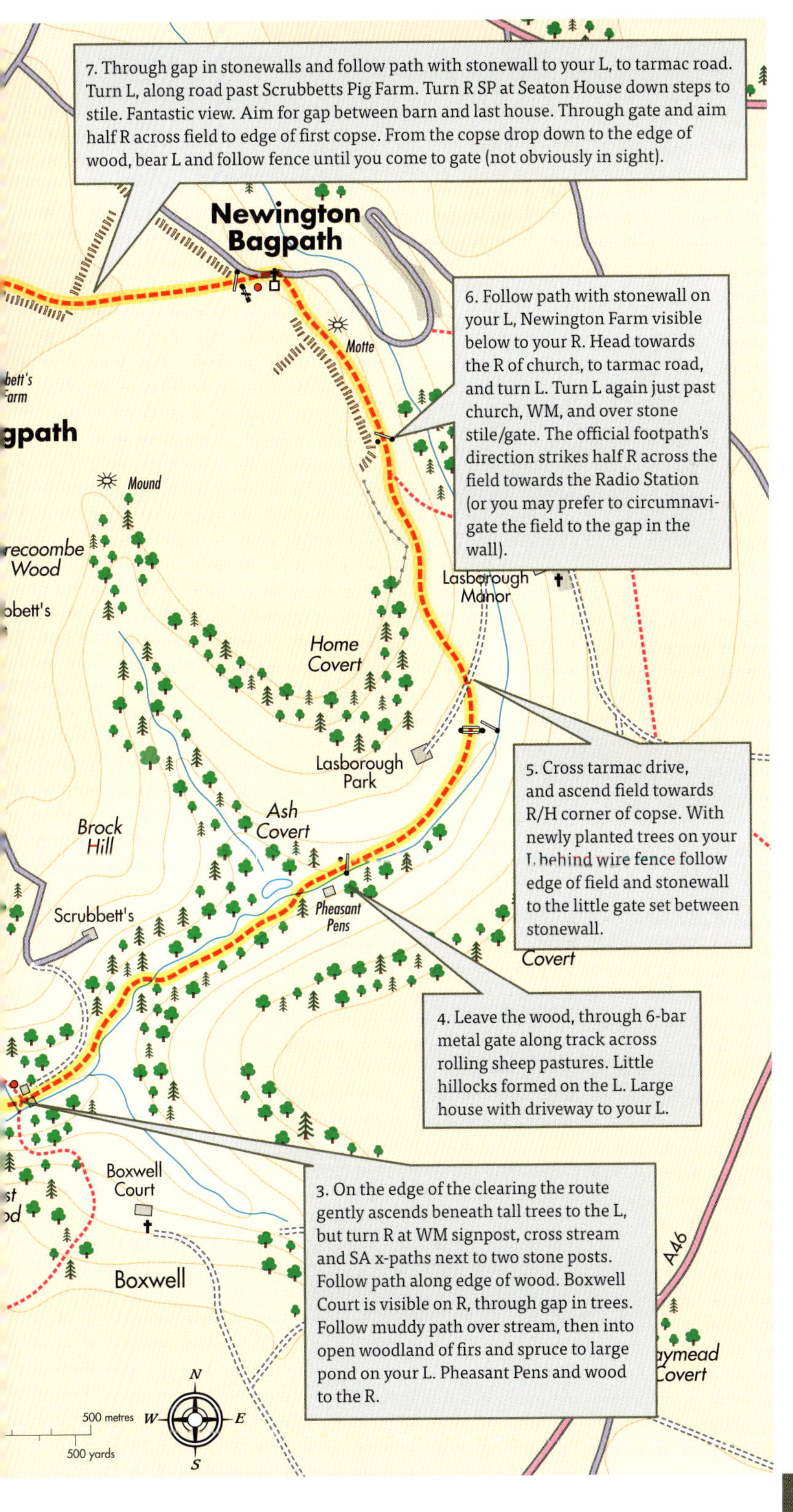

7. Through gap in stonewalls and follow path with stonewall to your L, to tarmac road. Turn L, along road past Scrubbetts Pig Farm. Turn R SP at Seaton House down steps to stile. Fantastic view. Aim for gap between barn and last house. Through gate and aim half R across field to edge of first copse. From the copse drop down to the edge of wood, bear L and follow fence until you come to gate (not obviously in sight).

Newington Bagpath

Motte

bett's Farm

gpath

Mound

recoombe Wood

obett's

Home Covert

Lasborough Manor

6. Follow path with stonewall on your L, Newington Farm visible below to your R. Head towards the R of church, to tarmac road, and turn L. Turn L again just past church, WM, and over stone stile/gate. The official footpath's direction strikes half R across the field towards the Radio Station (or you may prefer to circumnavigate the field to the gap in the wall).

Lasborough Park

Brock Hill

Ash Covert

Scrubbett's

Pheasant Pens

Covert

5. Cross tarmac drive, and ascend field towards R/H corner of copse. With newly planted trees on your L behind wire fence follow edge of field and stonewall to the little gate set between stonewall.

4. Leave the wood, through 6-bar metal gate along track across rolling sheep pastures. Little hillocks formed on the L. Large house with driveway to your L.

Boxwell Court

st od

Boxwell

A46

aymead Covert

3. On the edge of the clearing the route gently ascends beneath tall trees to the L, but turn R at WM signpost, cross stream and SA x-paths next to two stone posts. Follow path along edge of wood. Boxwell Court is visible on R, through gap in trees. Follow muddy path over stream, then into open woodland of firs and spruce to large pond on your L. Pheasant Pens and wood to the R.

500 metres
500 yards
N
W E
S

One of England's prettiest villages hidden away in a deep, wooded, combe. Take in the lovely old world cottages and follow the path, idly, through the woods with the shimmering By Brook below. The walk incorporates a section of the Colham Farm Trail, a circular trail that takes you through ancient woodland in Parsonage Wood and down into the By Brook valley where the meadow is a Site of Special Scientific Interest. Resident species include the green winged meadow orchid.

Distance
Walk One: 2.75 miles/4.4km.
Walk Two: 5.25 miles/8.4km.
Minimum Time
Walk One: 2.5 hours.
Walk Two: 1 hour.
Grade/Level of Difficulty
Easy.
Terrain/Paths
Woodland tracks, grass.
Landscape
Wooded combe.
Dogs
Well trod path with few stiles - fairly good for dogs.

Public Toilets
Below the bridge at Castle Combe.
Parking (P)
Car park at the top of Castle Combe.
Recommended Start/Finish
Opposite the Dower House in Castle Combe.
Location
Castle Combe is situated midway between Chippenham and Chipping Sodbury. It is best approached from Chippenham via the A420 (Chippenham to Bristol), or from the north via the A46 (Stroud to Bath) by the villages of Badminton/Acton Turville.

FEATURES OF INTEREST…

Castle Combe. One of the prettiest and most visited villages in the Cotswolds lies sheltered in a hidden valley surrounded by steep, wooded hills. It takes its name from the Norman castle on the hilltop above. In former times, it was an important medieval wool centre as evidenced by the weavers and clothiers' cottages that descend from the Market Cross to By Brook, and the three-arch bridge. Its great claim to fame followed its appearance in the 1966 film of Doctor Doolittle starring Rex Harrison, more recently as a backdrop for Spielberg's War Horse. You could be forgiven believing it to be a film set for there is no real life going on here. The Post Office and gift shops have closed and young families can ill afford to live here. The only life appears those sitting outside the pubs, or that of wandering tourists. castle-combe.com

Dower House. The finest house in the village built in the C17. Note the beautiful shell-hooded doorway.

Long Dean. A cluster of small cottages that were probably built for workers of the disused mill now a spacious home.

Ford. Village on the busy A420, but a welcome stop if you've developed a hunger and a thirst.

Motor Racing Circuit. Regular car and motorcycle race days take place through the summer at this circuit, one of the longest established race tracks in the UK. 01249 782417 castlecombecircuit.co.uk

St Andrew's Church, Castle Combe. Originally C13, the nave was added in the C14 and the tower completed in the C16. In the 1850s much of the church had to be rebuilt. Note the beautiful fan vaulting reminiscent of Bath Abbey. Also the medieval faceless clock, one of the most ancient working clocks in the country.

WHERE TO EAT, DRINK…SLEEP…

The Castle Inn Hotel. A pretty honey-coloured building set in the market place. Features of the original C12 construction remain thanks to over subtle restoration. The eleven bedrooms are individual in character. You can choose fine dining in the restaurant or more simple bar food in the bar itself. Elegant dining in a pleasant setting. 01249 783030 exclusive.co.uk

The White Hart, Market Place. C14 pub at the heart of the village with sunny conservatory, patio gardens and beautiful courtyard to the rear. 01249 782295 wadworth.co.uk

White Hart Inn, Ford. A rambling C16 coaching inn situated in the Wyvern Valley beside a trout stream and with a large beer garden. B&B. Children welcome. 01249 782213 whitehart-ford.com

WHERE TO STAY…

Fosse Farmhouse B&B. Set conveniently close to the north-west corner of this walk. Caron's home is beautifully furnished in English Vintage and French Brocante. You will be made very welcome, and your hostess is a source of abundant information. Dogs and children welcomed. Self-catering. 01249 782286 fossefarmhouse.com

The Manor House Hotel. More Surrey country club than Cotswold Manor, and with its fine golf course is probably not geared for walkers. However, it shadows the village lying hidden away in 365-acres of gardens and woodland. You can stay in the Mews Cottages if you prefer the simple life. 01249 782206 exclusive.co.uk/the-manor-house

Castle Combe

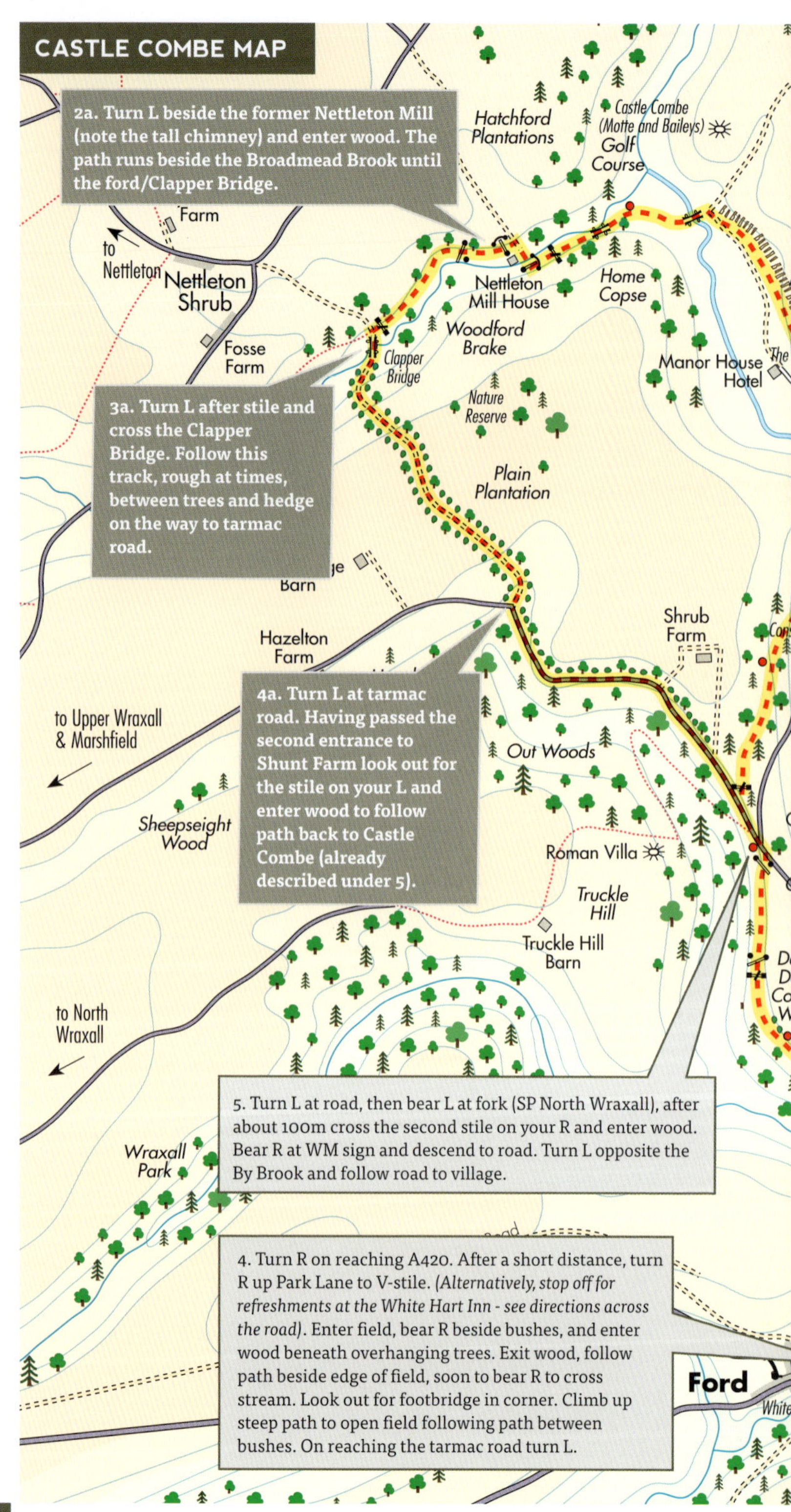
2a. Turn L beside the former Nettleton Mill (note the tall chimney) and enter wood. The path runs beside the Broadmead Brook until the ford/Clapper Bridge.
Hatchford Plantations
Castle Combe (Motte and Baileys)
Golf Course
Farm
to Nettleton
Nettleton Shrub
Fosse Farm
Nettleton Mill House
Home Copse
Woodford Brake
Clapper Bridge
Manor House Hotel
The C
3a. Turn L after stile and cross the Clapper Bridge. Follow this track, rough at times, between trees and hedge on the way to tarmac road.
Nature Reserve
Plain Plantation
Barn
Shrub Farm
Conse
Hazelton Farm
4a. Turn L at tarmac road. Having passed the second entrance to Shunt Farm look out for the stile on your L and enter wood to follow path back to Castle Combe (already described under 5).
to Upper Wraxall & Marshfield
Out Woods
Sheepseight Wood
Roman Villa
C
Truckle Hill
to North Wraxall
Truckle Hill Barn
Da
Do
Cott
Wo
5. Turn L at road, then bear L at fork (SP North Wraxall), after about 100m cross the second stile on your R and enter wood. Bear R at WM sign and descend to road. Turn L opposite the By Brook and follow road to village.
Wraxall Park
4. Turn R on reaching A420. After a short distance, turn R up Park Lane to V-stile. (Alternatively, stop off for refreshments at the White Hart Inn - see directions across the road). Enter field, bear R beside bushes, and enter wood beneath overhanging trees. Exit wood, follow path beside edge of field, soon to bear R to cross stream. Look out for footbridge in corner. Climb up steep path to open field following path between bushes. On reaching the tarmac road turn L.
Ford
White

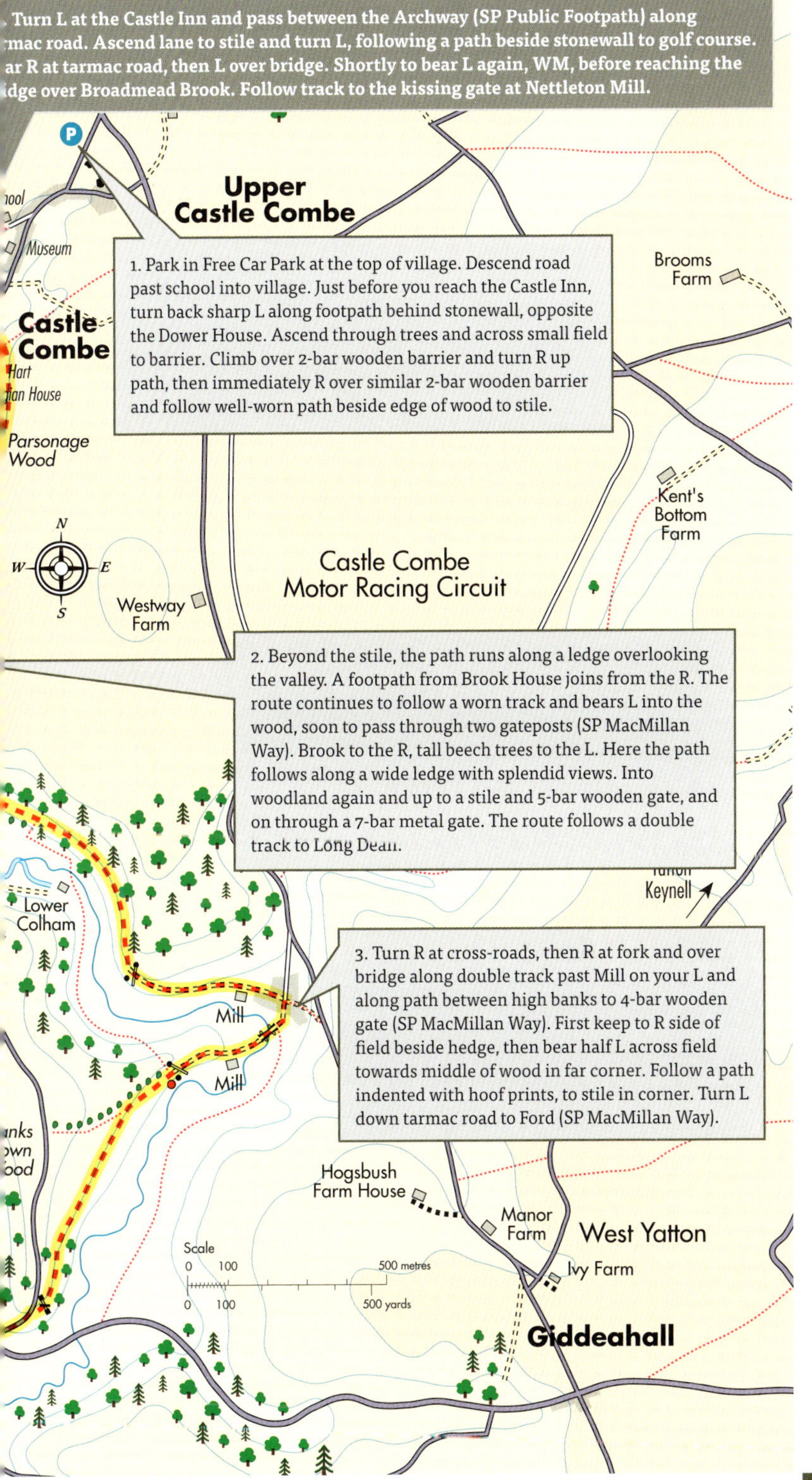

. Turn L at the Castle Inn and pass between the Archway (SP Public Footpath) along
rmac road. Ascend lane to stile and turn L, following a path beside stonewall to golf course.
ar R at tarmac road, then L over bridge. Shortly to bear L again, WM, before reaching the
idge over Broadmead Brook. Follow track to the kissing gate at Nettleton Mill.

P

Upper
Castle Combe

1. Park in Free Car Park at the top of village. Descend road
past school into village. Just before you reach the Castle Inn,
turn back sharp L along footpath behind stonewall, opposite
the Dower House. Ascend through trees and across small field
to barrier. Climb over 2-bar wooden barrier and turn R up
path, then immediately R over similar 2-bar wooden barrier
and follow well-worn path beside edge of wood to stile.

Brooms
Farm

ool
Museum

Castle
Combe
Hart
ian House

Parsonage
Wood

Kent's
Bottom
Farm

N
W E
S

Westway
Farm

Castle Combe
Motor Racing Circuit

2. Beyond the stile, the path runs along a ledge overlooking
the valley. A footpath from Brook House joins from the R. The
route continues to follow a worn track and bears L into the
wood, soon to pass through two gateposts (SP MacMillan
Way). Brook to the R, tall beech trees to the L. Here the path
follows along a wide ledge with splendid views. Into
woodland again and up to a stile and 5-bar wooden gate, and
on through a 7-bar metal gate. The route follows a double
track to Long Dean.

Keynell

Lower
Colham

3. Turn R at cross-roads, then R at fork and over
bridge along double track past Mill on your L and
along path between high banks to 4-bar wooden
gate (SP MacMillan Way). First keep to R side of
field beside hedge, then bear half L across field
towards middle of wood in far corner. Follow a path
indented with hoof prints, to stile in corner. Turn L
down tarmac road to Ford (SP MacMillan Way).

Mill

Mill

inks
own
ood

Hogsbush
Farm House

Manor
Farm   West Yatton

Ivy Farm

Scale
0   100   500 metres

0   100   500 yards

Giddeahall

Descending from Banbury Stone & Tower, Bredon Hill

Stand on a bridge over any of the motorways at a weekend, and count the cars topped with mountain bikes heading west or northwest from London and the Home Counties, or Birmingham and the Midlands. Destination North Wales, The Peak District, Yorkshire Dales or the Lakes - because that's where they've been conditioned to think the best off-road mountain biking is. Some of these cars will pass within 20 miles of the routes described here, but few will even give them a thought. The sad truth is that for mountain bikers, the Cotswolds suffer from an image problem - all Jilly Cooper, green wellies and horse-riding toffs. And, of course the countryside is green and lush, a land of rolling hills rather than rugged crags - and not being a National Park it doesn't suffer from the saturation advertising of those areas above. Now rugged crags may make for great scenery, but they also often equate with steep, bone-jarring descents and uphill pushes and carries - and if that's your main thing, then don't head for the Cotswolds. But, for the cross-country rider who wants long green lanes criss-crossing some of England's most beautiful landscapes, and linking some of her most beautiful villages, and all 100% rideable - then this is for you.

Some of these tracks are prehistoric in origin, though more owe their existence to the medieval wool-trade and the need to move herds of sheep to market. The wool trade made England rich, and many of the delightful honey-stoned villages and their pubs date from this period - often with huge churches

Riding the Cotswold Way near Wontley Farm, Charlton Abbots

that stand as memorials to the rich merchants who tried to buy their way into heaven - but perhaps even more to the hundreds of shepherds who spent so many cold, lonely nights up on the hills in order to produce such wealth. Though centres such as Broadway and Burford can be overrun by tourists at the height of the season, most tourists suffer panic attacks when more than a few hundred yards from their cars, and have an aversion to narrow lanes where they have to drive slowly or change gear. As a result you are unlikely to meet more than the occasional vehicle on the narrow lanes forming part of the rides, and the occasional walker or horse-rider off-road. As few of the hills are really steep, unless you are particularly unlucky with the weather you're unlikely to spend much time pushing - but with such smooth surfaces there are a number of excellent downhill runs. But, do keep a look-out for walkers, and particularly horse-riders - horses are very easily spooked by cyclists suddenly appearing in their field of vision with little audible warning. Bells may be out of fashion, but they remain by far the best way of signalling your approach, and I've always found both riders and walkers to be grateful - and somehow the ping of a bell seems guaranteed to bring a smile to faces - but do remember to give your warning in plenty of time. And, for anyone tempted to write-off horse-riders as toffs who's horses tear up the tracks - remember that we owe the fact that so many tracks are categorized as bridleways rather than footpaths, to the horse-riding community.

GRADING

1. (Easy). Almost flat routes, usually around 10 miles in length and on good surfaces that in all but extreme conditions should be 100% rideable. With easy navigation and any real climbs on tarmac, these are particularly suitable for beginners or family groups.

2. (Moderate). More challenging routes, generally of 12 to 15 miles over more undulating terrain and varied surfaces (possibly including mud when wet). More exciting downhills, and steeper climbs may need the occasional push.

3. More strenuous (and possibly longer routes) with significant ascents which will certainly need pushing or carrying. Steep and/or technical, and rough and rocky descents. May cross high, remote moorland, requiring appropriate equipment and experience.

These gradings are for average conditions, and many routes can be a grade harder in particularly harsh conditions. Sections which are particularly likely to become more difficult after bad weather are, whenever practical, mentioned in the text. Some harder routes are quite possible for less experienced riders as long as they are prepared to spend more time on them - pushing or carrying on the tougher sections when necessary. Personally, I'm never ashamed to get off and walk when I think there's a good chance of bending myself or my bike!

You are allowed to cycle OFF-ROAD on:- Bridleways, designated Cycle-Ways, RUPPS (Roads Used As Public Paths), Byeways and Unclassified Country Roads.

Unfortunately you may meet Scrambling Motorbikes or 4 x 4 drivers on the last three mentioned - these have caused more damage to our ancient network of tracks in a few years, than all the forces of nature and humanity have achieved in centuries, and one hopes this will not be allowed to continue indefinitely. They should give way to you, but more often will expect the opposite. In turn we should give way to horses and walkers, being prepared to dismount if necessary. Take particular care to avoid spooking horses when approaching from behind by giving ample audible warning in plenty of time - either by

voice or bell (both riders and walkers always seem to respond favourably to the ring of a bell). If there are more than four or five riders, split yourselves into two groups - and remember, a smile and a friendly greeting costs nothing, and can only help with relationships between different outdoor groups, which in some cases are badly strained. Cycling is also allowed on some Forestry tracks and Canal Towpaths, but NOT on footpaths.

Pushing a bike on footpaths is a "grey" area and so far only one each of our Cotswold and Lake District routes entail a short push along footpaths to avoid sections of main road.

Bridleways are often signed by blue arrows, and footpaths by yellow ones, though this is not universal.

WHAT TO CARRY

Essentials are:- a pump, puncture outfit and tyre levers, spare tube, coins/phone card for emergency phone calls or a mobile phone, and a small first-aid kit. Also worth carrying are a chain-breaker, allen keys, small spanners or an adjustable (all of which can be in the form of one of the various compact multi-tools), disposable gloves, screw driver (reversible ?), and a small screw-top container of oil (old dropper bottles are useful). A compass weighs little and though rarely needed, it can make all the difference on the odd difficult junction choice - particularly in bad weather and/or light. Cable locks are best - riding without a front wheel is not recommended - but try not to leave your bike unattended for any length of time.

If there's a chance of being caught by the dark, carry lights - a rear LED permanently in place is also valuable in fog etc., and a Petzl zoom headtorch in your pack not only supplies a front light (though technically illegal) but also leaves your hands free for those punctures that always occur just as its getting dark and starting to rain.

THE MOUNTAIN BIKE CLUB'S OFF-ROAD CODE

Only ride where you know you have a legal right.

Always yield to horses and pedestrians, and warn of your approach.

Avoid animals and crops. Where this is not possible, keep contact to a minimum.

Take all litter home.

Leave all gates as found.

Keep noise down.

Don't get annoyed with anyone, it never solves problems.

Always try to be self-sufficient, for yourself and your bike.

Never create a fire hazzard.

Harry testing a Hybrid E-Bike

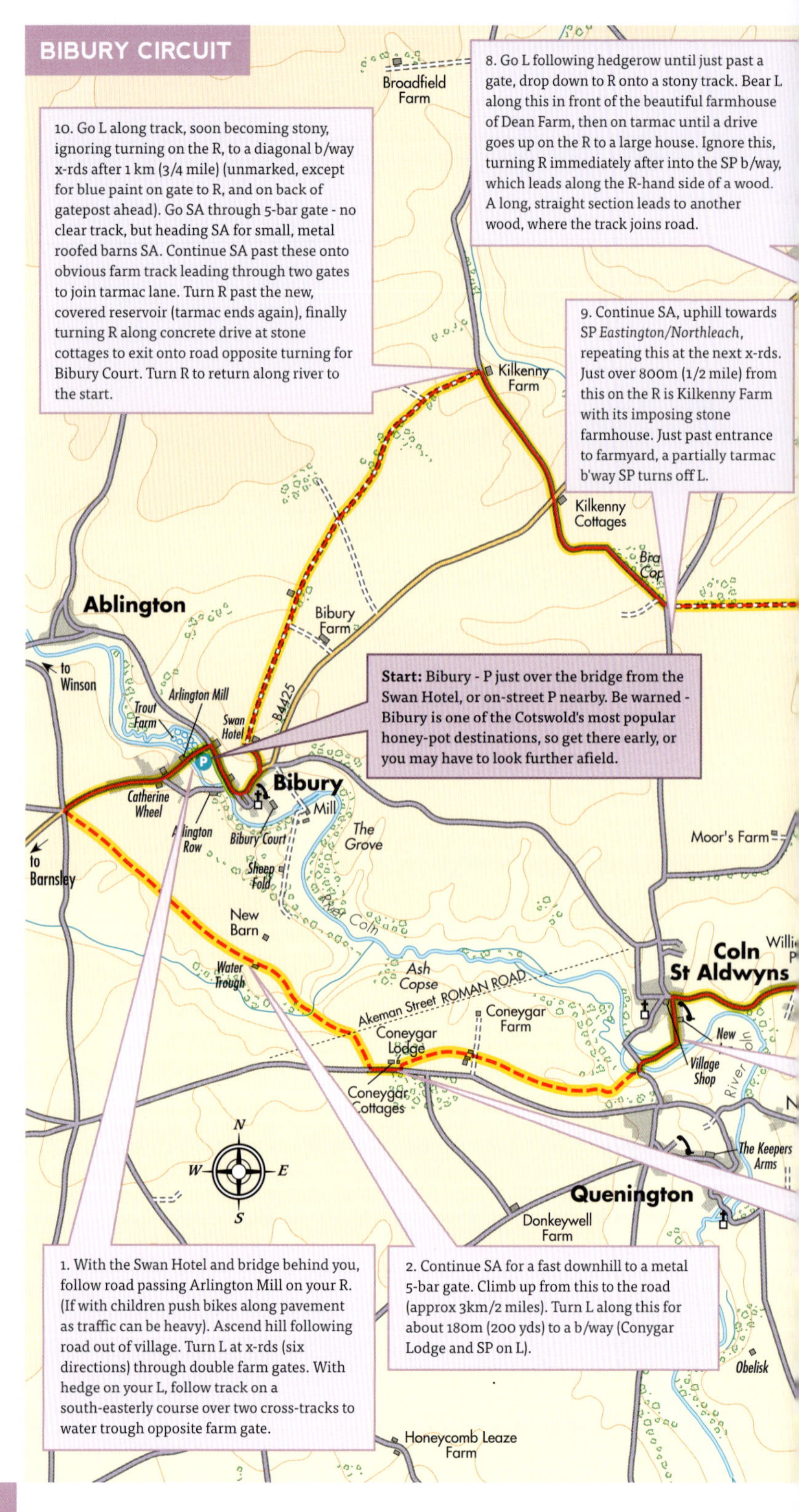

10. Go L along track, soon becoming stony, ignoring turning on the R, to a diagonal b/way x-rds after 1 km (3/4 mile) (unmarked, except for blue paint on gate to R, and on back of gatepost ahead). Go SA through 5-bar gate - no clear track, but heading SA for small, metal roofed barns SA. Continue SA past these onto obvious farm track leading through two gates to join tarmac lane. Turn R past the new, covered reservoir (tarmac ends again), finally turning R along concrete drive at stone cottages to exit onto road opposite turning for Bibury Court. Turn R to return along river to the start.

8. Go L following hedgerow until just past a gate, drop down to R onto a stony track. Bear L along this in front of the beautiful farmhouse of Dean Farm, then on tarmac until a drive goes up on the R to a large house. Ignore this, turning R immediately after into the SP b/way, which leads along the R-hand side of a wood. A long, straight section leads to another wood, where the track joins road.

9. Continue SA, uphill towards SP *Eastington/Northleach*, repeating this at the next x-rds. Just over 800m (1/2 mile) from this on the R is Kilkenny Farm with its imposing stone farmhouse. Just past entrance to farmyard, a partially tarmac b'way SP turns off L.

Start: Bibury - P just over the bridge from the Swan Hotel, or on-street P nearby. Be warned - Bibury is one of the Cotswold's most popular honey-pot destinations, so get there early, or you may have to look further afield.

1. With the Swan Hotel and bridge behind you, follow road passing Arlington Mill on your R. (If with children push bikes along pavement as traffic can be heavy). Ascend hill following road out of village. Turn L at x-rds (six directions) through double farm gates. With hedge on your L, follow track on a south-easterly course over two cross-tracks to water trough opposite farm gate.

2. Continue SA for a fast downhill to a metal 5-bar gate. Climb up from this to the road (approx 3km/2 miles). Turn L along this for about 180m (200 yds) to a b/way (Conygar Lodge and SP on L).

Distance: 26km (16 miles); 19 km (12 miles) off-road, 7 km (4 miles) road.

Grade: 1

Riding time: 2½ hours.

Direction: Anti-clockwise.

An easy route that would be hard to better. Though there are no real hills, the landscape undulates just enough to provide interest and views - a little like Suffolk. The off-road sections are easy to follow, and on good surfaces, and a few quiet miles of road pass through pretty villages. This route is one of the longest Grade 1s. Alternate sections of road are indicated for very wet conditions, or to make it a little easier for family parties or beginners (the first option also allows for a visit to the lovely village of Quenington). The route would easily split into two circuits of about 13 km (8 miles) by using the minor road running north from Coln St. Aldwyns.

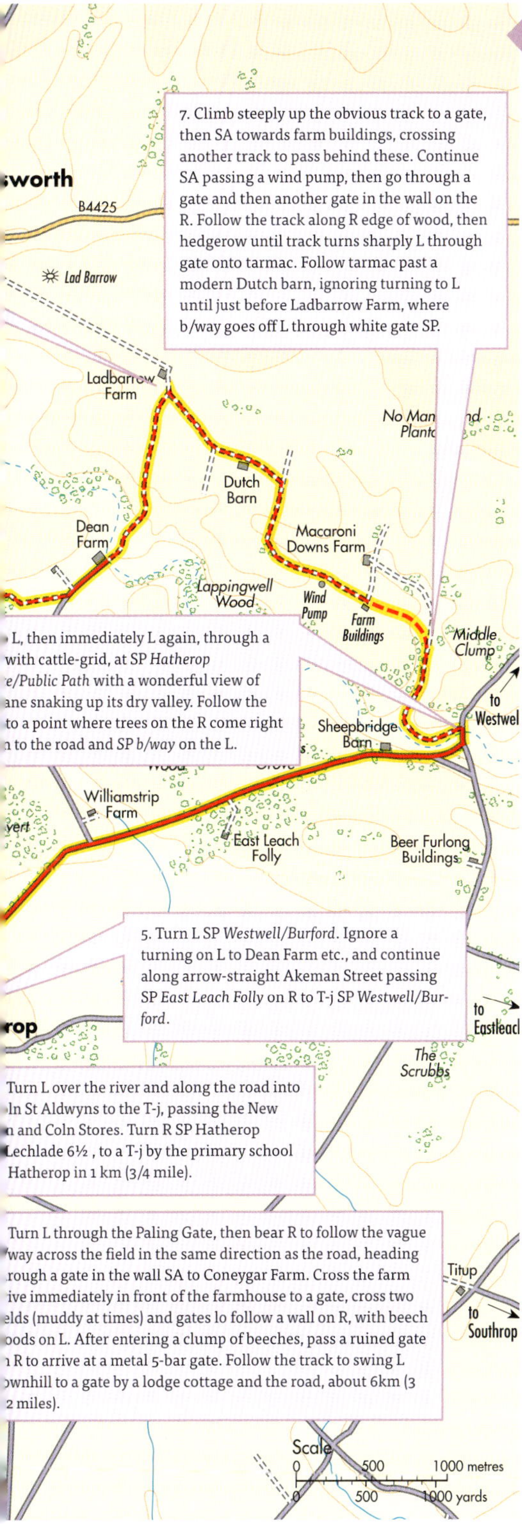
7. Climb steeply up the obvious track to a gate, then SA towards farm buildings, crossing another track to pass behind these. Continue SA passing a wind pump, then go through a gate and then another gate in the wall on the R. Follow the track along R edge of wood, then hedgerow until track turns sharply L through gate onto tarmac. Follow tarmac past a modern Dutch barn, ignoring turning to L until just before Ladbarrow Farm, where b/way goes off L through white gate SP.
L, then immediately L again, through a with cattle-grid, at SP *Hatherop* e/Public Path with a wonderful view of ane snaking up its dry valley. Follow the to a point where trees on the R come right n to the road and *SP b/way* on the L.
5. Turn L SP *Westwell/Burford*. Ignore a turning on L to Dean Farm etc., and continue along arrow-straight Akeman Street passing SP *East Leach Folly* on R to T-j SP *Westwell/Burford*.
Turn L over the river and along the road into ln St Aldwyns to the T-j, passing the New n and Coln Stores. Turn R SP Hatherop Lechlade 6½ , to a T-j by the primary school Hatherop in 1 km (3/4 mile).
Turn L through the Paling Gate, then bear R to follow the vague way across the field in the same direction as the road, heading rough a gate in the wall SA to Coneygar Farm. Cross the farm ive immediately in front of the farmhouse to a gate, cross two elds (muddy at times) and gates lo follow a wall on R, with beech oods on L. After entering a clump of beeches, pass a ruined gate R to arrive at a metal 5-bar gate. Follow the track to swing L ownhill to a gate by a lodge cottage and the road, about 6km (3 2 miles).
sworth
B4425
Lad Barrow
Ladbarrow Farm
Dutch Barn
Dean Farm
Macaroni Downs Farm
Lappingwell Wood
Wind Pump
Farm Buildings
Middle Clump
to Westwel
Sheepbridge Barn
Williamstrip Farm
East Leach Folly
Beer Furlong Buildings
rop
to Eastleacl
The Scrubbs
Titup
to Southrop
Scale
0 500 1000 metres
0 500 1000 yards

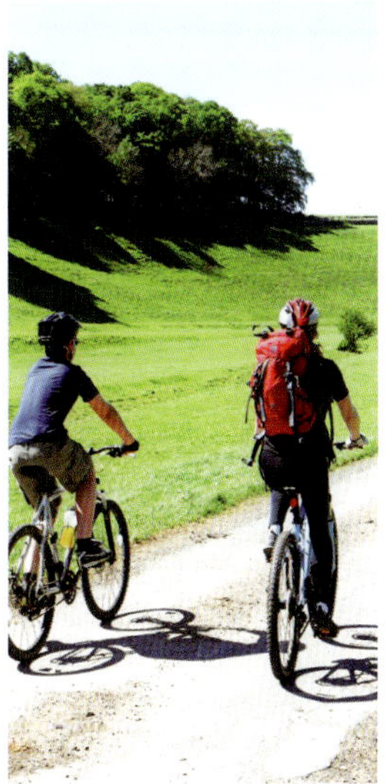

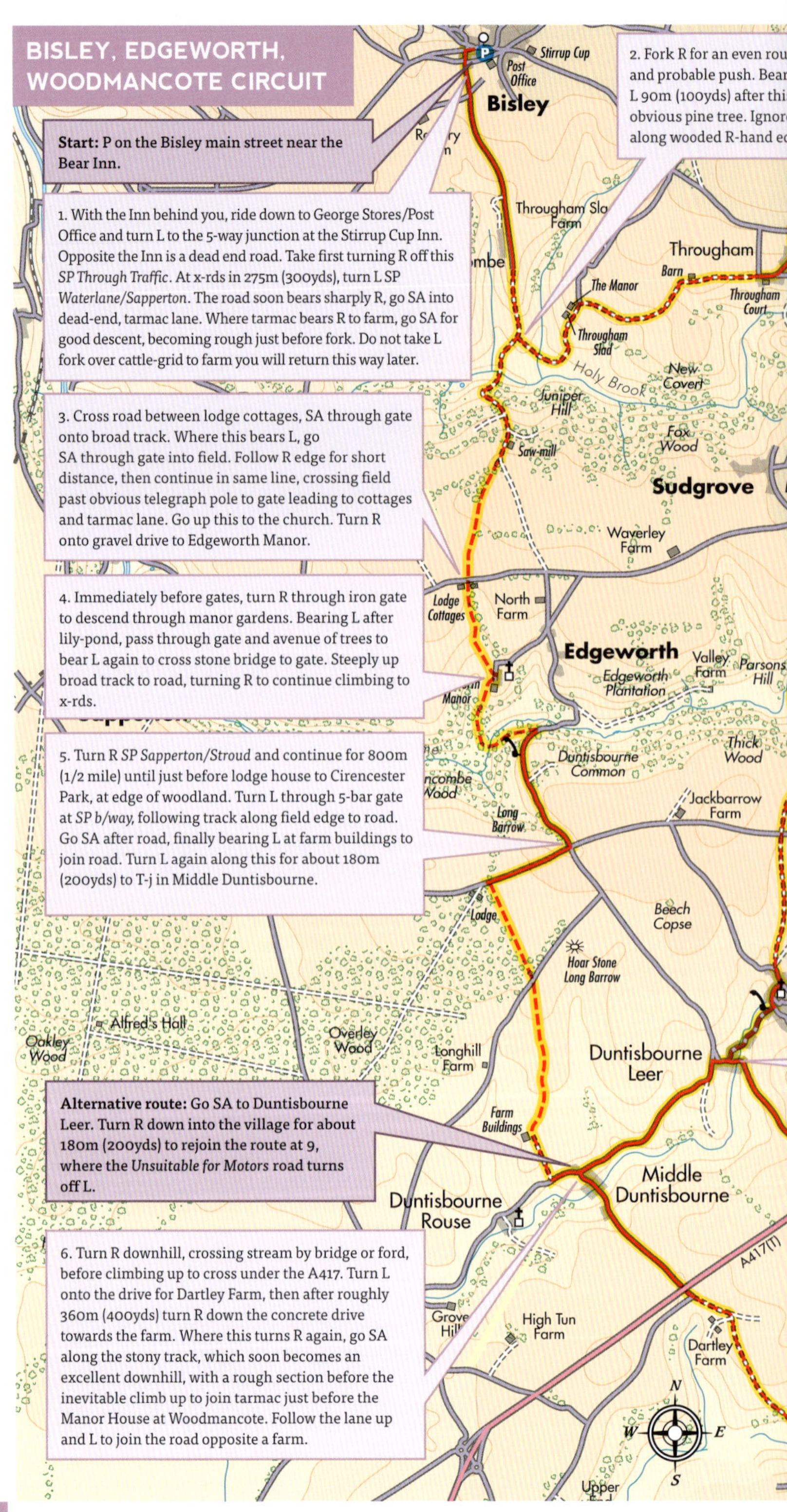

Start: P on the Bisley main street near the Bear Inn.

1. With the Inn behind you, ride down to George Stores/Post Office and turn L to the 5-way junction at the Stirrup Cup Inn. Opposite the Inn is a dead end road. Take first turning R off this *SP Through Traffic*. At x-rds in 275m (300yds), turn L SP *Waterlane/Sapperton*. The road soon bears sharply R, go SA into dead-end, tarmac lane. Where tarmac bears R to farm, go SA for good descent, becoming rough just before fork. Do not take L fork over cattle-grid to farm you will return this way later.

2. Fork R for an even roug[h] and probable push. Bear L 90m (100yds) after this obvious pine tree. Ignore [...] along wooded R-hand ed[ge]

3. Cross road between lodge cottages, SA through gate onto broad track. Where this bears L, go SA through gate into field. Follow R edge for short distance, then continue in same line, crossing field past obvious telegraph pole to gate leading to cottages and tarmac lane. Go up this to the church. Turn R onto gravel drive to Edgeworth Manor.

4. Immediately before gates, turn R through iron gate to descend through manor gardens. Bearing L after lily-pond, pass through gate and avenue of trees to bear L again to cross stone bridge to gate. Steeply up broad track to road, turning R to continue climbing to x-rds.

5. Turn R SP *Sapperton/Stroud* and continue for 800m (1/2 mile) until just before lodge house to Cirencester Park, at edge of woodland. Turn L through 5-bar gate at SP *b/way*, following track along field edge to road. Go SA after road, finally bearing L at farm buildings to join road. Turn L again along this for about 180m (200yds) to T-j in Middle Duntisbourne.

Alternative route: Go SA to Duntisbourne Leer. Turn R down into the village for about 180m (200yds) to rejoin the route at 9, where the *Unsuitable for Motors* road turns off L.

6. Turn R downhill, crossing stream by bridge or ford, before climbing up to cross under the A417. Turn L onto the drive for Dartley Farm, then after roughly 360m (400yds) turn R down the concrete drive towards the farm. Where this turns R again, go SA along the stony track, which soon becomes an excellent downhill, with a rough section before the inevitable climb up to join tarmac just before the Manor House at Woodmancote. Follow the lane up and L to join the road opposite a farm.

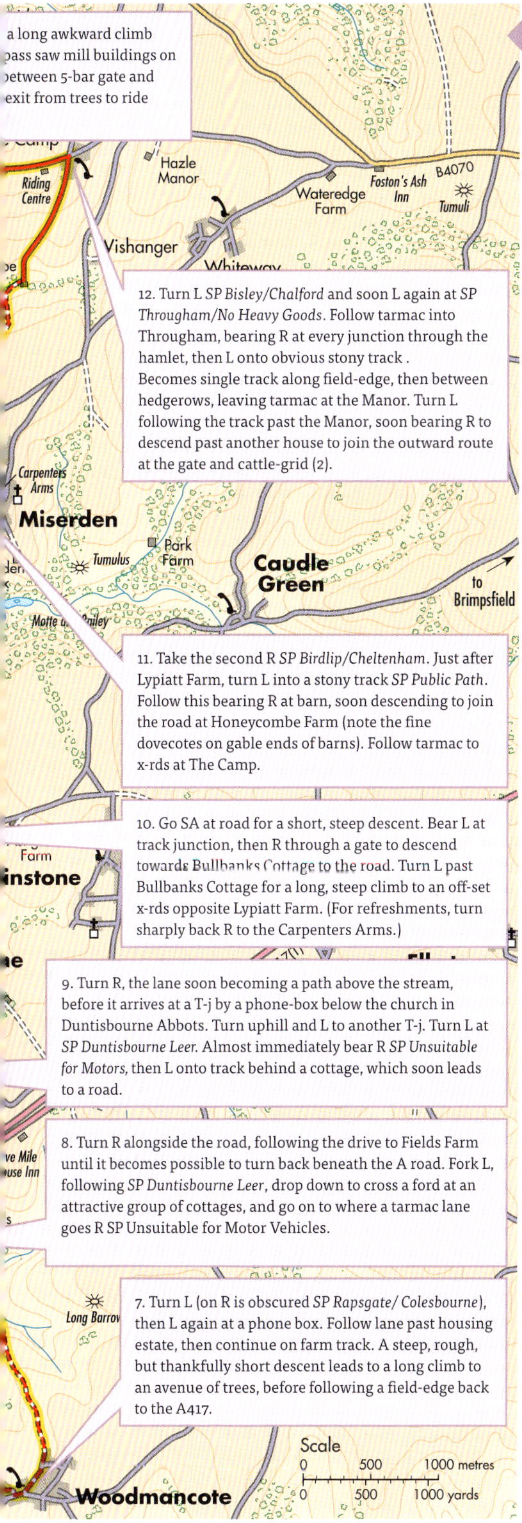

a long awkward climb
pass saw mill buildings on
between 5-bar gate and
exit from trees to ride

12. Turn L *SP Bisley/Chalford* and soon L again at *SP Througham/No Heavy Goods*. Follow tarmac into Througham, bearing R at every junction through the hamlet, then L onto obvious stony track .
Becomes single track along field-edge, then between hedgerows, leaving tarmac at the Manor. Turn L following the track past the Manor, soon bearing R to descend past another house to join the outward route at the gate and cattle-grid (2).

11. Take the second R *SP Birdlip/Cheltenham*. Just after Lypiatt Farm, turn L into a stony track *SP Public Path*. Follow this bearing R at barn, soon descending to join the road at Honeycombe Farm (note the fine dovecotes on gable ends of barns). Follow tarmac to x-rds at The Camp.

10. Go SA at road for a short, steep descent. Bear L at track junction, then R through a gate to descend towards Bullbanks Cottage to the road. Turn L past Bullbanks Cottage for a long, steep climb to an off-set x-rds opposite Lypiatt Farm. (For refreshments, turn sharply back R to the Carpenters Arms.)

9. Turn R, the lane soon becoming a path above the stream, before it arrives at a T-j by a phone-box below the church in Duntisbourne Abbots. Turn uphill and L to another T-j. Turn L at *SP Duntisbourne Leer*. Almost immediately bear R *SP Unsuitable for Motors*, then L onto track behind a cottage, which soon leads to a road.

8. Turn R alongside the road, following the drive to Fields Farm until it becomes possible to turn back beneath the A road. Fork L, following *SP Duntisbourne Leer*, drop down to cross a ford at an attractive group of cottages, and go on to where a tarmac lane goes R SP Unsuitable for Motor Vehicles.

7. Turn L (on R is obscured *SP Rapsgate/ Colesbourne*), then L again at a phone box. Follow lane past housing estate, then continue on farm track. A steep, rough, but thankfully short descent leads to a long climb to an avenue of trees, before following a field-edge back to the A417.

Distance: 26km (16 miles); 13 km 18 miles) off-road, 13 km (8 miles) road. Including Woodmancote extension: 32km (20 miles), 17 km (10½ miles) off-road, 15 km (9½ miles) road.

Grade: 2

Riding time: 3 to 4½ hours.

Direction: Anti-clockwise.

The southern Cotswolds is by far the hilliest part of the area, and though this route tackles some of the gentle terrain to the east of the really steeply wooded combes, it is still quite strenuous with several good climbs. Surfaces are generally firm, with only a short section east of Edgeworth likely to give any problems with mud, and the many woods en route make this a particularly good choice for spring and autumn. Edgeworth with its lovely church and manor house, is a hidden jewel, and the route actually takes you through the gardens of the house. Two alternatives are given for the eastern part of the route, but it would be just as simple to shorten the route by using one of the other north to south roads which cross it.

Two pubs and a Post Office in Bisley, plus the Carpenters Arms, just off route at Miserden.

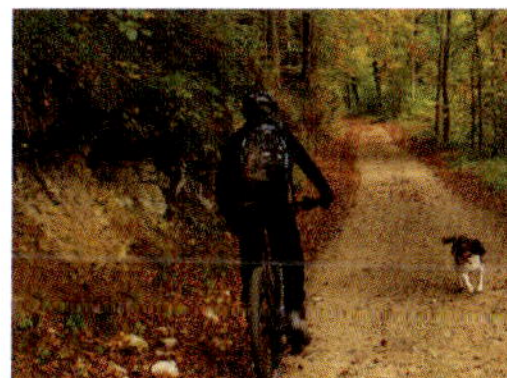

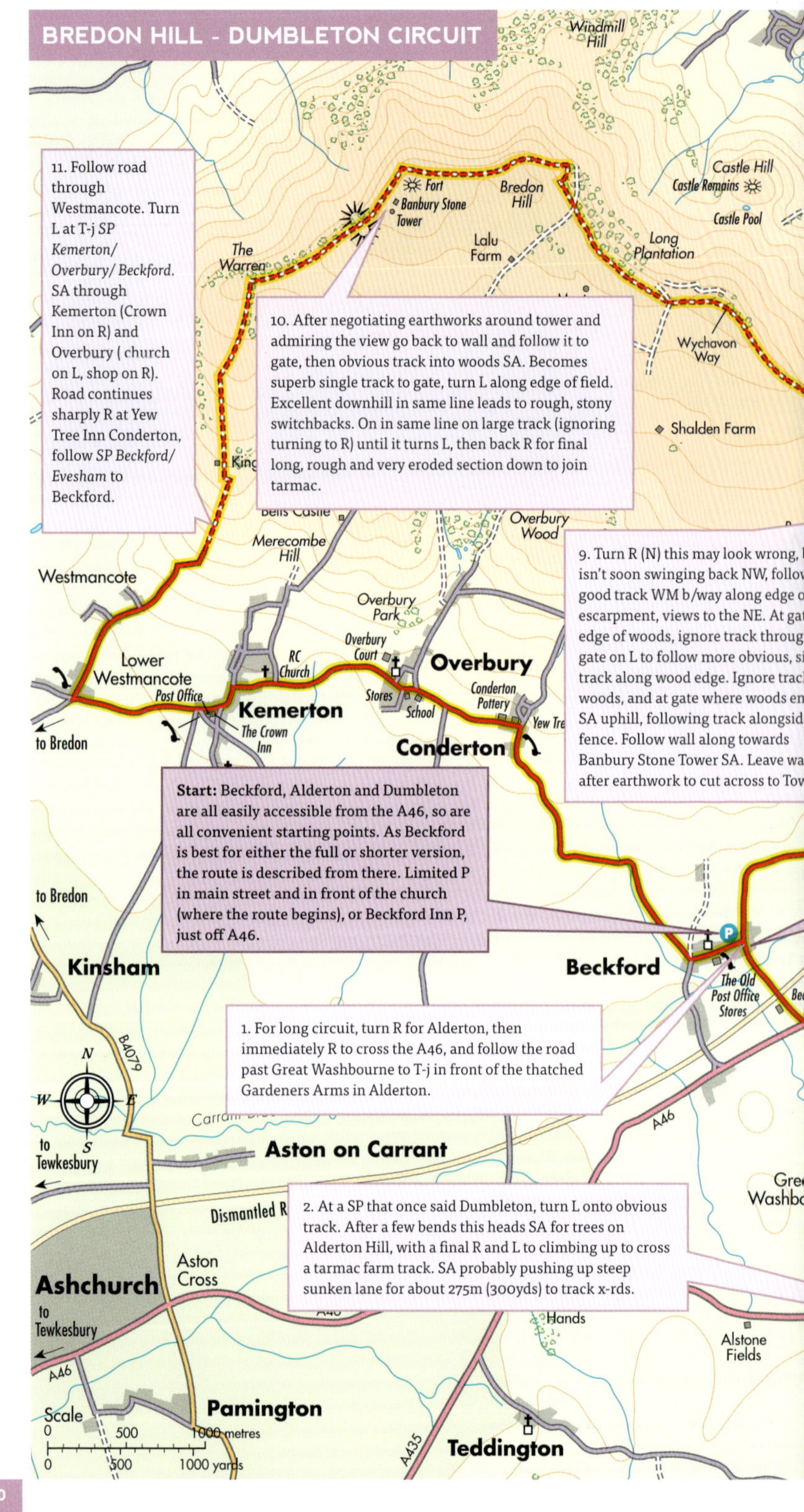

11. Follow road through Westmancote. Turn L at T-j SP *Kemerton/ Overbury/ Beckford.* SA through Kemerton (Crown Inn on R) and Overbury (church on L, shop on R). Road continues sharply R at Yew Tree Inn Conderton, follow *SP Beckford/ Evesham* to Beckford.

10. After negotiating earthworks around tower and admiring the view go back to wall and follow it to gate, then obvious track into woods SA. Becomes superb single track to gate, turn L along edge of field. Excellent downhill in same line leads to rough, stony switchbacks. On in same line on large track (ignoring turning to R) until it turns L, then back R for final long, rough and very eroded section down to join tarmac.

9. Turn R (N) this may look wrong, isn't soon swinging back NW, follow good track WM b/way along edge of escarpment, views to the NE. At gate edge of woods, ignore track through gate on L to follow more obvious, si track along wood edge. Ignore trac woods, and at gate where woods en SA uphill, following track alongsid fence. Follow wall along towards Banbury Stone Tower SA. Leave wa after earthwork to cut across to Tow

Start: Beckford, Alderton and Dumbleton are all easily accessible from the A46, so are all convenient starting points. As Beckford is best for either the full or shorter version, the route is described from there. Limited P in main street and in front of the church (where the route begins), or Beckford Inn P, just off A46.

1. For long circuit, turn R for Alderton, then immediately R to cross the A46, and follow the road past Great Washbourne to T-j in front of the thatched Gardeners Arms in Alderton.

2. At a SP that once said Dumbleton, turn L onto obvious track. After a few bends this heads SA for trees on Alderton Hill, with a final R and L to climbing up to cross a tarmac farm track. SA probably pushing up steep sunken lane for about 275m (300yds) to track x-rds.

es below a gate. DO NOT go through this, but contour R for
n (1/4 mile) along line of fence to complex of gates and sheep
L through this, into field on L, and take the most obvious
h leads diagonally L uphill towards tallest tree. Flattens out
ar gate with b/way arrow. Follow obvious track, soon leaving
arrow to bear R, SA up hillside to gate in fence WM.

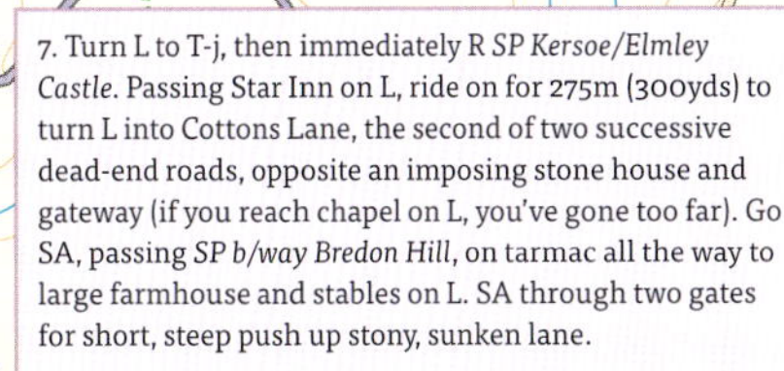

7. Turn L to T-j, then immediately R SP *Kersoe/Elmley Castle*. Passing Star Inn on L, ride on for 275m (300yds) to turn L into Cottons Lane, the second of two successive dead-end roads, opposite an imposing stone house and gateway (if you reach chapel on L, you've gone too far). Go SA, passing *SP b/way Bredon Hill*, on tarmac all the way to large farmhouse and stables on L. SA through two gates for short, steep push up stony, sunken lane.

6. Pass to L of caravan site, and follow b/way to gate, go R to old railway bridge, then L on track to join tarmac lane into Ashton under Hill.

4. Turn L, and L again past the entrance to Dumbleton Hall Hotel and the church. Continue for 2km (11/4 miles) to where a tarmac drive goes off L beside a solitary house.

Alternative route: For shorter circuit, turn L at T-j after church into Ashton d *SP Grafton/ Ashton* der Hill and continue from step 7.

5. Turn R follow grassy track *SP b/way* to cross A46. Go R of a house drive to enter narrow b/way to tarmac drive.

3. Turn L following b/way WM, until immediately the track forks again. (Turning L into trees is a short cut possibly muddy descending directly to join the Wychavon Way, and our route at 5). Turn R, out of trees and through gateway to descend to Hill Farm. Then tarmac drive swooping down through open parkland to the road.

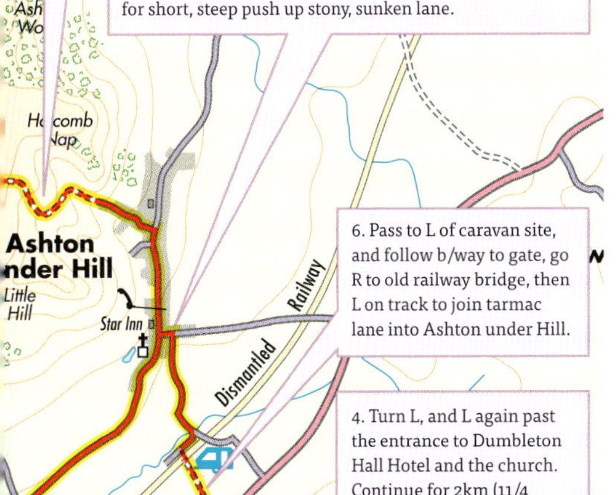

Distance: 226km (16 miles); 13 km (8 miles) off-road, 13 km (8 miles) road. Bredon Hill only: 18km (11 miles); 8 km (5 miles) off-road, 10 km (6 miles) road.

Grade: 2

Riding time: 3 to 3½ hours.

Direction: Anti-clockwise.

An excellent route and good for all weathers. Fabulous views from Bredon Hill, but care needed with navigation, particularly the first mile above Ashton. Follow the instructions, even when they seem to be against common sense. After a steep road section and a short, steep push, the climb up Bredon Hill is actually quite easy, and the downhill superb.

Refreshment available in pubs in all villages on route. Also village stores in Beckford and Kemerton.

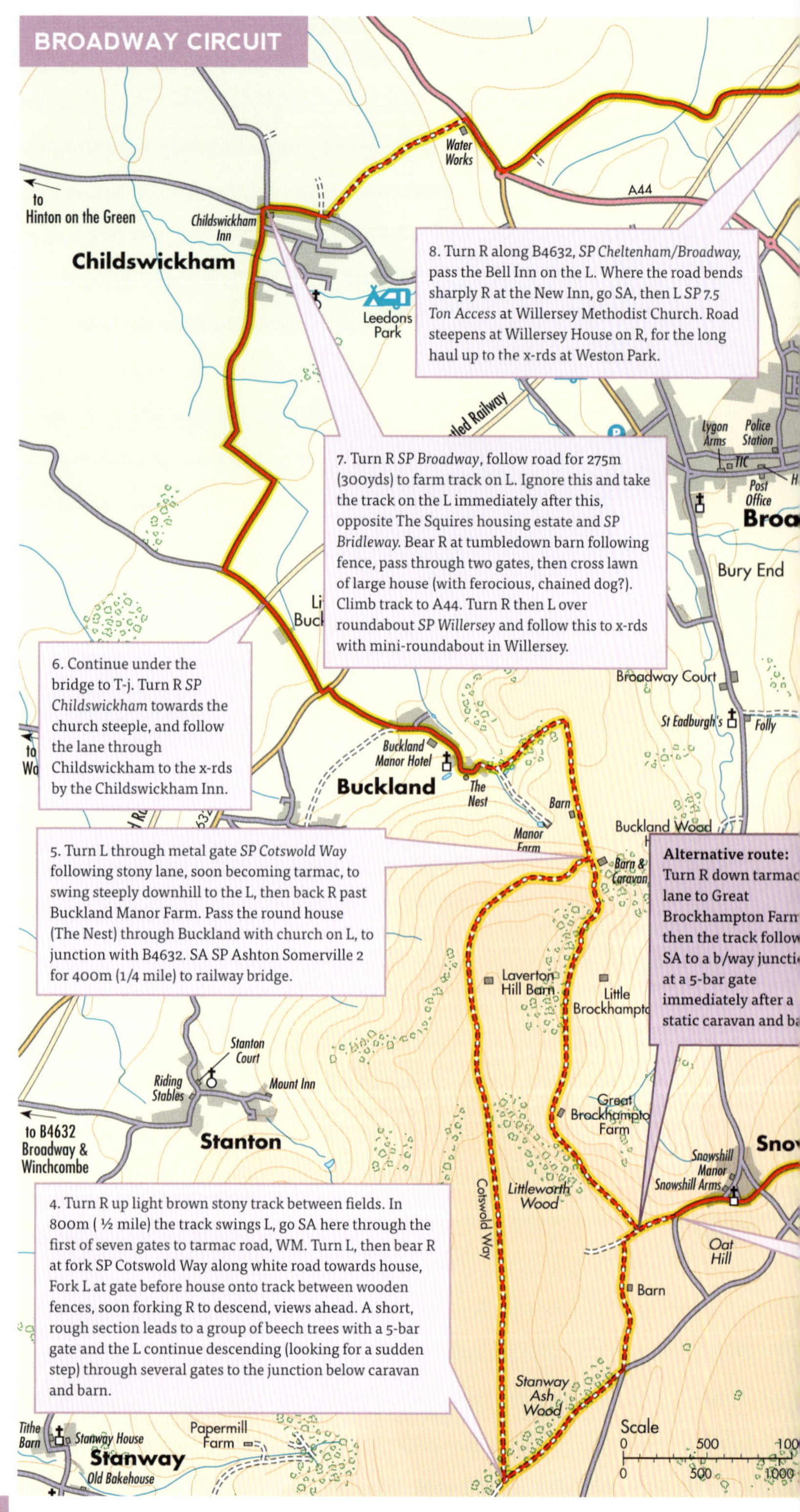

to
Hinton on the Green
Childswickham
Inn
Childswickham
Leedons
Park
Water
Works
A44
8. Turn R along B4632, *SP Cheltenham/Broadway*, pass the Bell Inn on the L. Where the road bends sharply R at the New Inn, go SA, then L *SP 7.5 Ton Access* at Willersey Methodist Church. Road steepens at Willersey House on R, for the long haul up to the x-rds at Weston Park.
...led Railway
Lygon Police
Arms Station
TIC
Post
Office
Broa
Bury End
7. Turn R *SP Broadway*, follow road for 275m (300yds) to farm track on L. Ignore this and take the track on the L immediately after this, opposite The Squires housing estate and *SP Bridleway*. Bear R at tumbledown barn following fence, pass through two gates, then cross lawn of large house (with ferocious, chained dog?). Climb track to A44. Turn R then L over roundabout *SP Willersey* and follow this to x-rds with mini-roundabout in Willersey.
Li...
Buc...
Broadway Court
St Eadburgh's Folly
6. Continue under the bridge to T-j. Turn R *SP Childswickham* towards the church steeple, and follow the lane through Childswickham to the x-rds by the Childswickham Inn.
to
Wo
Buckland
Manor Hotel
Buckland
The
Nest
Barn
Buckland Wood
Manor
Farm
Alternative route:
Turn R down tarmac lane to Great Brockhampton Farm then the track follow... SA to a b/way juncti... at a 5-bar gate immediately after a static caravan and ba...
5. Turn L through metal gate *SP Cotswold Way* following stony lane, soon becoming tarmac, to swing steeply downhill to the L, then back R past Buckland Manor Farm. Pass the round house (The Nest) through Buckland with church on L, to junction with B4632. SA SP Ashton Somerville 2 for 400m (1/4 mile) to railway bridge.
Barn &
Caravan
H R...
632
Laverton
Hill Barn
Little
Brockhampt...
Stanton
Court
Riding
Stables
Mount Inn
Great
Brockhampto...
Farm
to B4632
Broadway &
Winchcombe
Stanton
Snowshill
Manor
Snowshill Arms
Sno
4. Turn R up light brown stony track between fields. In 800m (½ mile) the track swings L, go SA here through the first of seven gates to tarmac road, WM. Turn L, then bear R at fork SP Cotswold Way along white road towards house, Fork L at gate before house onto track between wooden fences, soon forking R to descend, views ahead. A short, rough section leads to a group of beech trees with a 5-bar gate and the L continue descending (looking for a sudden step) through several gates to the junction below caravan and barn.
Littleworth
Wood
Oat
Hill
Barn
Cotswold Way
Stanway
Ash
Wood
Scale
0   500   100
0   500   1000
Tithe
Barn
Stanway House
Papermill
Farm
Stanway
Old Bakehouse

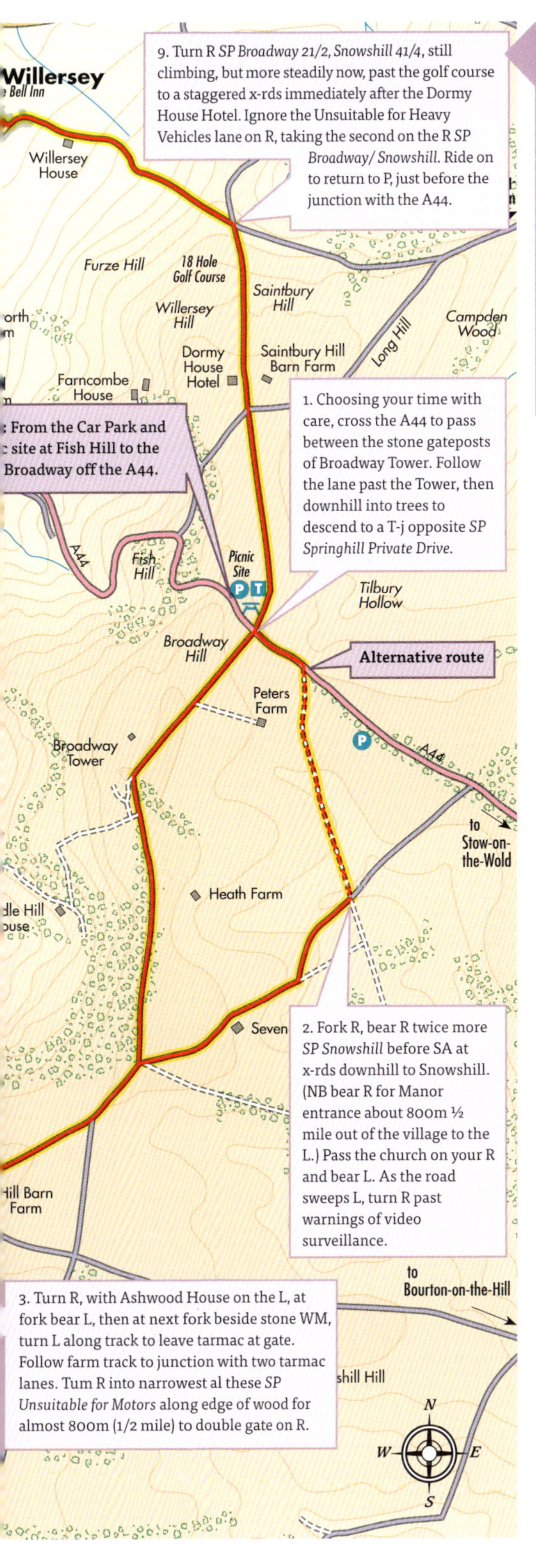

1. Choosing your time with care, cross the A44 to pass between the stone gateposts of Broadway Tower. Follow the lane past the Tower, then downhill into trees to descend to a T-j opposite *SP Springhill Private Drive.*

9. Turn R *SP Broadway 21/2, Snowshill 41/4,* still climbing, but more steadily now, past the golf course to a staggered x-rds immediately after the Dormy House Hotel. Ignore the Unsuitable for Heavy Vehicles lane on R, taking the second on the R *SP Broadway/ Snowshill.* Ride on to return to P, just before the junction with the A44.

2. Fork R, bear R twice more *SP Snowshill* before SA at x-rds downhill to Snowshill. (NB bear R for Manor entrance about 800m ½ mile out of the village to the L.) Pass the church on your R and bear L. As the road sweeps L, turn R past warnings of video surveillance.

3. Turn R, with Ashwood House on the L, at fork bear L, then at next fork beside stone WM, turn L along track to leave tarmac at gate. Follow farm track to junction with two tarmac lanes. Tum R into narrowest al these *SP Unsuitable for Motors* along edge of wood for almost 800m (1/2 mile) to double gate on R.

Distance: 24km (15½ miles); 7km (4½ miles) off-road, 17km (11 miles) road.
Disused railway line variant; 23 km (14½ miles) - 11km (7 miles) off-road, 12 km 17½ miles) road.

Grade: 2

Riding time: 3 hours.

Direction: Clockwise.

The circuit does not actually visit the famous village of Broadway, though it would be easy to start there, or make a simple diversion to do so. The off-road part of the route is packed into an enjoyable section between the pretty villages of Snowshill and Buckland. The rest of the route follows quiet lanes, which normally carry little traffic. Apart from the big climb up Willersey Hill - thankfully on tarmac - this is one of those unusual routes where you seem to spend more time going downhill than uphill, though you may disagree!

Broadway Tower is always in sight, and the view from its top is worth paying for. There is an alternative section of off-road to the east that misses out Broadway Hill.

Other atractions nearby: Snowshill Manor (NT) and the small village church at Buckland. Pubs in Snowshill and Childwickham (cafe at Snowshill Manor), plus a variety of pubs, tea-rooms and cafés in Broadway.

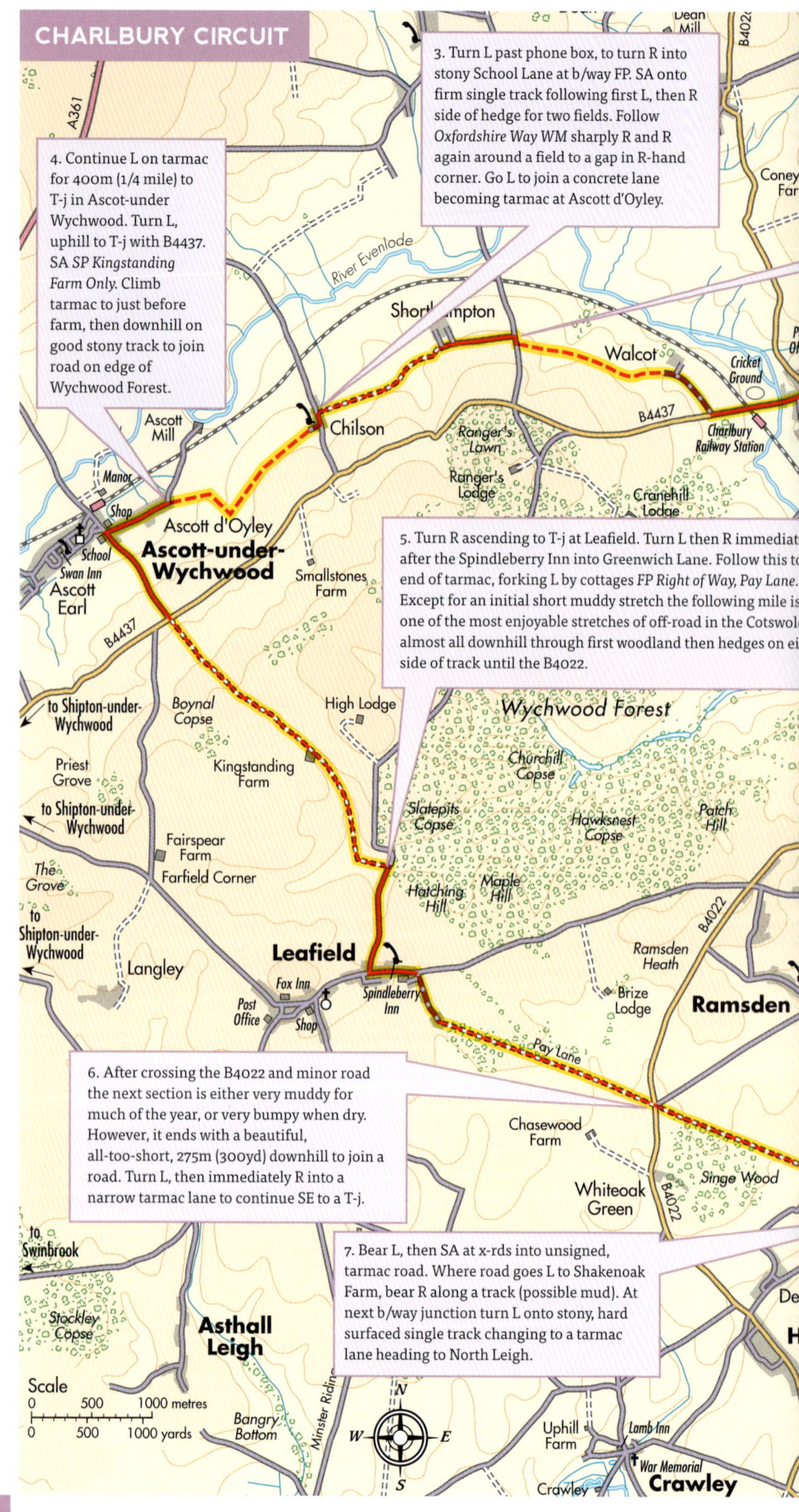

A361
A4021
Dean Mill
B4021
3. Turn L past phone box, to turn R into stony School Lane at b/way FP. SA onto firm single track following first L, then R side of hedge for two fields. Follow Oxfordshire Way WM sharply R and R again around a field to a gap in R-hand corner. Go L to join a concrete lane becoming tarmac at Ascott d'Oyley.
Coney Far
4. Continue L on tarmac for 400m (1/4 mile) to T-j in Ascot-under Wychwood. Turn L, uphill to T-j with B4437. SA SP Kingstanding Farm Only. Climb tarmac to just before farm, then downhill on good stony track to join road on edge of Wychwood Forest.
River Evenlode
Short Hampton
Walcot
Cricket Ground
Chilson
B4437
Ranger's Lawn
Ascott Mill
Charlbury Railway Station
Ranger's Lodge
Manor
Cranehill Lodge
Shop
Ascott d'Oyley
School
Ascott-under-Wychwood
5. Turn R ascending to T-j at Leafield. Turn L then R immediat after the Spindleberry Inn into Greenwich Lane. Follow this to end of tarmac, forking L by cottages FP Right of Way, Pay Lane. Except for an initial short muddy stretch the following mile is one of the most enjoyable stretches of off-road in the Cotswol almost all downhill through first woodland then hedges on ei side of track until the B4022.
Swan Inn
Ascott Earl
Smallstones Farm
B4437
to Shipton-under-Wychwood
Boynal Copse
High Lodge
Wychwood Forest
Churchill Copse
Priest Grove
Kingstanding Farm
Slatepits Copse
Hawksnest Copse
Patch Hill
to Shipton-under-Wychwood
Fairspear Farm
B4022
The Grove
Farfield Corner
Hatching Hill
Maple Hill
Ramsden Heath
to Shipton-under-Wychwood
Langley
Leafield
Spindleberry Inn
Brize Lodge
Ramsden
Fox Inn
Post Office
Shop
Pay Lane
6. After crossing the B4022 and minor road the next section is either very muddy for much of the year, or very bumpy when dry. However, it ends with a beautiful, all-too-short, 275m (300yd) downhill to join a road. Turn L, then immediately R into a narrow tarmac lane to continue SE to a T-j.
Chasewood Farm
Singe Wood
Whiteoak Green
B4022
to Swinbrook
7. Bear L, then SA at x-rds into unsigned, tarmac road. Where road goes L to Shakenoak Farm, bear R along a track (possible mud). At next b/way junction turn L onto stony, hard surfaced single track changing to a tarmac lane heading to North Leigh.
De
H
Stockley Copse
Asthall Leigh
Scale
0   500   1000 metres
0   500   1000 yards
Bangry Bottom
Minster Riding
N
W   E
S
Uphill Farm
Lamb Inn
War Memorial
Crawley
Crawley

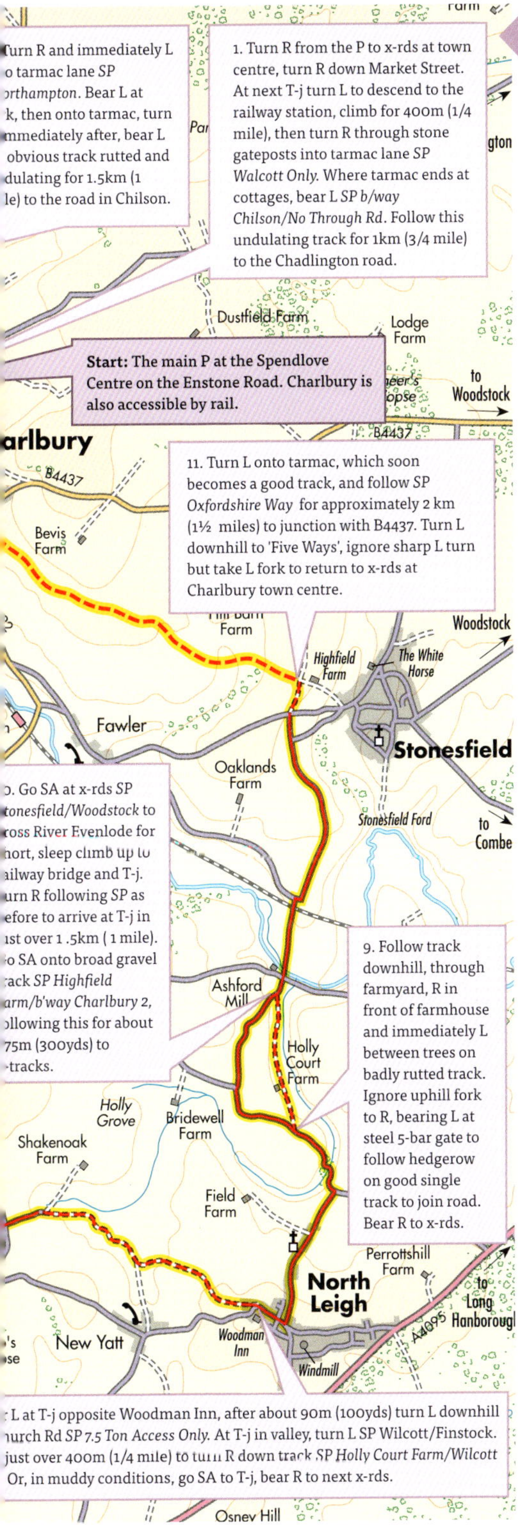
Turn R and immediately L
o tarmac lane SP
orthampton. Bear L at
k, then onto tarmac, turn
mmediately after, bear L
obvious track rutted and
dulating for 1.5km (1
le) to the road in Chilson.
1. Turn R from the P to x-rds at town centre, turn R down Market Street. At next T-j turn L to descend to the railway station, climb for 400m (1/4 mile), then turn R through stone gateposts into tarmac lane SP Walcott Only. Where tarmac ends at cottages, bear L SP b/way Chilson/No Through Rd. Follow this undulating track for 1km (3/4 mile) to the Chadlington road.
Dustfield Farm
Lodge Farm
Start: The main P at the Spendlove Centre on the Enstone Road. Charlbury is also accessible by rail.
to Woodstock
B4437
arlbury
B4437
Bevis Farm
11. Turn L onto tarmac, which soon becomes a good track, and follow SP Oxfordshire Way for approximately 2 km (1½ miles) to junction with B4437. Turn L downhill to 'Five Ways', ignore sharp L turn but take L fork to return to x-rds at Charlbury town centre.
Farm
Woodstock
Highfield Farm
The White Horse
Fawler
Stonesfield
Oaklands Farm
Stonesfield Ford
to Combe
0. Go SA at x-rds SP
tonesfield/Woodstock to
ross River Evenlode for
hort, sleep climb up to
ailway bridge and T-j.
urn R following SP as
efore to arrive at T-j in
ist over 1 .5km (1 mile).
o SA onto broad gravel
ack SP Highfield
arm/b'way Charlbury 2,
ollowing this for about
75m (300yds) to
-tracks.
Ashford Mill
Holly Court Farm
9. Follow track downhill, through farmyard, R in front of farmhouse and immediately L between trees on badly rutted track. Ignore uphill fork to R, bearing L at steel 5-bar gate to follow hedgerow on good single track to join road. Bear R to x-rds.
Holly Grove
Bridewell Farm
Shakenoak Farm
Field Farm
Perrottshill Farm
North Leigh
to Long Hanborough
A4095
New Yatt
Woodman Inn
Windmill
L at T-j opposite Woodman Inn, after about 90m (100yds) turn L downhill
urch Rd SP 7.5 Ton Access Only. At T-j in valley, turn L SP Wilcott/Finstock.
just over 400m (1/4 mile) to turn R down track SP Holly Court Farm/Wilcott
Or, in muddy conditions, go SA to T-j, bear R to next x-rds.
Osney Hill

Distance: 30km (18½ miles); 23km (14½ miles) off-road,
7 km (4 miles) road.

Grade: 2

Riding time: 2½ to 3 hours.

Direction: Anti-clockwise.

The rides in the Charlbury area are among my favourite in the Cotswolds, and this circuit has a good claim for the number one spot. It's almost all off-road, but as with all the best mountain bike routes, the climbs are all on tarmac. Good for most weather, serious mud problems after prolonged wet weather are only on the two short sections, where there are obvious road alternatives. There are various possibilities to shorten the route, and several alternative finishes.

There are plenty of opportunities for refreshments: pubs in Ascott-under-Wychwood, Leafield, North Leigh, and just off route at Ramsden and Stonesfield. Charlbury itself also offers a good choice of pubs and cafés. There is a campsite just to the north of Charlbury.

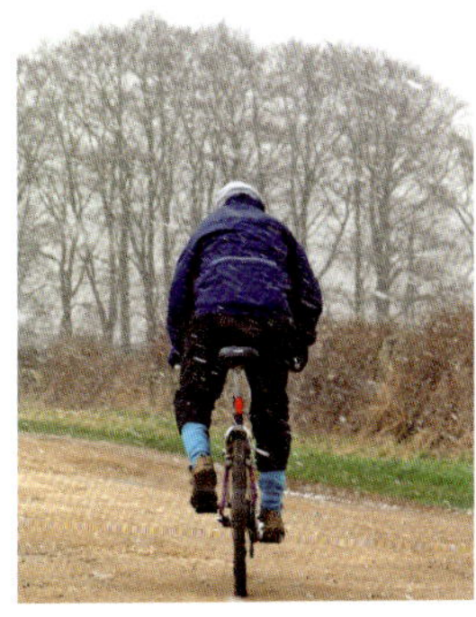

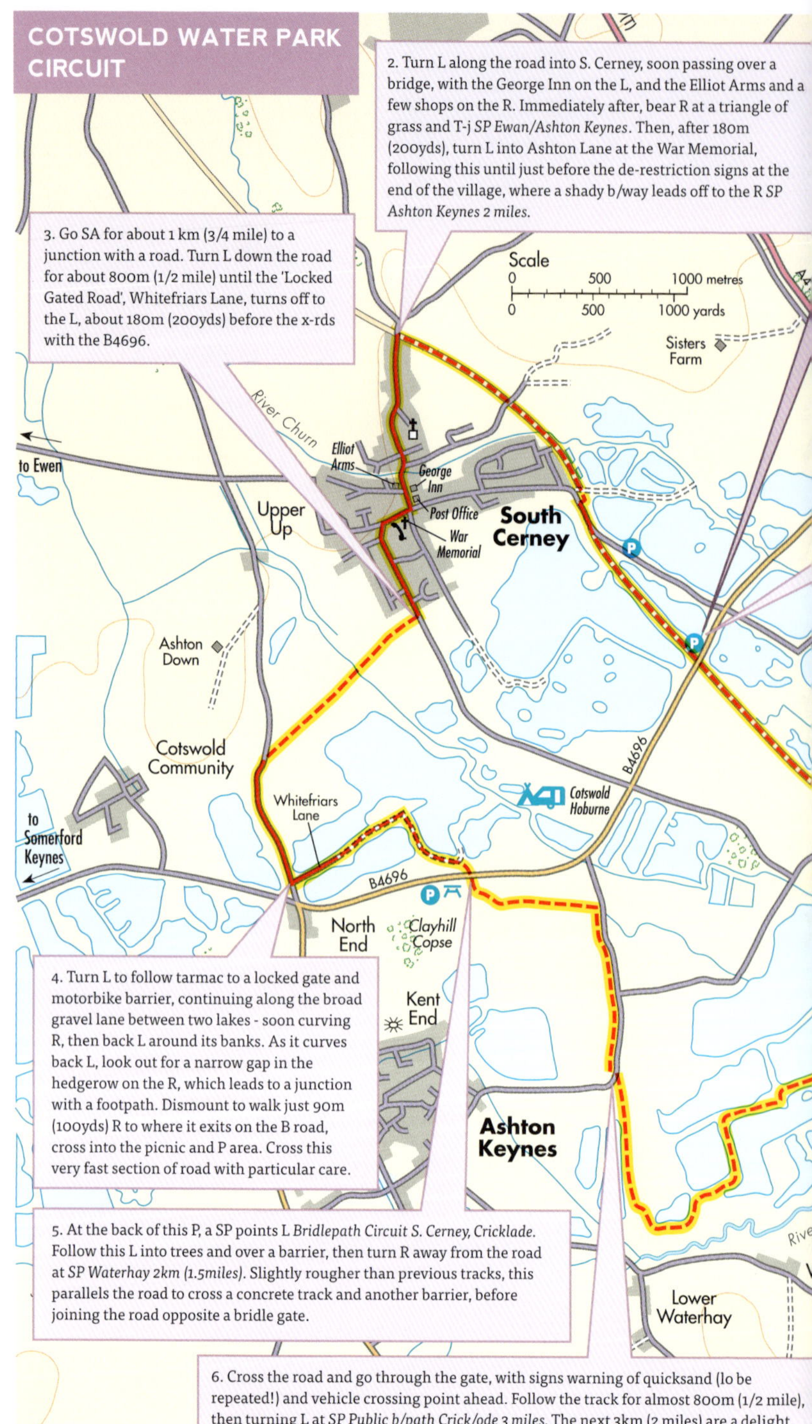

2. Turn L along the road into S. Cerney, soon passing over a bridge, with the George Inn on the L, and the Elliot Arms and a few shops on the R. Immediately after, bear R at a triangle of grass and T-j *SP Ewan/Ashton Keynes*. Then, after 180m (200yds), turn L into Ashton Lane at the War Memorial, following this until just before the de-restriction signs at the end of the village, where a shady b/way leads off to the R *SP Ashton Keynes 2 miles*.

3. Go SA for about 1 km (3/4 mile) to a junction with a road. Turn L down the road for about 800m (1/2 mile) until the 'Locked Gated Road', Whitefriars Lane, turns off to the L, about 180m (200yds) before the x-rds with the B4696.

4. Turn L to follow tarmac to a locked gate and motorbike barrier, continuing along the broad gravel lane between two lakes - soon curving R, then back L around its banks. As it curves back L, look out for a narrow gap in the hedgerow on the R, which leads to a junction with a footpath. Dismount to walk just 90m (100yds) R to where it exits on the B road, cross into the picnic and P area. Cross this very fast section of road with particular care.

5. At the back of this P, a SP points L *Bridlepath Circuit S. Cerney, Cricklade*. Follow this L into trees and over a barrier, then turn R away from the road at *SP Waterhay 2km (1.5miles)*. Slightly rougher than previous tracks, this parallels the road to cross a concrete track and another barrier, before joining the road opposite a bridle gate.

6. Cross the road and go through the gate, with signs warning of quicksand (lo be repeated!) and vehicle crossing point ahead. Follow the track for almost 800m (1/2 mile), then turning L at *SP Public b/path Crick/ode 3 miles*. The next 3km (2 miles) are a delight, as the trail weaves its way between the different lakes and its anglers. The track eventually meets a gate with *SP Private Road*. Turn R as directed by a linger post to cross a footbridge, and then another barrier to a track junction *SP S. Cerney L/Cricklade ½ miles R*.

: There are a number of useful P's on the B469 W of the A4 l 9
:cester - Swindon Rd. The first is about 1 .5km (1 mile) from the
:dabout on the R *SP Lakeside Parking*. About 180m (200yds) further
:so on the R, is another small P under a set of red-brick railway
:s. As this gives direct access to the route, it is described from here.
:here are Height Restriction bars across the arches, so remember to
:and remove bikes carried on roof racks before entering. It would be
:ly useful to start from the picnic-area/P situated about 1.5km (1
: further on the L or at the converted railway track in Cricklade.
:gh strangely not signposted at all from Cricklade. The converted
:ay track begins behind the Cricklade Leisure Centre, NW of the
: Follow the lane along the side of the Centre, turn L through a gate,
:immediately R onto the trail, which soon passes beneath a bridge
:r the road.

Down Ampney

1. From the railway arches, go through the bridle gate at the
back of the P *SP South Cerney Lakes*, and continue through trees
for almost 800m (1/2 mile) to a gate and road. Turn L along the
road for about 360m (400yds) to a bridle gate on the R, just
after the *South Cerney SP*, and immediately before a turning on
the R. Go through the gate to rejoin the trail, which leads under
more arches and round an estate. A gate leads lo another mile
of pleasant, flat riding, until a slight climb gives warning of a
sudden descent to a road (and barrier!).

To return to the start, turn L along the
railway path, crossing the B4696 in about
1.5km (l mile) to return to the railway
arches P.

Latton

Turn R for Cricklade, follow the railway
path to the Leisure Centre.

to Castle Eaton

Hailstone Hill

Cricklade

Cricklade Leisure Centre

L to ride on to another junction - not
way path, but a parallel track (often
er). Turn R again to yet another
n - this time with the raised railway

N
W — E
S

Chelworth
Lower Green

Distance: 16 or 21km (10 or 13 miles); all except 2 km (1½ miles) off-road.

Grade: 1

Riding time: 1½ to 2 hours.

Direction: Anti-clockwise.

Though pretty-much dead-flat, and certainly the easiest of the set, this is still a route with plenty of interest - for families, or anyone wanting a leisurely ride in very different surroundings. The conversion of this complex of flooded gravel-pits into a resource for leisure and wildlife is a fine example of what can be achieved.

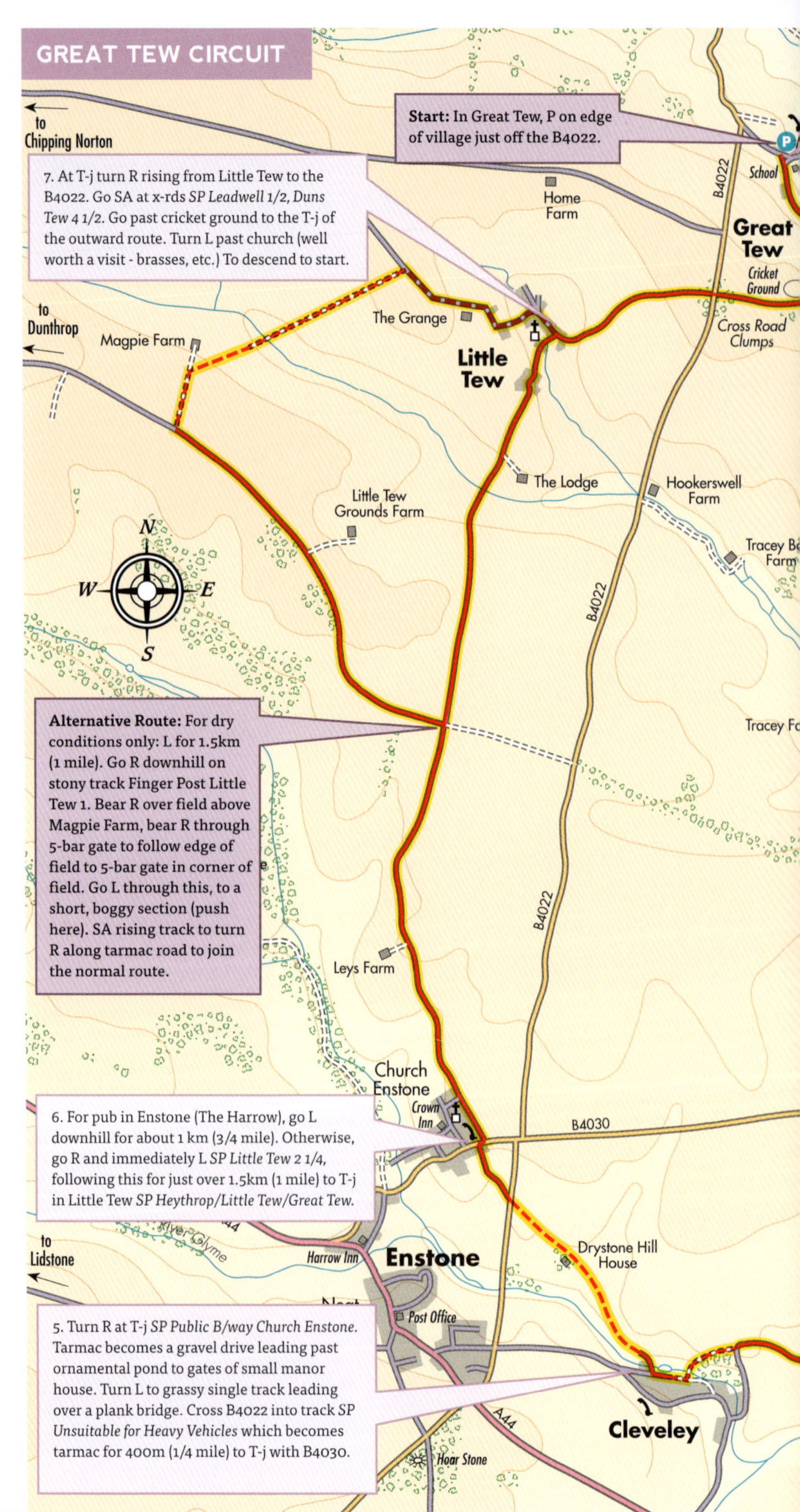

to Chipping Norton
Start: In Great Tew, P on edge of village just off the B4022.
7. At T-j turn R rising from Little Tew to the B4022. Go SA at x-rds SP Leadwell 1/2, Duns Tew 4 1/2. Go past cricket ground to the T-j of the outward route. Turn L past church (well worth a visit - brasses, etc.) To descend to start.
to Dunthrop
Magpie Farm
Home Farm
The Grange
Little Tew
School
Great Tew
Cricket Ground
Cross Road Clumps
The Lodge
Hookerswell Farm
Tracey Barn Farm
Little Tew Grounds Farm
B4022
N
W   E
S
Tracey Farm
Alternative Route: For dry conditions only: L for 1.5km (1 mile). Go R downhill on stony track Finger Post Little Tew 1. Bear R over field above Magpie Farm, bear R through 5-bar gate to follow edge of field to 5-bar gate in corner of field. Go L through this, to a short, boggy section (push here). SA rising track to turn R along tarmac road to join the normal route.
Leys Farm
B4022
Church Enstone
Crown Inn
6. For pub in Enstone (The Harrow), go L downhill for about 1 km (3/4 mile). Otherwise, go R and immediately L SP Little Tew 2 1/4, following this for just over 1.5km (1 mile) to T-j in Little Tew SP Heythrop/Little Tew/Great Tew.
B4030
to Lidstone
River Glyme
Harrow Inn
Enstone
Drystone Hill House
Post Office
5. Turn R at T-j SP Public B/way Church Enstone. Tarmac becomes a gravel drive leading past ornamental pond to gates of small manor house. Turn L to grassy single track leading over a plank bridge. Cross B4022 into track SP Unsuitable for Heavy Vehicles which becomes tarmac for 400m (1/4 mile) to T-j with B4030.
A44
Cleveley
Hoar Stone

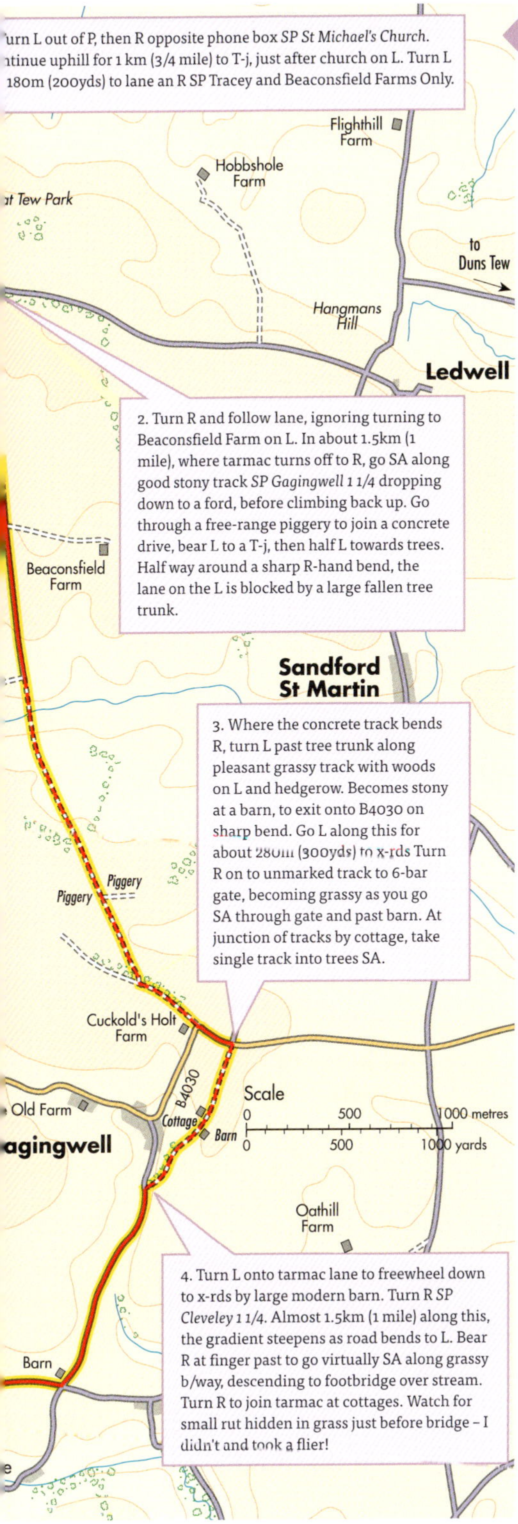

urn L out of P, then R opposite phone box *SP St Michael's Church*.
ntinue uphill for 1 km (3/4 mile) to T-j, just after church on L. Turn L
180m (200yds) to lane an R *SP Tracey and Beaconsfield Farms Only.*

2. Turn R and follow lane, ignoring turning to Beaconsfield Farm on L. In about 1.5km (1 mile), where tarmac turns off to R, go SA along good stony track *SP Gagingwell 1 1/4* dropping down to a ford, before climbing back up. Go through a free-range piggery to join a concrete drive, bear L to a T-j, then half L towards trees. Half way around a sharp R-hand bend, the lane on the L is blocked by a large fallen tree trunk.

3. Where the concrete track bends R, turn L past tree trunk along pleasant grassy track with woods on L and hedgerow. Becomes stony at a barn, to exit onto B4030 on sharp bend. Go L along this for about 280m (300yds) to x-rds Turn R on to unmarked track to 6-bar gate, becoming grassy as you go SA through gate and past barn. At junction of tracks by cottage, take single track into trees SA.

4. Turn L onto tarmac lane to freewheel down to x-rds by large modern barn. Turn R *SP Cleveley 1 1/4*. Almost 1.5km (1 mile) along this, the gradient steepens as road bends to L. Bear R at finger past to go virtually SA along grassy b/way, descending to footbridge over stream. Turn R to join tarmac at cottages. Watch for small rut hidden in grass just before bridge – I didn't and took a flier!

Distance: 16km (10 miles); 6 km (3½ miles) off-rood, 10km (6½ miles) road.

Grade: 1

Riding time: 1½ to 3 hours.

Direction: Clockwise.

A pleasant country ride, mostly on very quiet lanes, but with some good off-road sections. Leave some time to look around the tiny villages of Little and Great Tew, two of the prettiest in the Cotswolds. Great Tew Church is also well worth a visit.

There are refreshments at the Falkland Arms and the cafe next door, and 800m (1/2 mile) off-route in Enstone.

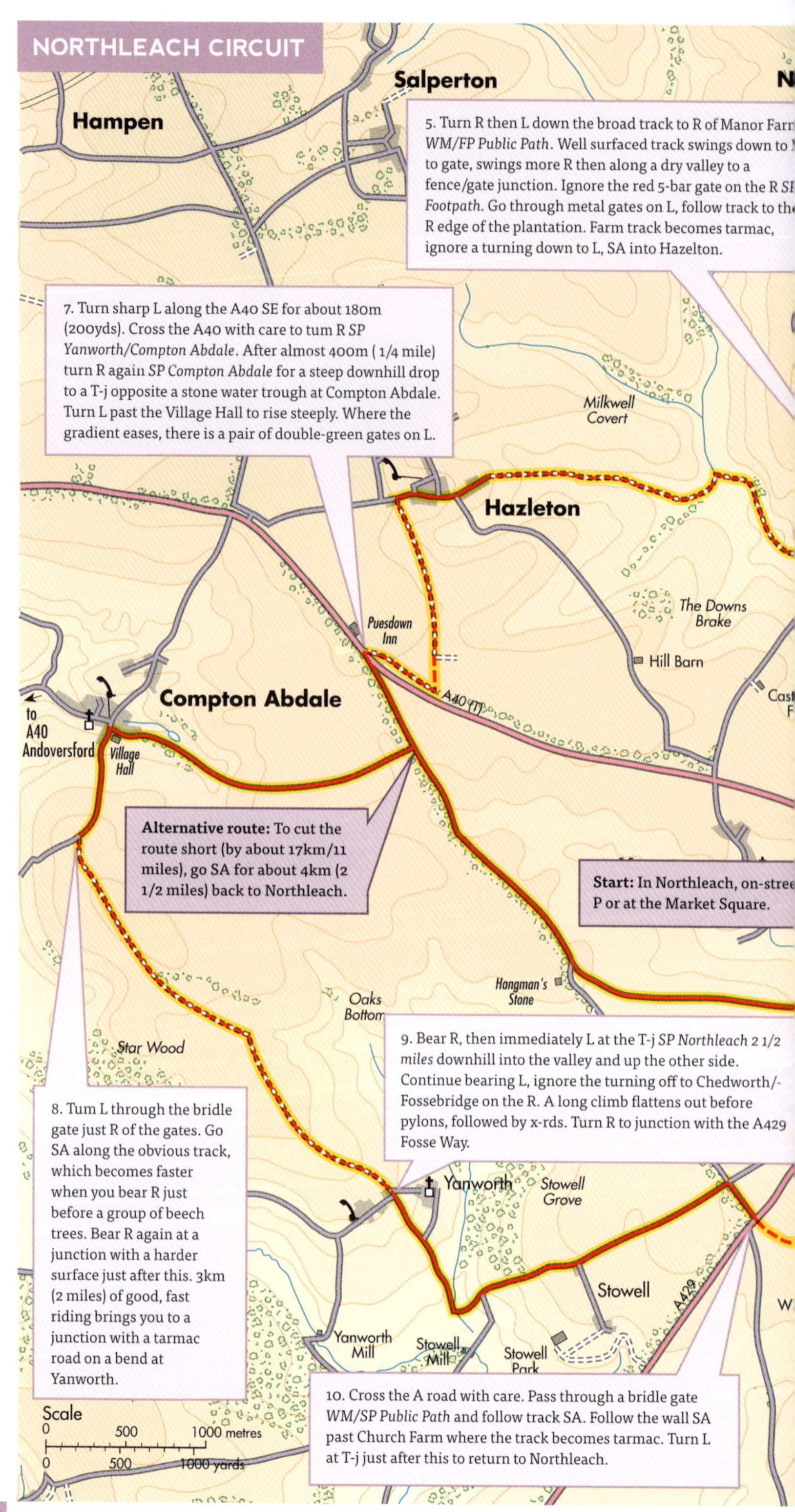
Hampen
Salperton
N

5. Turn R then L down the broad track to R of Manor Farm
WM/FP Public Path. Well surfaced track swings down to
to gate, swings more R then along a dry valley to a
fence/gate junction. Ignore the red 5-bar gate on the R SP
Footpath. Go through metal gates on L, follow track to the
R edge of the plantation. Farm track becomes tarmac,
ignore a turning down to L, SA into Hazelton.

7. Turn sharp L along the A40 SE for about 180m
(200yds). Cross the A40 with care to tum R SP
Yanworth/Compton Abdale. After almost 400m (1/4 mile)
turn R again SP Compton Abdale for a steep downhill drop
to a T-j opposite a stone water trough at Compton Abdale.
Turn L past the Village Hall to rise steeply. Where the
gradient eases, there is a pair of double-green gates on L.

Hazelton

Milkwell
Covert

The Downs
Brake

Puesdown
Inn

Hill Barn

Compton Abdale

Cast
F

to
A40
Andoversford
Village
Hall

A40 (T)

Alternative route: To cut the
route short (by about 17km/11
miles), go SA for about 4km (2
1/2 miles) back to Northleach.

Start: In Northleach, on-stree
P or at the Market Square.

Hangman's
Stone

Oaks
Bottom

9. Bear R, then immediately L at the T-j SP Northleach 2 1/2
miles downhill into the valley and up the other side.
Continue bearing L, ignore the turning off to Chedworth/-
Fossebridge on the R. A long climb flattens out before
pylons, followed by x-rds. Turn R to junction with the A429
Fosse Way.

Star Wood

8. Tum L through the bridle
gate just R of the gates. Go
SA along the obvious track,
which becomes faster
when you bear R just
before a group of beech
trees. Bear R again at a
junction with a harder
surface just after this. 3km
(2 miles) of good, fast
riding brings you to a
junction with a tarmac
road on a bend at
Yanworth.

Yanworth
Stowell
Grove

Stowell

A429

W

Yanworth
Mill
Stowell
Mill
Stowell
Park

10. Cross the A road with care. Pass through a bridle gate
WM/SP Public Path and follow track SA. Follow the wall SA
past Church Farm where the track becomes tarmac. Turn L
at T-j just after this to return to Northleach.

Scale
0   500   1000 metres
0   500   1000 yards

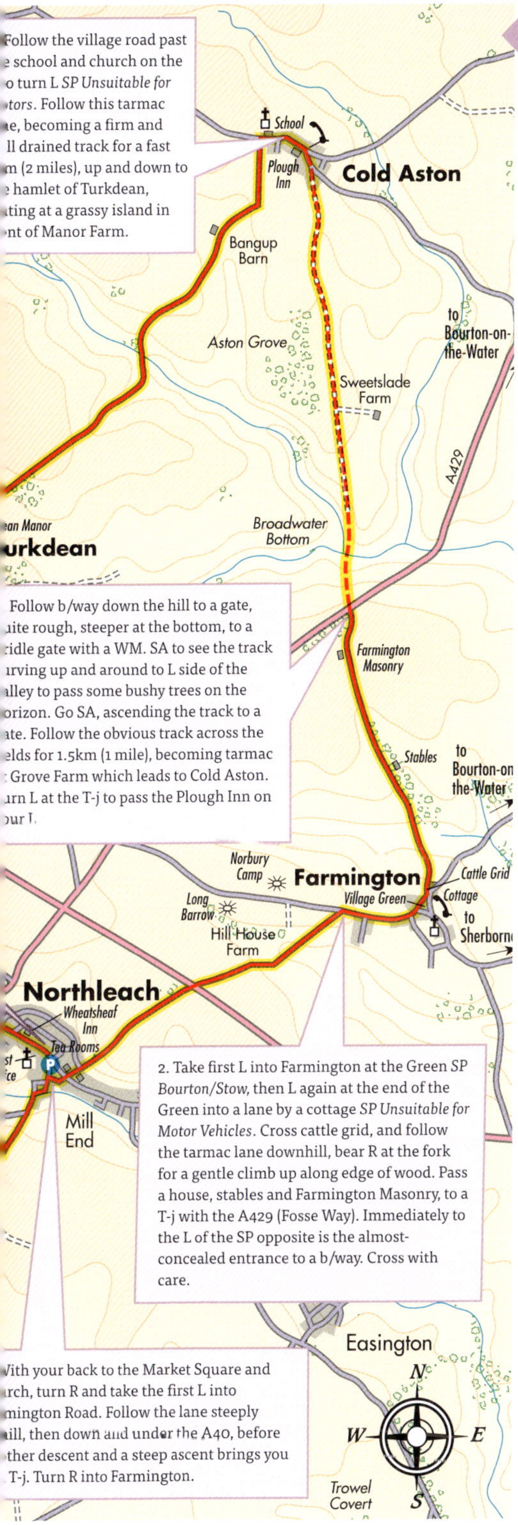

Follow the village road past e school and church on the o turn L *SP Unsuitable for otors*. Follow this tarmac ie, becoming a firm and ll drained track for a fast m (2 miles), up and down to e hamlet of Turkdean, iting at a grassy island in ont of Manor Farm.

Follow b/way down the hill to a gate, uite rough, steeper at the bottom, to a ridle gate with a WM. SA to see the track urving up and around to L side of the alley to pass some bushy trees on the orizon. Go SA, ascending the track to a ate. Follow the obvious track across the elds for 1.5km (1 mile), becoming tarmac Grove Farm which leads to Cold Aston. urn L at the T-j to pass the Plough Inn on our L.

2. Take first L into Farmington at the Green *SP Bourton/Stow*, then L again at the end of the Green into a lane by a cottage *SP Unsuitable for Motor Vehicles*. Cross cattle grid, and follow the tarmac lane downhill, bear R at the fork for a gentle climb up along edge of wood. Pass a house, stables and Farmington Masonry, to a T-j with the A429 (Fosse Way). Immediately to the L of the SP opposite is the almost-concealed entrance to a b/way. Cross with care.

Vith your back to the Market Square and irch, turn R and take the first L into mington Road. Follow the lane steeply iill, then down and under the A40, before ther descent and a steep ascent brings you T-j. Turn R into Farmington.

Distance: 28 km (17½ miles); 16 km (10 miles) off-road, 12 km) 7½ miles) road.

Grade: 2

Riding time: 3 to 3½ hours.

Direction: Anti-clockwise.

Mostly on good, firm tracks, there is little evidence of the infamous Cotswold mud on this route, so it is good for all year round. The only significant climbs are on tarmac, although there are some good off-road downhills.

Refreshments are available from the Old Prison Cafe on the Fosse Way, Northleach, the Black Cat Café in Northleach's Town Square and the Plough Inn, Cold Aston.

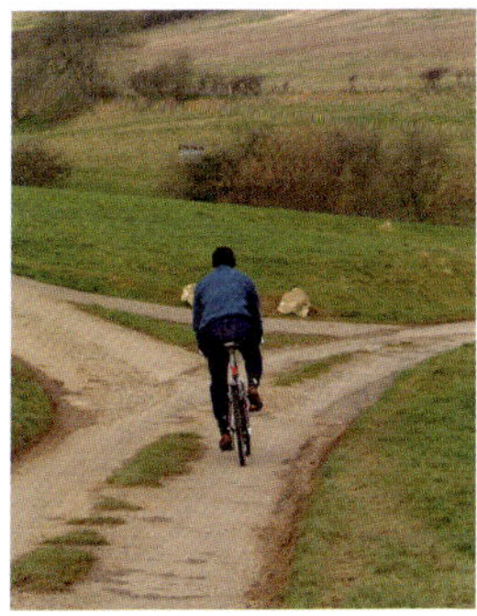

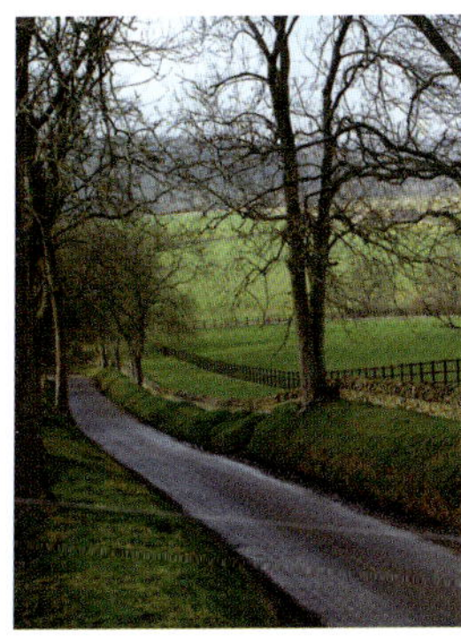

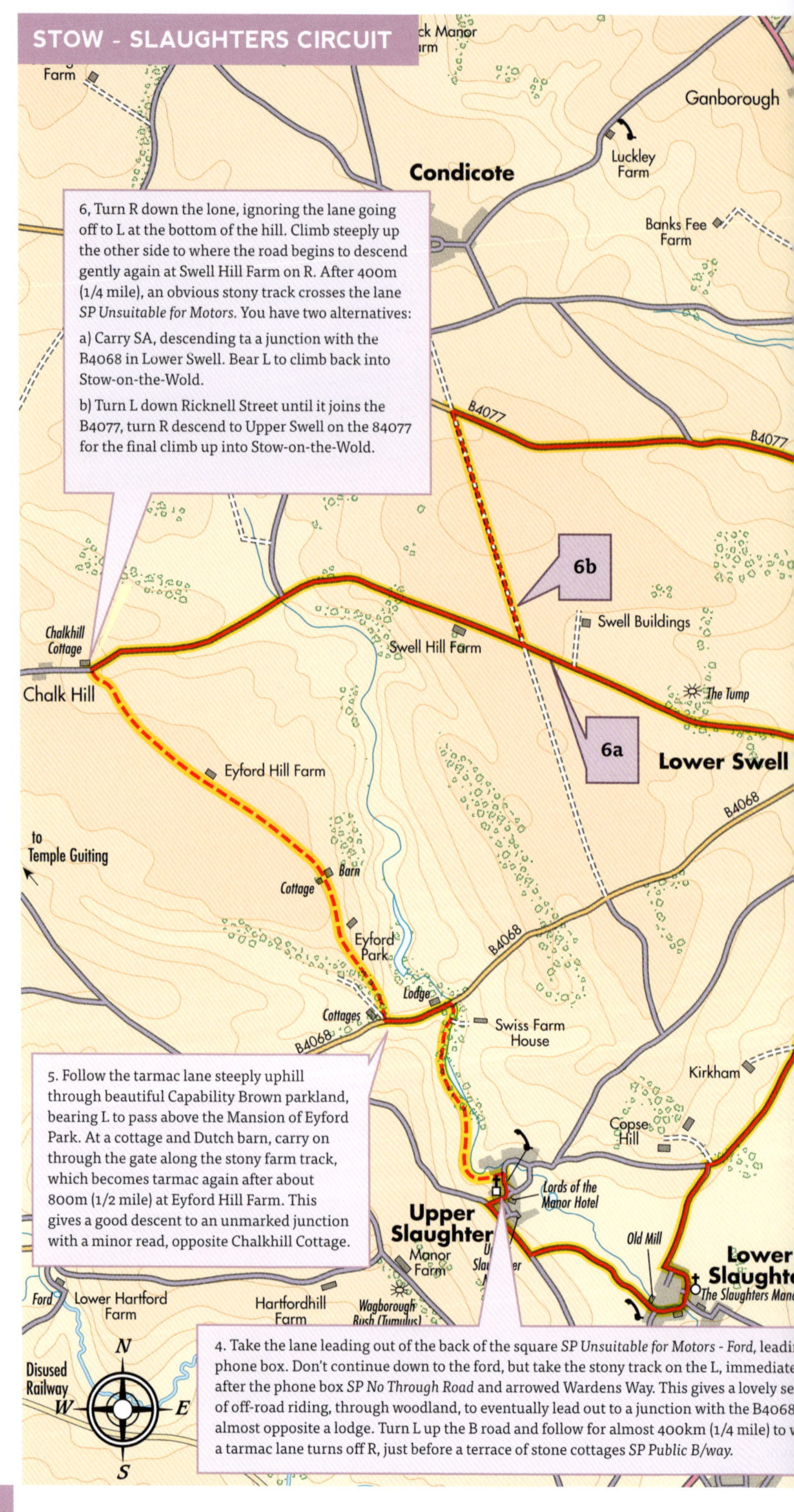

Ganborough
Condicote
Luckley Farm
Banks Fee Farm
k Manor rm
Farm
6, Turn R down the lone, ignoring the lane going off to L at the bottom of the hill. Climb steeply up the other side to where the road begins to descend gently again at Swell Hill Farm on R. After 400m (1/4 mile), an obvious stony track crosses the lane SP Unsuitable for Motors. You have two alternatives:
a) Carry SA, descending ta a junction with the B4068 in Lower Swell. Bear L to climb back into Stow-on-the-Wold.
b) Turn L down Ricknell Street until it joins the B4077, turn R descend to Upper Swell on the 84077 for the final climb up into Stow-on-the-Wold.
B4077
B4077
6b
Swell Buildings
Chalkhill Cottage
Swell Hill Farm
The Tump
Chalk Hill
6a
Lower Swell
Eyford Hill Farm
B4068
to Temple Guiting
Barn
Cottage
Eyford Park
B4068
Lodge
Cottages
B4068
Swiss Farm House
Kirkham
Copse Hill
5. Follow the tarmac lane steeply uphill through beautiful Capability Brown parkland, bearing L to pass above the Mansion of Eyford Park. At a cottage and Dutch barn, carry on through the gate along the stony farm track, which becomes tarmac again after about 800m (1/2 mile) at Eyford Hill Farm. This gives a good descent to an unmarked junction with a minor read, opposite Chalkhill Cottage.
Lords of the Manor Hotel
Upper Slaughter
U Sla er
Old Mill
Lower Slaughte
The Slaughters Man
Manor Farm
Ford
Lower Hartford Farm
Hartfordhill Farm
Wagborough Bush (Tumulus)
Disused Railway
N
W
E
S
4. Take the lane leading out of the back of the square SP Unsuitable for Motors - Ford, leadi phone box. Don't continue down to the ford, but take the stony track on the L, immediate after the phone box SP No Through Road and arrowed Wardens Way. This gives a lovely se of off-road riding, through woodland, to eventually lead out to a junction with the B4068 almost opposite a lodge. Turn L up the B road and follow for almost 400km (1/4 mile) to a tarmac lane turns off R, just before a terrace of stone cottages SP Public B/way.

Distance: 21km (13 miles); 7km (4 miles) off-road, 14km (9 miles) road.

Grade: 1

Riding time: 2 to 2½ hours.

Direction: Clockwise.

Starting at the beautiful market town of Stow-on-the-Wold, this route takes in one of the prettiest honey-pot villages of Lower Slaughter and the Capability Brown landscape of Eyford Park.

There are numerous hotels on the route in both Upper and Lower Slaughter, as well as pubs and cafés in Stow-on-the-Wold itself.

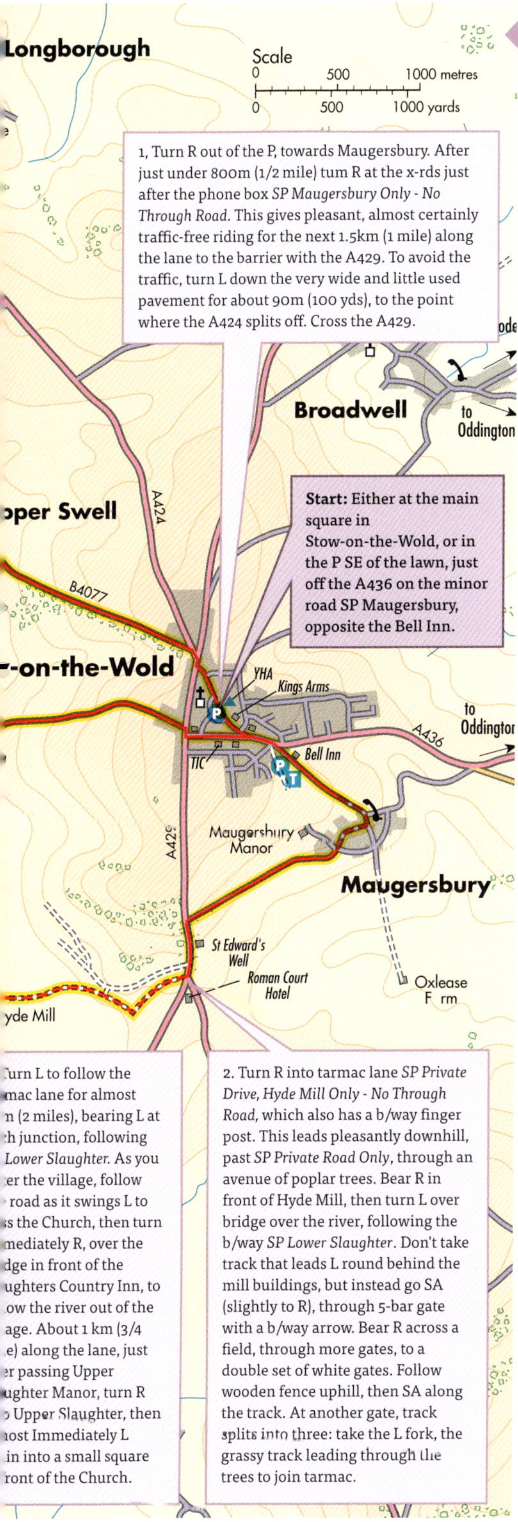

Map labels

1, Turn R out of the P, towards Maugersbury. After just under 800m (1/2 mile) turn R at the x-rds just after the phone box *SP Maugersbury Only - No Through Road*. This gives pleasant, almost certainly traffic-free riding for the next 1.5km (1 mile) along the lane to the barrier with the A429. To avoid the traffic, turn L down the very wide and little used pavement for about 90m (100 yds), to the point where the A424 splits off. Cross the A429.

Start: Either at the main square in Stow-on-the-Wold, or in the P SE of the lawn, just off the A436 on the minor road SP Maugersbury, opposite the Bell Inn.

Turn L to follow the [ta]rmac lane for almost [3k]m (2 miles), bearing L at [eac]h junction, following [SP] Lower Slaughter. As you [ent]er the village, follow [the] road as it swings L to [pas]s the Church, then turn [imm]ediately R, over the [bri]dge in front of the [Sla]ughters Country Inn, to [foll]ow the river out of the [vill]age. About 1 km (3/4 [mil]e) along the lane, just [afte]r passing Upper [Sla]ughter Manor, turn R [SP] Upper Slaughter, then [alm]ost Immediately L [aga]in into a small square [in fr]ont of the Church.

2. Turn R into tarmac lane *SP Private Drive, Hyde Mill Only - No Through Road*, which also has a b/way finger post. This leads pleasantly downhill, past *SP Private Road Only*, through an avenue of poplar trees. Bear R in front of Hyde Mill, then turn L over bridge over the river, following the b/way *SP Lower Slaughter*. Don't take track that leads L round behind the mill buildings, but instead go SA (slightly to R), through 5-bar gate with a b/way arrow. Bear R across a field, through more gates, to a double set of white gates. Follow wooden fence uphill, then SA along the track. At another gate, track splits into three: take the L fork, the grassy track leading through the trees to join tarmac.

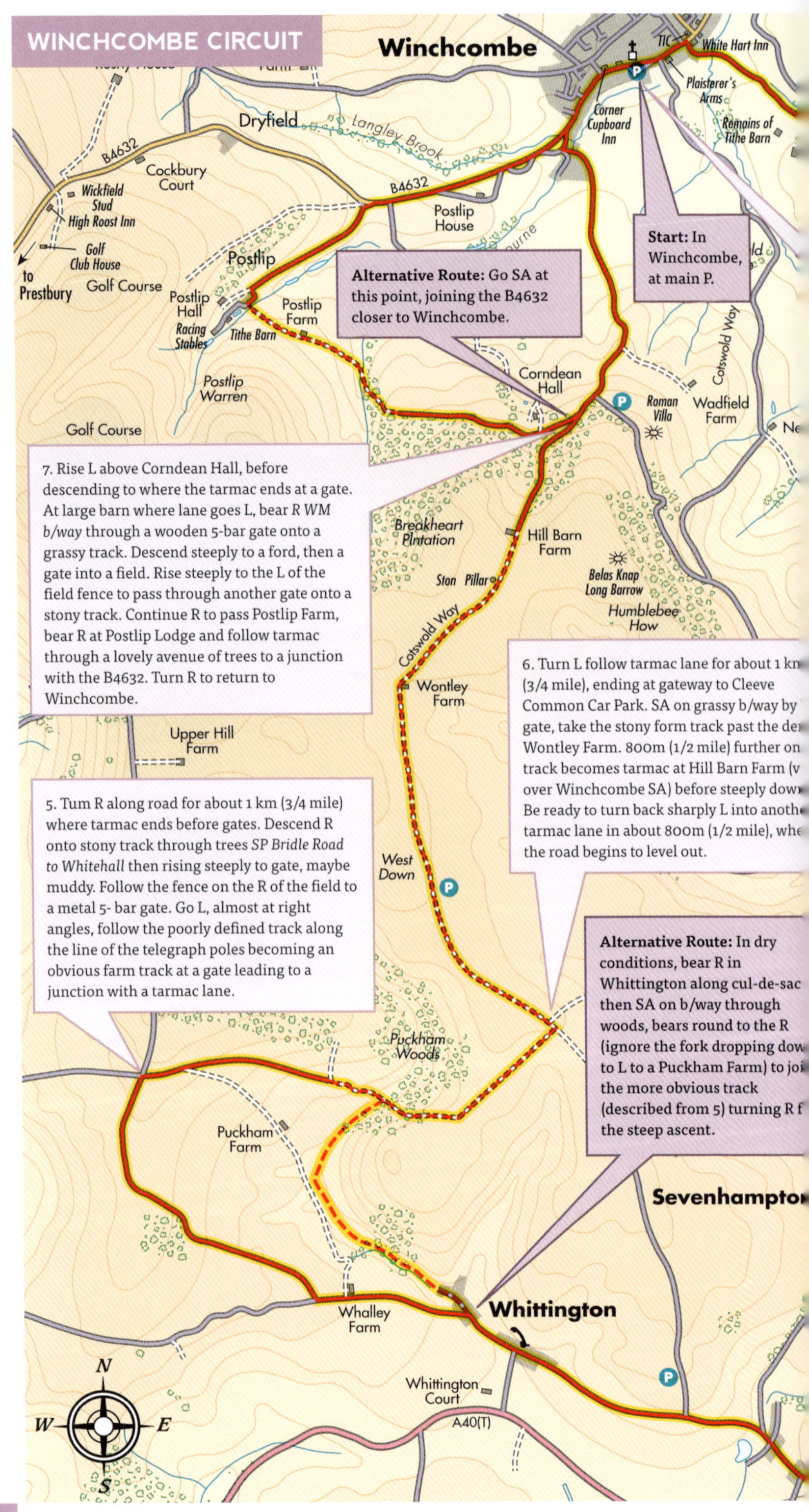
Winchcombe
TIC
White Hart Inn
Plaisterer's Arms
Corner Cupboard Inn
Remains of Tithe Barn
Dryfield
Langley Brook
B4632
Postlip House
Postlip
Cockbury Court
Wickfield Stud
High Roost Inn
Golf Club House
to Prestbury
Golf Course
Postlip Hall
Postlip Farm
Racing Stables
Tithe Barn
Postlip Warren
Golf Course
Corndean Hall
Roman Villa
Wadfield Farm
Ne
Cotswold Way
Start: In Winchcombe, at main P.
Alternative Route: Go SA at this point, joining the B4632 closer to Winchcombe.
Breakheart Plntation
Hill Barn Farm
Ston Pillar
Belas Knap Long Barrow
Humblebee How
7. Rise L above Corndean Hall, before descending to where the tarmac ends at a gate. At large barn where lane goes L, bear R WM b/way through a wooden 5-bar gate onto a grassy track. Descend steeply to a ford, then a gate into a field. Rise steeply to the L of the field fence to pass through another gate onto a stony track. Continue R to pass Postlip Farm, bear R at Postlip Lodge and follow tarmac through a lovely avenue of trees to a junction with the B4632. Turn R to return to Winchcombe.
Upper Hill Farm
Cotswold Way
Wontley Farm
6. Turn L follow tarmac lane for about 1 km (3/4 mile), ending at gateway to Cleeve Common Car Park. SA on grassy b/way by gate, take the stony form track past the der Wontley Farm. 800m (1/2 mile) further on track becomes tarmac at Hill Barn Farm (v over Winchcombe SA) before steeply dow Be ready to turn back sharply L into anothe tarmac lane in about 800m (1/2 mile), whe the road begins to level out.
5. Tum R along road for about 1 km (3/4 mile) where tarmac ends before gates. Descend R onto stony track through trees SP Bridle Road to Whitehall then rising steeply to gate, maybe muddy. Follow the fence on the R of the field to a metal 5- bar gate. Go L, almost at right angles, follow the poorly defined track along the line of the telegraph poles becoming an obvious farm track at a gate leading to a junction with a tarmac lane.
West Down
Alternative Route: In dry conditions, bear R in Whittington along cul-de-sac then SA on b/way through woods, bears round to the R (ignore the fork dropping dow to L to a Puckham Farm) to joi the more obvious track (described from 5) turning R f the steep ascent.
Puckham Woods
Puckham Farm
Sevenhampto
Whalley Farm
Whittington
Whittington Court
A40(T)
N
W   E
S

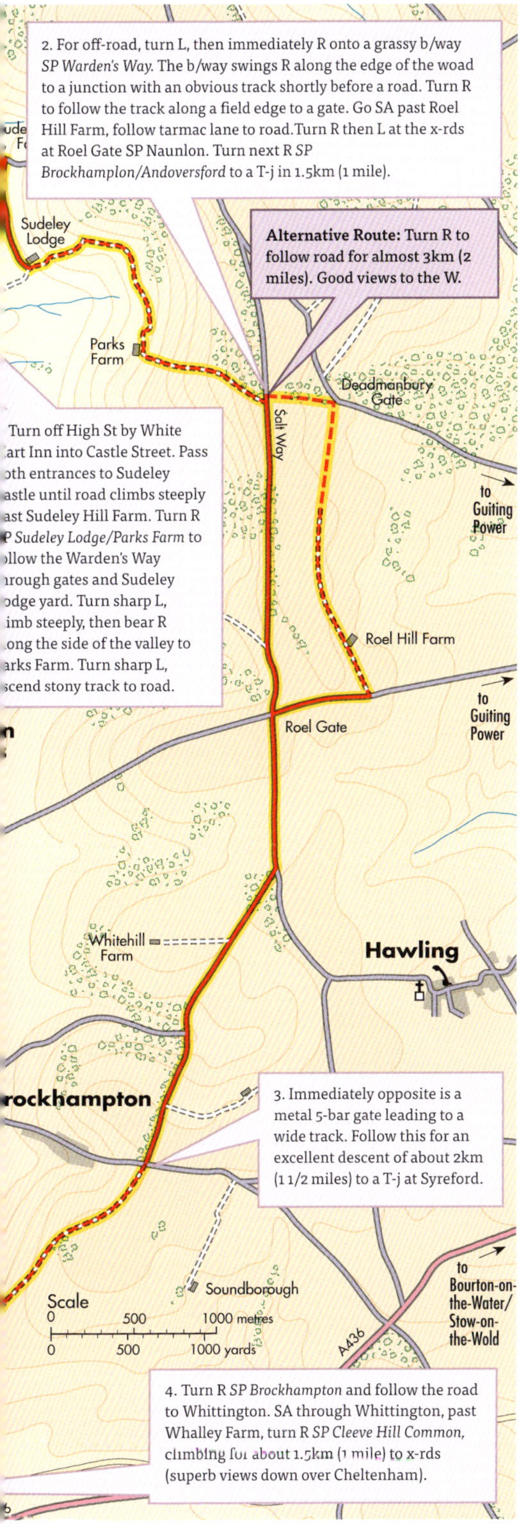

2. For off-road, turn L, then immediately R onto a grassy b/way *SP Warden's Way*. The b/way swings R along the edge of the woad to a junction with an obvious track shortly before a road. Turn R to follow the track along a field edge to a gate. Go SA past Roel Hill Farm, follow tarmac lane to road. Turn R then L at the x-rds at Roel Gate *SP Naunlon*. Turn next R *SP Brockhamplon/Andoversford* to a T-j in 1.5km (1 mile).

Alternative Route: Turn R to follow road for almost 3km (2 miles). Good views to the W.

Turn off High St by White art Inn into Castle Street. Pass oth entrances to Sudeley astle until road climbs steeply ast Sudeley Hill Farm. Turn R *P Sudeley Lodge/Parks Farm* to llow the Warden's Way hrough gates and Sudeley odge yard. Turn sharp L, imb steeply, then bear R ong the side of the valley to arks Farm. Turn sharp L, scend stony track to road.

3. Immediately opposite is a metal 5-bar gate leading to a wide track. Follow this for an excellent descent of about 2km (1 1/2 miles) to a T-j at Syreford.

4. Turn R *SP Brockhampton* and follow the road to Whittington. SA through Whittington, past Whalley Farm, turn R *SP Cleeve Hill Common*, climbing for about 1.5km (1 mile) to x-rds (superb views down over Cheltenham).

Distance: 27 km (17 miles); 11km (7 miles) off-road, 16 km (10 miles) road.

Grade: 2

Riding time: 2½ hours.

Direction: Clockwise.

With the highest point in the Cotswolds only just off-route, you can expect both good views and a few stiff climbs. In fact, the climbs are not really that bad, and are well worth it for the descents. With the exception of the short section of B road to return to Winchcombe, the roads normally carry little traffic, and the tracks are generally firm and well drained.

There are pubs off-route in Andoversford and Brockhampton.

ABOUT THE AUTHOR & PHOTOGRAPHER

William Fricker was born in Somerset and educated at Stonyhurst College, Lancashire, and in various places of learning in Austria and Germany. He has worked in publishing for many years. William first worked for William Collins (now Harper Collins) in London, where he became a Creative Director in their paperback division before taking a sabbatical to make a 4,000 mile trek across Europe (France-The Alps-Italy, to Greece) along the old mule tracks, footpaths and pilgrim's routes. Inspired by Patrick Leigh Fermor's A Time of Gifts, and Laurie Lee's As I Walked Out One Midsummer Morning. On reaching Greece, his original plan was to then head south and walk up the Nile, but he believes his better judgement prevailed, and returned on a bicycle via North Africa, Spain and France. For the past thirty-five years he has built up Goldeneye compiling the research, editorial and photography, for more than two hundred UK travel guides and books; on cycling, touring and walking. For many years the Cotswold Hills were William's base. He played cricket in many of the villages, visited many a hostelry and introduced his young family to the wonders of the countryside. More recently, he has been re-developing his Guidebook series to The Cotswolds, Cornwall, Devon and The Lake District.

THE E-BIKE ROUTES AUTHOR

Al Churcher has many years, world-wide, experience in a wide range of adventurous activities: from climbing, road cycling and mountain biking, hiking, downhill skiing and ski mountaineering. He is the author of Classic Climbs in the Dolomites and Selected Climbs in Northern Italy (Cicerone Press), and Al has devised many cycling routes for Goldeneye, too numerous to catalogue. He regularly contributes articles and photographs to a wide range of outdoor magazine. More recently he has been competing in the Olympic Triathlon events (cycling, swimming and running) for the Over-70s.